Extracting Goats

Extracting Goats from Jean-Claude's Kitchen

*And Other Essential Tips from Seven Years of Musical and
Family Life in Rural France*

Dan Jones

Copyright © Dan Jones
Cover Design by Dan Jones
First Published 2019

ISBN: 9781095150122

Acknowledgements

In choosing a dedicatee for my book, I am faced with a conundrum. The overriding experience of this chapter in our lives was one of great personal enrichment, yet I must recognise there were moments when we were royally up the creek. We were always bailed out both emotionally and practically by those who surrounded us. Indeed, we owe much to family and friends.

I thank Carol, for her tolerance in accepting our dreams and for being an honorary mum to me. I also acknowledge my father-in-law Dave, mother-in-law Jan, brother-in-law Ian and sister-in-law Lucy. All of the above embraced our adventure without judgement or question, like magical mystery tour day trippers being flown by a pilot with a map scrawled on the back of a beer mat.

I'd like to express my thanks and love to my co-pilot, Kirsty. Without her drive and courage, the adventure would never have taken off. I also acknowledge my son Matthew, a measured, intelligent and assured young man who must, in the small hours, wonder what madcap scheme his father will embark on next. I must express my gratitude and constant amazement of my other children, Flo and Sam. They unwittingly throw new adventures at Kirsty and me with alarming regularity, ensuring that, thankfully, life can never settle into a sensible routine.

I owe much to Carol Jones, John Jones, Avril Hamley and Tony Flower (he's a great author – check him out) for giving their time, energy, encouragement, expertise and feedback during the creation of this book. Sometimes a few insightful words can make a world of difference. Of course, the responsibility for any errors or inaccuracies lands firmly at my doorstep. I'd like to thank John Lindsay of Alyth Photography for the author photo, his glamorous assistants, Jenny Scott and Dave Stanghon, and Mary and John at The River Edge Lodges in Bridge of Earn, Scotland for their good humour and the loan of their highly-photogenic goats, Archie and Tim.

So, my conundrum remains unsolved. Who should enjoy the dubious honour of becoming this book's dedicatee? My late mum who caused me to fall in love with the guitar springs to mind, as does my late younger brother 'Little' Paul, whose free spirit and healthy disregard for authority hinted at the possibility of an alternative lifestyle, or even my stepfather 'Big' Paul, whose love of the outdoor life may have seeped into my consciousness during my formative and ill-tempered teenage years?

All of the above are folk to whom I owe everything and more, yet I would like to dedicate this book to the man who introduced me to the country which attracts my spirit like an irrepressible magnetic force; the person I came to know and identify with during those happy, destiny-shaping summers in France in the 1980's and 1990's.

For Dad, with thanks and love

Contents

(i) Prologue

The water is wide, I cannot get over
Neither have I wings to fly
Give me a boat that can carry two
And both shall row, my love and I

The Water is Wide - Traditional (Scotland)

"Now, grasp his head with your right armpit, pass your left forearm under his tummy and lift up his rear end towards me."

"Errr… Okay, I think I've got it."

"Hold him still for heaven's sake man! It's impossible to grasp anything with them wobbling around like jellified ping pong balls!"

"Well, you can hardly blame him, given the circumstances…"

"It would be helpful if you opened your eyes and looked towards me."

"I'm not certain I can do that… As a fellow male, I feel a certain empathy."

"Look do you want me to wrap a rubber band around his testicles or not?"

"Now, you put it like that, I can only declare the jury to be well-and-truly out."

"You're going to faint aren't you?" observed my partner-in-crime, with an unerringly accurate insight into my state of well-being.

"*Kirsty!*" she bellowed in withering tones, "come and take over… he's going to pass out!"

"What, the goat?" responded my spouse quizzically, and with some concern for the creature undergoing this distinctly rustic surgical intervention.

"No, your husband. Now, hurry up otherwise we're going to wind up hoisting him out of the hay rack."

This exchange took place in our back garden on a pleasant spring evening in 2016. It was one I'd wholly failed to anticipate some six years previously when we lived a comfortable existence in South Wales, unfettered by everyday countryside tasks, such as goat castration.

It was in August 2010 when we - *la Famille Jones* - embarked on a life-changing journey. We had made the decision to leave our home in Pontypridd, near Wales' capital city of Cardiff, to experience life in a sleepy, rural village in South-West France. Over the previous nine years we'd built an agreeable lifestyle and enjoyed relatively-secure employment; Kirsty was an orchestral violinist, and I was teaching in a national music conservatoire. We had two children young enough to embrace radical change: Flo, who was then five years old, and Sam, who was just four months. My older son Matt, having just earned his first degree, was forging his own path in the world. There was a window of opportunity, a chance to take a radical step, a now-or-never moment. We took the plunge.

Like most people undertaking emigration to new country and culture, we did a decent amount of research before setting sail. I dutifully swotted up on employment practices, health care, schooling, home ownership, taxation rules, pensions, inheritance law, and all those grown-up things which apparently formulate the necessities of life. As I reflect many years later, and with the glorious benefit of hindsight, I realise we were totally ignorant of skills which I now understand as being essential to becoming fully-integrated, functional and settled members of our modest corner of *la Patrie des Droits de l'Homme*. Forget Brexit for a moment and allow us to muse upon some of the unlikely questions we have been required to ponder. How does one act, for example, if your neighbour phones to say your goat is in his kitchen… again? At what hour of the day is it appropriate to offer friends an *aperitif* or, more to the point, is such a proposition ever inappropriate? Can the wrong choice of swimwear really lead to a decade-long ban from your local *piscine?* How might you juggle an unlikely combination of fireworks, naked flames and live rabbits at a junior school fete? And finally, writing from a male perspective, at what moment can you kiss a fellow man without being punched in the face?

These yawning gaps in our knowledge, and many others like them, were acquired through oft-painful experience, trial-and-error and no small degree of humiliation. If you wish to flourish in such a society, the offerings to be found within these pages may give you an invaluable edge, a springboard, a sense of *déjà vu,* which your relocation agent would most-likely see as being beyond his/her remit.

It strikes me it is a sense of belonging, inclusion and shared experience which define human happiness and identity. Nowhere are these values held in higher esteem than in our adopted corner of France. Many of the ethics and principles which formed the basis of our daily existence reminded me of bygone times in the country of my birth: those of courtesy, adventure, reasonable risk, independence and trust. As you will read, I found uncanny similarities between our new life and my childhood experiences of yesteryear. *La Famille Jones* experienced seven years of joy and sadness, victories and catastrophes, laughter and despair but, throughout the whole journey, we were ingrained with a deep sense of fellowship and brotherhood with our friends across *la Manche.* We learned to be enraptured and amazed at the cultural habits of our near-neighbours, and to both discover and share in their eccentricities. The passions held by those whose paths we crossed caused us to fall in love with this country and the lifestyle it holds dear. There were times when I felt like ripping my hair out in frustration, yet at other moments, I had the peculiar urge to kiss the ground and wondered how anyone could ever consider settling anywhere else.

I'd like to invite you to sit back, relax, uncork a Bordeaux *Grand Cru* and read on. I hope you'll learn some valuable lessons but more-so, share a laugh or two with me. Who knows, maybe one day, you too will be ensnared by the spell of rural France.

1. The Thirty-Year Journey

Ffarweliwch, rwy'n madal â'm gwlad
Mae mwriad am fynad i'r môr
Ffarweliwch, fy mam a fy nhad
Sy'n teimlo fy hiraeth ar ôl...
Mae amcan a bwriad y bard
Am fynad I belter y byd

Farewell, for I'm leaving my land
Intending to go off to sea
Farewell to my mother and father
Who feel such longing for me...
The purpose and plan of the poet
Is to go to the ends of the world

Traditional - *Ffarweliwch, Rwy'n Madal â'm Gwlad*
(Farewell, For I'm Leaving My Land - Wales)

***

La France est belle, ses destins sont bénis
Vivons pour elle, vivons unis
Passez les monts, passez les mers
Visitez cent climats divers
Loin d'elle, au bout de l'univers, Vous chanterez fidèle

France is beautiful, its destinies are blessed
Live for her, live united
Pass the mountains, pass the seas
Visit one hundred different climates
Far from her, at the end of the universe, you will loyally sing

George Nageli (18th-Century) – *La France est Belle*
(France is Beautiful - France)

July 1984. Contrary to Orwell's disquieting predictions, those who had travelled to this perfect, sun-kissed corner of France passed a carefree and idyllic day. Here, where the seemingly-endless expanse of fine, golden sand met the Atlantic, both the youthful and age-wizened shared the moment with an abundance of *joie de vivre.* Life's meaning had simplicity and clarity.

The ocean cast regular rushes of white foam onto the beach, beating out a symphony of nature's sonorities - rhythmic, reassuring, like the sounds of the womb. Crabs exposed to an alien world scuttled for shelter and jellyfish waited helplessly to be reclaimed by the waters. Wonderstruck toddlers discovered shells, millennia in their creation, and placed them lovingly into buckets. The advance of the tide, each push gaining an extra few inches of ground, stole the occasional towel and flip-flop of the rookie traveller; seasoned veterans installed their belongings just beyond the high-tide line with the smug confidence of the expert.

The majority of bathers indulged in horseplay at the point where water met land. Teenagers threw balls, athletically plunging to the left and right in a desperate effort to make *that* spectacular catch; girlfriends found themselves dumped unceremoniously into the breakers, little aware that this moment of frivolity would be reflected upon with wistful nostalgia in future decades. Infants smacked spades in the shallows and older, wiser couples ambled, hand in hand, with the remnants of the swirl lapping between their toes.

More pensive *vacanciers* gazed out to sea, the tang of salt on their lips, as if trying to spot the Americas some five thousand miles to the west. The observant may have spotted a tiny, black dot bobbing up and down in the surf. Minuscule against the huge, undulating rises of water, it became frequently concealed from those on the shore by the swell which surrounded it before being lifted back into view, as if raised as an offering to the ever-beating sun.

Closer inspection revealed this to be the head of a boy poking out of the waves, staring out to sea. He'd found himself well out of his depth but, being a competent and confident swimmer, the lad seemed at ease with his situation.

The boy swam with the surfers. They all awaited the same prize - the perfect wave. The group scanned the horizon, each individual an expert at recognising from afar a breaker with true potential. Occasionally, someone would waste their efforts on a wave with no true riding power; his reward - a trip akin to sitting in the back seat of Grandad's Austin Allegro on a Sunday afternoon rather than a Saturday-night joy ride in a Ferrari. The boy's sun-burnt face cracked a derisive grin at such amateurs.

Suddenly, a ripple of expectation. A surge of water approached - substantial, broad, robust and not too high. Yet. The experienced surfers jockeyed for position, alert, focused, yet always respectful of the space of others. The boy too found a line which would, in turn, allow the riders free passage. The mound advanced, ever-swelling, monstrous, increasing in speed. Others at the shoreline detected its presence and tried frantically to jump onto inflatable boats, airbeds, tyres – any floating body which would yield the thrill of the ride. The boy though sought no flotation aids. He was going commando. With the beast roaring towards the shore, the surfers inched bodies and boards towards the invisible line which they anticipated would be directly below the salty, rolling mass as it broke. Some probed too far into the sea and infuriatingly bobbed benignly over the wave's crest, their role reduced to that of disgruntled spectators. Conversely, those who had positioned themselves with perfection found themselves dwarfed by the massive arch of water, just at the point of its collapse. For a split second of awe and fear, the assembly was frozen in time, then, with an imperceptible flick of the body, the surfers shot off like torpedoes, attempting the coolest moves on their boards and hoping to catch the eyes of the girls tanning themselves on the beach. The boy though indulged in an altogether less commonly-witnessed practice. He placed his body in front of the approaching monster, like a gorilla protecting his harem from a young pretender, and spreading his arms wide emitted an animalistic battle cry.

"*Aaaaiiieeee!*"

He allowed the wave to crash delightfully down on his head.

The boy felt his feet instantly swept from underneath him and the familiar adrenalin-thrill of being wondrously out-of-control shot through his veins. Carried along with a noise like a thousand tons of TNT exploding in his ears, he found himself losing his sense of orientation, the mystery only resolved when his backside grazed against the sandy, submerged seabed as it passed beneath him at considerable pace. He had been holding his breath for a good thirty seconds, but he felt no fear. He knew that imminently, the ride would be over and the wave conquered. Moments later he found himself lying flat on his back in three inches of water, staring at the blazing sun, a jet of foul-tasting sea water spurting from his mouth. Another victory notched up. He punched the air with one hand and dislodged wriggling shrimps from his Speedos with the other. The impossibly-cool beach lifeguard had learned to ignore this peculiar fifteen-year-old some days ago. The boy was quirky, *Anglais*-speaking (albeit with an indecipherable accent) and had not yet drowned on his shift. Therefore, he deemed him harmless.

A voice called out.

"Dan, would you like to go and watch the fishermen?"

"Just one more wave Dad."

"OK."

I am the boy, many moons on, and this was the beginning of my love affair with *la France.*

The journey towards finding the ideal holiday for an adult and two lively boys had been a long and challenging one for my father. As I turned eleven years of age, my parents divorced. As a kind of 'sorry-that-we're-getting-divorced' compensatory gift, my Dad took my brother John and me to Blackpool for a long weekend. I remember we made a decent fist of the experience, mainly due to the fact that we siblings had been given licence to imbibe unrestrained quantities of sugar and food colouring. These dietary irregularities were coupled with unlimited visits to the Pleasure Park which, by the name alone, implies the experience should have been, well... pleasurable. I recall that the little B&B which hosted us enjoyed a view of a brick wall from the window. My Dad found this very funny. I was too young to understand irony but I laughed along with him anyway. Each morning, we wrapped ourselves up in jumpers and raincoats - the grey, relentless drizzle being a feature suspiciously absent from the tourist brochures – and ventured out to stroll along the promenade. Surreally, I vaguely remember taking a trip on a tram and running over a guy leaning out at a stop. A little too far so it appears.

The next year, Dad increased the scope of his ambition and took us to Magaluf (now charmingly nicknamed 'Shagaluf') in Majorca. This was a marked improvement for a boy approaching his teens. Whereas my compatriots apparently indulged in activities of a lustful and salubrious nature, we ate chicken basted in olive oil followed by pint glasses filled with fresh strawberries and cream. I found a set of false teeth in our hotel's swimming pool and it never rained.

Dad was clearly a tolerant and understanding man. Born in Aberystwyth at the beginning of the Second World War, he lost his own father at just six years of age. He was raised by his Mum in a council house on the Penparcau Council Estate. As an adult, I was genuinely surprised by the reaction of friends originating from this West-Wales seaside town when chatting about family origins.

"Your Nan lived in Beirut!" they would exclaim.

Against all odds, Dad excelled academically and studied Classics at Cambridge. He had a deeply powerful intellect, yet he smilingly tolerated his sons' purchases of souvenirs of dubious taste from Spain's sun-kissed isle (with his hard-earned money). Enormous straw sombreros (which I earnestly believed would serve as practical headwear for the approaching Welsh winter) and almost life-sized plastic donkeys (originating from Taiwan rather than Spain one suspects) made their way to the baggage-reclaim carousel at Heathrow upon our return. They were inevitably destined for the attic within three months of arrival in

South Wales, yet for us, such things represented unspeakable exoticism. For Dad, they must have been agonisingly tacky and boy, he hit the nail on the head.

Spanish holiday resorts boomed at a wholly unsustainable rate in the 1980's resulting in some accommodation providers bypassing inconveniences such as basic hygiene precautions and other tedious matters in order to drive prices down. A wave of sun seekers returned with distinctly disagreeable ailments, legionnaires' disease being a favourite. Therefore, when upon our return I developed a temperature and other unpleasant symptoms, my mum had a meltdown, calling a doctor to the house before I had a chance to mention that my illness was probably brought on due to my having consumed ten packets of Space Dust as a dare.

But Dad scored a bullseye when, one year, we stayed in a caravan in Brittany. I think it was 1983. I can remember very little detail of the holiday and I have no idea in which *departement* the site was situated, yet the feelings I experience when I visualise the setting remain to this day undiminished: warmth, excitement, joy, belonging even. We by no means enjoyed wall-to-wall sunshine, but it didn't matter. Even the night when John's upper bunk collapsed painfully onto my head at 3.00am just added to the thrill of it all. I recall the effortless *chic* of the older teenagers camping in small groups. One had a guitar. We discovered *pain au chocolat,* jellyfish-infested beaches, *moules, croissants,* melon with a little *Pineau de Charente* drizzled on top and other riches which have become cornerstones of our pleasure as adults, except for the jellyfish, although in 2004 I was obliged to eat jellyfish two nights in a row when on tour as a musician in Japan. We were 'treated' to this speciality after a concert yet the other musicians and dancers in our group refused to touch this highly prized and expensive treat. Consequently, I took one for the team and consumed a portion sufficient for four grown men. It was grim. The following night, our hosts, seeing how much I had 'enjoyed' the previous evening's meal provided me with another portion as a special gift.

The following year, we travelled further south to Saint-Palais-sur-Mer. *En route,* we camped in the Loire Valley where our tent became spectacularly flooded during a flash storm. I awoke to find the bottom of my airbed floating in my own personal pond. I loved every second of the experience.

In the holiday town of Saint-Palais-sur-Mer, I truly discovered the joy of the Atlantic Coast. After several hours of being pulverised by waves, my dad (who would have read at least three *Conan the Barbarian* novels during the day), brother John (my real brother rather than a random monk) and I would amble pleasantly along the waterfront, stopping to watch the fishermen. This group gathered daily at around 5.00pm at a rocky area protruding into the surf. Here, they shared gossip, drank an *aperitif* and, as an afterthought, did a spot of fishing. They were kitted out with impressive rods several metres long, held in specially-created pipes set in the concrete, leaving hands free for the all-important activities of eating and drinking. The prize they sought was conger eel. Some days would pass with no catch but occasionally, there would be the special moment when a pole twitched and then jolted violently. The owner would hurl back his *Ricard* in one, spring into action (well, as much as a retired gentleman with a fondness for the *Fruits des Vignes* as well as *Fruits de Mer* can be expected to) and an all-consuming battle would ensue. The fisherman wouldn't necessarily emerge the victor. There were moments when his line became snagged on the submerged labyrinth of rocks in the shallows, or he might haul his line from the ocean only to discover the remnants of his bait with a conger-eel-mouth-shaped bite taken from it. Good-natured mirth and banter from co-fishermen and watching public alike would ease the fisherman's mock disappointment. On the occasions when man vanquished eel, he would haul the beast from the sea and friends would trap it in a net. It was dispatched efficiently and, within half-an-hour, would be sizzling in olive oil and made available to diners along the seafront. If you enjoy eating warm blubber using utensils more often encountered in the toolkit of a neurosurgeon, and plucking tiny shards of bone and cartridge from your gums, seafront dining in Saint-Palais-sur-Mer is for you. At least the conger eel you'll have battled your way through will be indisputably fresh and locally sourced.

France is a country where I have always had a sense of belonging – a kind of spiritual affinity. Every time I set foot on its soil, I feel I am *Chez Moi.* In a school career dominated by an overriding, if not academically-relevant interest in the guitar, the only subject I really excelled at was French.

When we were in our twenties, Kirsty, our friend Andy and I drove through France on our way to visit friends in Barcelona. I had a yearning to recapture the feelings of my formative teenage years and, during our journey south, persuaded our little party to stop in the areas I had known and loved. I talked them into making elaborate detours, dragging them around small towns and their adjoining seafronts, scrambling unwisely over jagged rocks protruding into the Atlantic, always certain that the little bays I'd known would be 'just around the next corner'. My party indulged me with admirable patience, yet many of the places were unrecognisable from the images which inhabited the hazy depths of my brain. I felt more than a small tinge of disappointment, but the diversity and sheer oddness of the country, particularly the rural areas, continued to fascinate.

On our way down south, we camped in a bewildering range of environments, from a sleepy forest in Normandy where we shared the site with just two other tents, to the chaos of a tourist site on the Île de Ré. At the latter venue, campers were packed so closely together I could hear the nocturnal snorts of a chubby Belgian gentleman as if he were sharing my own pillow. I momentarily wondered if he'd unwittingly ambled into our tent in error following a vigorous evening's ale consumption in the site's feisty bar.

One particular evening of the trip has stayed in our minds. We had spent a memorable day in Barcelona and, before setting off for the three-day homeward journey towards Calais via the back roads, had indulged in a lazy lunch with friends and their families. Upon returning to Andy's little Peugeot 205, we found, with some dismay, a window smashed and the vehicle completely emptied with the exception of Andy's one-man tent (perhaps the thieves had plenty of one-man tents I mused). They took absolutely everything else: clothes, ball games, air beds, tinned food, a gas cooker, a copy of Hector Berlioz' memoirs, CDs of obscure 16th-Century viol consort music (I was, and still am, a geek), and all my dirty underwear stuffed into a plastic bag at the bottom of my rucksack. I pity the poor soul who dug that out; it had been thirty-five degrees all week.

We decided to cut the trip short and make for Calais at full speed. Armed with newly-purchased toothbrushes and underwear, and harbouring a peculiar mental image of a gang of Catalan hoodlums listening to their newly-pilfered music collection, comparing the imitative counterpoint of Orlando Gibbons and William Byrd, we headed through Central France. At about 7.00pm, we sought out a *Camping Municipale*. France's splendid *Camping Municipale* culture means many towns, small or large, will have cheap and clean campsites which one can choose spontaneously, and be confident of finding a pitch. These are usually financially subsidised by the local *commune* (council). We eventually found a suitable site in a beautiful, remote hamlet, miles from any serious human civilisation. I recall it being set on a slope running towards a fabulous lily-ridden lake which had 'Monet' written all over it. Andy had typically volunteered Kirsty and me his tiny tent and he nobly opted to sleep in the car. We had no airbeds, sleeping bags or pillows, these having all been stolen. We decided, given the trials of the day, a beer was in order, so we set out on what we suspected would be a fruitless search for an alcohol-vending institution. Having walked for about fifteen minutes, the light started to fade and we found ourselves alongside a graveyard which had the peculiar tradition of setting little glass houses above the deceased. It was otherworldly, odd, and a little bit scary. As we turned a slight bend in the road, spirits drooping, there appeared before us a restaurant with the illuminated *Pelforth* symbol glowing welcomingly in the star-dotted skies. Our collective morale reinstated, we entered the humble establishment in delicious anticipation of a cool *demi-pression*. Upon opening the door, a notable pause in the collective conversation was discernible and I sensed a sea of heads turning our way. Had there been a dartboard in the room, I'm sure the thrower would have missed. A kindly lady wearing clothing which seemed to come from the Amish tradition welcomed us. She had donned a bonnet, apron, long voluminous skirt and boots. The male staff sported loose shirts, waistcoats and knee-length shorts, somewhat at odds with my smelly T-shirt (the clean ones having been pinched), flip-flops and garish Bermuda shorts. The owners offered us a table amongst the similarly-attired diners who collectively resembled a Waltons' Family reunion but, in a rather British fashion, we explained we had already eaten and requested a beer apiece. They graciously obliged, and thus commenced an evening of unwisely-rapid *Pelforth* consumption - the fruity, sweet beer so popular in France which has the dangerous combination of being easy-to-drink yet very strong. Some empty bottles later, and fuelled by the false courage offered by the rich ale, I decided to try out a little schoolboy *Français*. Sporting a grin which suggested trapped wind rather than amicability, and an accent which resembled something out of a gloriously politically-incorrect 1980's TV sitcom I approached the bar.

"Why *are* you wearing these crazy clothes?" I asked our host. *Pourquoi portez-vous ces vêtements folles?*

The lady to whom I had addressed my enquiry briefly sported a look which suggested she had found a turd on the underside of her shoe. Admirably, she swiftly regained her composure and professional demeanour.

"Sir," she replied in notably tight-lipped French. "We always wear these clothes."

An awkward silence ensued after which I reimbursed the good lady, took the *Pelforths* and slunk back to our corner where my future wife held her head in her hands.

That night, the air became damp and the temperature plummeted. Kirsty and I half-froze to death in that tiny tent. With no pyjamas, sleeping mat or sleeping bags, our defences against the elements were damp T-shirts, mirror shades and a brand-new toothbrush. I suspect our state of inebriation contributed to the apparent loss of body heat. At 3.00am we went for a jog in an attempt to warm up, to little effect. This experience taught us that the so-called 'beer jacket' is indeed, a myth.

The following morning, we once again passed the little restaurant. In the light of day, it looked like any other modest country abode with no indicators as to the mysteries of the previous evening. The whole experience took on the facade of a reality-bending dream. The next night, we stayed in a B&B.

In 1998, my dad and stepmother invited Kirsty and me to share a holiday with them in Brittany. I had just completed a critical chapter in my life - having been supported through music college by my parents, I'd justified their faith in me by returning a first-class honours undergraduate degree and a distinction in my master's degree. This time, I revisited France with Dad and we shared adult pursuits - good food, great wine, beautiful buildings, much laughter and precious company. I recall his being troubled by an irritating cough which, unbeknownst to us, was cancer. It had silently penetrated much of his body. A little over three months later, he was gone. Our happy days in France are like bookends in my life's relationship with him. I felt I had truly come to know Dad in the country and had effectively said goodbye there as well.

The years passed. In 2003, Kirsty and I married and in 2005, our daughter Florence was born. A couple of years later, we were invited to enjoy a holiday in the beautiful area of Chabottes, in the Hautes-Alpes region of South-East France, where friends have a caravan. We leapt at the opportunity as it was another unknown area of France ripe for exploration. The breath-taking mountains of this wonderful region surrounded lakes in which we splashed and swam daily. I watched Florence tucking into melon (without the *Pineau de Charente*) and *pain au chocolate,* once again marvelling at how the French in small towns treat children as a delightful presence rather than an irritating inconvenience. It seemed that everyone wanted her to be part of their holiday. She created a bridge which led to conversation, unity, and a recognition of shared values between cultures.

When we returned home, Kirsty and I started having conversations about moving to France, initially as a retirement pipe-dream but subsequently, as a 'do-it-now' project. We had bought a modest but charming little end-of-terrace cottage in the working town of Pontypridd which enjoyed spectacular views over the Rhondda Valley. There we had a great community of friends and Florence was flourishing, chatting effortlessly with our neighbours in the Welsh language. Kirsty and I enjoyed good, yet sporadic work; she was a freelance violinist, often with The Welsh National Opera Orchestra, and I taught in the conservatoire where I had studied. We had no burning desire to run away from the UK but we sensed that other opportunities and experiences awaited us, if we dared to take them. I had grown up and studied in South Wales and am naturally cautious; Kirsty though was more widely travelled - she had lived and worked in the US, Romania and South Africa. I sensed that if I'd have suggested we departed the next morning, she wouldn't have batted an eyelid.

There was the inconvenient question of how we would make a living. Thankfully, music-teaching, particularly instrumental teaching, is a universal skill which one can employ with relatively little knowledge of the local language. Of course, in music performance, the shared language is the music itself. Kirsty and I shared a vision of running a complementary business which would celebrate the outdoors in the summer months. Our experiences in the Hautes-Alpes had been an inspiration so we considered the possibility of running a campsite. An initial challenge was that we'd need to find several hundred thousand euros of capital in order to purchase a private site. I wrote to a number of English speakers running such camps and their universally-discouraging responses took the wind from our sails. Some told tales of marital collapse, nervous breakdowns, twenty-hour working days and other such disagreeable elements. We identified though that these sites were situated in tourist resorts and catered for vast numbers. It seems there is big money to be earned for three months of living hell.

The primary motivation for relocating to a rural area of France was to improve our quality of life, so we abandoned this path for others to tread (we still needed to find that several hundred thousand euros too). Next, we decided to explore the more modest world of the *Camping Municipale.* We suspected, correctly, that the kind of client who would patronise a *Camping Municipale* would be more interested in nature, conversation and conviviality than, *Europop,* competing over sunbeds, and *Stella Artois.* There was a notable dearth in hard cash to be made, but the wealth of lasting memories of an agreeable nature which appeared to accompany such a vocation more than compensated for that minor inconvenience. On a whim, I contacted a British couple who ran a business called *Breton Bikes.* Their response was warm and encouraging; they put us in contact with their Anglophone friends, David, a former French teacher, and Marion. They ran a *Camping Municipale* in Central Brittany alongside the Nantes-Brest Canal. To discover whether we were cut out for the job, we volunteered to work on the site for a few weeks in the summer of 2009.

They say that jumping in at the deep end is the best education. I soon learned that years of sitting on my backside playing classical guitar and teaching 16th-Century Species Counterpoint had left a certain dent in my practical skills. On one particularly challenging day, David asked me to chain up his canoes for the night on the banks of the adjacent canal. As I fiddled with an awkward knot, a canoe escaped, floating agonisingly out of reach of my perilously-outstretched arms. Therefore, I had to untie the other canoes (ensuring no further escapees) and jump into canoe number two in order to rescue canoe number one. Like a guilty schoolboy, I glanced over my shoulder to see if David had noticed this farce and in a truly fantastic moment, I saw him observing the entire debacle in the company of two nuns. I actually believed that I was in a surreal dream for three glorious seconds but no, he really was chatting with a pair of nuns who'd popped out of the local convent for a stroll. With reddening cheeks, I observed them graciously giving thanks for the unexpected entertainment with which they'd been blessed, in the form of a piece of spontaneous, comic street-theatre offered by a kindly *Gallois*.

David and Marion demonstrated a great depth of kindness and generosity of heart, giving us all the information we'd ever need and more. They encouraged local businesses to use their site as an outpost for their wares, recognising that the well-being of the community held greater importance than snatching every available euro to line their own pockets. Most importantly, they understood the value of treating people well. David kept a little fridge full of light beers and juice in his office which he would offer to new arrivals by means of welcome. I learned that you could take a full twenty minutes finishing a task in hand and your waiting client would still feel valued and at-ease – who wouldn't while quaffing a leisurely beer in a camp chair after a long journey whilst watching one's children tearing across the field to a sandpit.

David was incredibly adept with his hands. He would go to junk shops and buy decrepit old children's bicycles which looked, to the untrained eye, only fit for the landfill. Within twenty-four hours, they would be sitting proudly alongside dozens of others, free for all the children on the site to enjoy. I loved the fact that a prerequisite was for the kids to ask permission before borrowing a bike – a requirement which they universally fulfilled. He would never have dreamed of refusing them but he understood the importance of courtesy in the French countryside. On a grander scale, many cyclists attempted the bike ride from Nantes to Brest and a good proportion of campers were passing traffic. I witnessed David repairing a young man's rather second-rate hired bike with a rare and generous spirit. He accepted nothing but the fellow's smile in return for his efforts.

We must have done something right as David and Marion entrusted us with the site for a few days when they went to the UK for a family wedding. They also explained that they intended to move on in a couple of years and would recommend us to the village's *maire* as their replacements. We took this as a great compliment. I felt overawed with responsibility once *la Famille Jones* had been placed in sole command; I prayed fervently that nothing involving electrics or plumbing would malfunction. Soon after though, we both experienced a sensation of being trapped on-site and severe bouts of cabin-fever. Had we taken the role on board, I feel we would have run a looser ship that our hosts and left the campers to their own devices for much of the day. David would rarely leave the site unattended whereas many other *camping municipales* often only receive the boss morning and night. The region of Brittany also attracts more than its fair share of rain. On the frequent days when we awoke to the heart-sinking sound of raindrops tapping on canvas, the atmosphere became flat and depressing; Kirsty and I felt terrible for the families trying to entertain their children under such circumstances. Shallow though it may be, we realised that if we were going to go to the trouble of emigration, we might as well chase the sunshine.

We reached a juncture in our lives when a window was obviously wide-open, inviting us to make the move. Florence would still be young enough to accept the change, Kirsty was pregnant with Sam, and Matthew was forging his own path in the world as a young adult. We explored Southern Brittany, the Loire Valley and eventually chose the Dordogne on the basis that I'd applied for some guitar teaching work online and had been offered a post. Our disturbingly-vague plans for a second income could be devised once we had safely installed and established ourselves in the area.

We were unable to afford a removal company or a relocation agent, so we did everything ourselves. We lugged our belongings - from the fridge/freezer to bundles of socks - down the garden steps into our borrowed van belonging to wonderful friends, Jim and Jess, who have a place near the beautiful town of Confolens in the Charente. I sought out work from adverts I'd found on *Pole Emploi* - the French employment service - participating in job interviews, in French, over the telephone. The limited space available for luggage made us reconsider what material goods we truly needed and we gave away most of our bulky furniture. To add spice to the recipe, we also had a young child and baby in tow. Happily for us, friends and family rose to the occasion and nobly helped out. The day before our departure, I was loading the groaning-at-the-seams van with our remaining worldly goods when friends turned up with a takeaway curry. I felt touched by the beautiful gesture, but all our plates and cutlery had been packed up days before, jammed between a jazz guitar and a box of toys. I sat wearily on the floor, constantly clock-watching, picking up pieces of chicken-tikka masala with my fingers.

So, in August 2010, Kirsty, Florence, our new-born baby boy Sam, Badger and Olive (the cats) and I set off in our Vauxhall Astra, in convoy with our dear friend Adrian who drove the van. We knew and trusted Adrian as we had employed him to build an extension on our home in Pontypridd some years previously. When seeking a driver, he seemed like the right person to ask. Strong, friendly, reliable and positive. A good man. We set out at 2.50am with Adrian taking the lead. He nearly caused us to miss the ferry when, to my absolute horror, he casually breezed past the Portsmouth turn-off from the M4. We were forced to catch up with him and overtake, flashing our lights and gesticulating madly, only to be answered by a broad grin and cheery wave by our friend who thought we were participating in some motorway-banter, like excited families setting out on a summer holiday. Our detour cost us thirty minutes of journey time but we had left plenty of contingency. It was a good thing too as within striking distance of the port, I stopped at a café to see if the cats would use the litter tray before boarding the vessel. With misplaced confidence, I ushered the family out of the car and, having closed the doors, smilingly released Badger and Olive from their carriers. Perhaps I mentally-envisaged them enjoying a casual stretch and *gentile* pee in the carefully-placed receptacle on the suitcase but, *au contraire,* there ensued a frenzy of fur and claws as our moggies tore around the interior of the vehicle in an anti-clockwise direction, their centrifugal force permitting them to use the windows as would a pair of wall-of-death motorcyclists.

"Why did Daddy let the pussy cats out of the box?" asked Florence of a bemused Kirsty from the sanctuary of the car park, as I sat on the passenger seat, arms flailing in the feline vortex and Adrian held his sides, lost in the throes of laughter.

I recall a journey rich with emotion. We'd left behind our culture, families, friends and jobs, and had started a venture into the unknown. My stomach was a heady cocktail of fear, excitement, concern, regret even. Some called us foolish, others humorously expressed jealousy.

We have photos of us on the ferry, *en route,* on the brink of this new, defining chapter in our lives. Adrian can be seen gleefully opening a picnic box groaning with sandwiches. His wife Alaine had seemingly packed enough food to satisfy the whole boat. Kirsty, as always, looks calm and serene. I am caught with a vacant stare, pointlessly anxious about everything from whether the car would make it to the South West of France to the well-being of the two cats in the hold. Flo, in a bizarrely prophetic moment, won the ferry's dance competition.

Once we arrived at our first stop - the home of van-owners Jim and Jess in Confelons - they spotted a winner and employed Adrian to renovate their barn. It is said that France is like a disease which, once it's got a grip on you, won't let go. A few years later, Adrian and Alaine bought their own French hideaway in Central France as a direct result of this experience which they are presently restoring as time and life allow.

The years which followed have been challenging, hilarious, frightening and heart-warming. I have changed. I am better and stronger. I believe with a passion that my children have had an amazing start in life. This is what happened. This is what we've learned. This is what I'd like to share with you.

***

The Thirty-Year Journey – The Essential Tips

(1) If you take your children to France for their summer holidays, you may unintentionally change the direction of their lives.

(2) It is prudent to keep comments about your hosts' clothing to yourself.

(3) Canoes have a mind of their own.

(4) French Nuns have a wicked sense of humour.

(5) It's wise practice to keep your cats in their carrier *en route.*

Figure 1 The view from the upper deck of the ferry as we leave the UK for a new life in France.

2. Friend, Foe or *Fonctionnaire?*

Oh the farmer is the man, the farmer is the man
Lives on credit 'til the fall
Then they take him by the hand
And they lead him from the land
And the middle man's the one that gets them all

Traditional - *The Farmer is the Man* (America)

Upon arrival in any new country, an immigrant will face an admin-fest. If like me you have an aversion to bureaucracy, you should take a deep breath, brace yourself, buy several bottles of good Saint Emilion and make some friends who understand the system.

France is renowned as an administrative dinosaur and has a reputation for being archaic and obtrusive. In the majority of civilised countries, relocation procedures have been made more bearable by the online revolution. Frustratingly though, the administrative conveniences offered by the internet have been slow to take off in France. This may be, in part, due to the reluctant demise of *Minitel* which was eventually dragged offstage in 2012, kicking and screaming like a reluctant *Diva* unwilling to accept her relevance is over.

Minitel was an extraordinarily innovative idea for a country in love with old-school practices. Rolled out experimentally in 1978, *Minitel* preceded the internet by around a decade. Using telephone lines, the French recognised they had a huge network which they figured could be employed to do useful things. Users were given - yes, you read correctly - *given* a black and white monitor with a keyboard attached. This meant that everyone from a young techno-savvy high-flyer in Parisian finance to a rural baker in an isolated Breton village could use *Minitel* to... well, initially look up other people's *Minitel* numbers. It was a kind of electronic telephone directory. Soon after though, *les Français* could order train tickets, shop and even check their bank balances.

Sadly though, like the internet, *Minitel* became a hotbed of more questionable activities involving isolated single men and financially-reimbursed ladies employed in call centres. Gentlemen unwisely accepted invitations to disclose in text their innermost fantasies; the ladies on the other end of the line appearing surprisingly receptive of these. As the good menfolk of *la France* were encouraged to reveal more and more of their deepest (and no-doubt questionable) desires, their chat partners watched the francs-per-minute counter rack up the revenue. I can imagine the employees typing a stock of well-tried and worn clichés whilst filing their nails and sharing an *espresso*. The service was text-only so I suspect the scantily-clad models appearing in the publicity posters were otherwise engaged at the moment of contact, and that ladies and gentlemen of all ages, shapes and sizes occupied their clients with their dialogue *de préférence*.

Once the internet took off in the 1990's, *Minitel's* doom had been set in stone. Incredibly though, when we arrived in 2010, I recall being perplexed by the *Minitel* communication option which still adorned the heads of our bills and administrative letters. There was rarely an email address or website. Sadly, I sold the equipment required to access *Minitel* along with my ZX Spectrum in 1985 when I grew out of playing *Chuckie Egg*. In France, *Minitel* was still pushed as a serious option until 2012 before someone decided *'OK, OK, c'est perdu. Zut!'* Incidentally, our wonderful elderly neighbours, of whom you will read much of in later chapters, have never used a PC or the internet, and see little use in doing so.

This resistance to change remains perceptible to the present day. In 2017, I needed to contact CAF *(Caisse d'Allocations Familials*. It's Family Allowance and much more) regarding our family allowance. I found their website (they have one!) and went to my own personal 'space'. We had apparently created an online account sometime in the past and I was required to enter a password which, needless to say, I had forgotten. I clicked on the little *mot de passe oublié* (forgotten password) link and entered my email address. I anticipated, reasonably I believe, that an email would instantly zip into my inbox providing me with the necessary steps to reset it. I found myself laughing out loud when a message popped up reading 'Your password will be sent to you by post within the next twelve days'.

We had a similar experience in 2015. Kirsty had set up an online *Etsy* shop selling her hand-made goods, and wanted to add a second activity to her employment status. This required a degree of interaction with the bureaucratic powers-that-be so, as that kind of task was allocated to me, I was to be found one Tuesday morning bracing myself adjacent to the telephone as I knew 'administration time' loomed. This had the potential to induce much gnashing of teeth and repeated bashing of one's head against the wall.

I needed to contact the *Chambre des Métiers.* Such an activity could go one of two ways: either convivial mutual satisfaction or a telling-off which would make me feel like a naughty schoolboy. These exchanges had the power to plunge me into a deep depression - a state of mind only resolved by sharing a generous lunchtime *aperitif* with André next door.

After a few minutes of being passed around *fonctionnaires*, I spoke to a friendly young gentleman who made a proud announcement.

"But *Monsieur!* Do you know that this is possible to do on the internet now?"

I dropped the phone in astonishment.

"Really!" I replied, having retrieved the handset from under the fridge.

Hoping for a rapid conclusion to this affair so I could get on with doing important things like messing around with my guitar or playing with the goats, I tried my luck.

"I have my computer at my side this very moment. If you have two minutes, perhaps you'd be kind enough to guide me to the correct page?" I cheekily ventured.

"Bien sur!" my new friend replied, who was beginning to take on saint-like status in my mind's eye. *"On y va!"*

He directed me through many pages, during which I found myself making those daft, unnecessary quips one says when waiting for a page to load on a slow computer.

"Sorry, I need to put more coal in it… I think my computer's going on strike, like the rest of your country…"

Monsieur Nice-Guy on the other end obligingly tittered at the appropriate moments which further elevated my highly-favourable view of this magnificent human being. Eventually, we arrived at the correct section of the site and filled in the document together. At the end of the page, I searched for the *envoyer* (send) button when my new-found demi-god buddy on the other end of the line said (and I have friends who think I'm making this up).

"Merci Monsieur Jones. Now all you have to do is print it off and send it in the post."

Many Brits go to France with dreams of simplifying life, setting up a business and being their own boss in the sunshine. Like anything, this is possible where there is a will, but one will find administrative obstacles at every corner. It is this which inspired the legendary alleged utterance of George W Bush.

"The French don't have a word for *entrepreneur.*"

Even the most simple of actions appear to conjure up incomprehensible administrative hoops which must be leapt through. For example, Kirsty had the idea of taking her *Etsy* goods and organic products to markets during the tourist season. This, being *la France* bless her cotton socks, necessitated an application for a *carte ambulante.* The French administration believes that selling anything at a market - from watercolours to tissue-bags; lobsters to lamp-shades - requires a licence. Quite why is anyone's guess.

Once we had settled in the Dordogne, we needed to sort out a *Carte Vitale*. This looks like a credit card but in fact, gives you access to the health-care system so it is quite important. Health-care is managed by a number of different bodies. Which body depends on factors such as where you live and particularly, whether you are employed or self-employed. I never meant it to be this way but I am the *fonctionnaire's* nightmare. I am employed by various sources, have a number of self-employed activities and, just to top it off, have revenue from more than one country. In the UK I would be described as 'having a portfolio career'. Fellow musicians will identify this as 'doing whatever you can to make ends meet'. It was necessary to visit a large, rectangular office in Perigueux, home to URSSAF, (the exotically-entitled *Unions de Recouvrement des Cotisations de Sécurité Sociale et d'Allocations Familiales)* to start the application process for a *Carte Vitale*. I had befriended a piano teacher called Jean-Marie, and he chirpily volunteered to come along with me.

Together, we sped our way into Perigueux. Jean-Marie's appalling driving made me feel sick to the core due to the combination of jerky motions and pure terror; his licence had acquired more points than a second-hand dartboard. Once he'd parked across an old lady's driveway, ignoring hoots of protest with a careless wave of the hand and a Gallic shrug, we marched purposefully into the grey, faceless headquarters of URSSAF. Despite thus far painting you a picture of a bureaucratic nightmare, the observant reader will have noted that one actually *can* go to an office and speak to a human being. There are many things I'd rather be doing with my Thursday morning, but being able to talk to a real-life person in order to rectify an administrative quibble is one element of 1980's-inspired practice I truly cherish in rural France.

We took a ticket and awaited the appearance of our number on the little digital board, installing ourselves in one of those plastic bucket chairs designed to prevent people from settling comfortably. In the ensuing few minutes, I learned a key lesson about handling administration in France: the outcome of your meeting is down to the individual you encounter. This day, we pulled the short straw.

The lady who addressed our queries spent forty-five seconds, speaking like an auctioneer on speed, staring at a fictional spot about thirty metres behind my right shoulder. At the close of her monologue, she pressed her little 'next ticket' button to indicate our time in her presence was over. A little shaken, Jean-Marie and I left the grey box building.

"What did she say?" I asked.

"I haven't a clue," Jean-Marie replied, which was quite something as he had been born and raised in the area.

Later, over a reviving glass of *Pelforth,* we deduced that she had concluded my multiple employment statuses were impossible in France as they failed to conveniently respond to the pre-requisite document 182b, sub-section 17 (or something like that) so I'd better just pack up my bags and hop on to the next *bateau* home. At this point, I was all ready to book the next flight, but Jean-Marie advised me to hold my nerve. Experienced as he was in these situations, he knew it would be, quite simply, a case of trying again on our next day off - and hopefully being interviewed by a different *fonctionnaire.*

There is a breed of *fonctionnaire* wholly unaccepting of anything which fails to fit into a prerequisite set of circumstances. Any sense of flexibility is alien to such a beast. As they are in a position of power and even worse, in control of your healthcare, they make a formidable enemy. I sometimes wonder if their existence has its roots in elements of schooling I've witnessed in France. Within the French education system, there is often a deeply-ingrained sense of 'it's right' or 'it's wrong' with little space to breathe or manoeuvre in between.

When teaching guitar, I had pupils obsessed with the concept of *'j'arrive'.* As you will read in 'Learning the Lingo', *'arriver'* is a verb with many meanings, as well as the English 'to arrive'.

It can translate as: to complete, to win, to satisfy, to meet a requirement and all-importantly, to succeed. As a guitar teacher, I became disturbed by pupils, not yet in high school, repeatedly saying *'je n'arrive pas'*. It derived from the early tagging of everything as 'right' or 'wrong'; 'able' or 'not able'. It drove me so mad, I put up a notice in my room.

Je n'arrive pas – INTERDIT!

I proposed a light-hearted system of parental fines every time it was uttered. It worked. Such a mentality drips through to the world of administration and must be combatted with vigour and industry if one is to advance.

Another phrase which really rattles my cage is *'il faut'*. This translates as 'it is necessary' but in an argument or healthy debate, it carries an all-consuming power to which there is no response. Hearing *'il faut'* is rather like being blackballed by a man in an apron at a masonic meeting; arguing back is futility in the extreme. If a doctor announces that your left leg needs to be amputated when you went to the surgery with a cold, stating *'il faut'* may well be the sole explanation offered for such a radical course of treatment. These two doom-laden and disproportionately-powerful words are wheeled out habitually in administrative interviews. Similar in its linguistic potency is the word *'obligatoire'*, obviously linked to our 'obligatory'. It is stated slowly, syllable by syllable, in order to emphasise its absolute authority - a bit like Craig Revel Horwood on *Strictly Come Dancing* with his catchphrase *'Fa-bu-lous'*. It is nearly as strong as *'il faut'*.

"You have seen my marriage certificate twice, kissed my children and given me a mortgage. Must I really ask a lawyer to sign three copies of my passport in order to receive a bank card?" I might beg the lady behind the counter in our local bank.

"Oui. *Ob-li-ga-toire,"* she'd reply with authority.

"Ouf!" would be my response (this being the French for 'Ouch!')

In an agonising display of old-school sexism, I was granted a bank card months before Kirsty. I have no idea why, especially as she deals with all the finances *Chez Jones.*

So, some weeks later, armed with employment contracts, passports, birth certificates, marriage certificate, next-door neighbour's aunt's shoe size and the like, Jean-Marie and I returned to URSSAF with new-found confidence, dragging a suitcase of documentation behind us. This time, a different *fonctionnaire* greeted us with a warm smile. For starters, she treated me better than one would a rabid dog in an infant's school playground - which is more than I can say for her colleague.

It was upon this *rendezvous* though that I first came to understand the all-encompassing power of possessing an electricity bill. That morning I had been enjoying an altogether more constructive discourse with a different *Madame Admin.*

"So, you have your work contract?" *Madame Admin* asked.

"Oui!" I replied.

"All four passports, copied in triplicate?" she ventured.

"The very same!" I was gaining confidence by the second.

"Signed photos of your children?" tested *Madame Admin.*

"Bien sur! *Il faut!* " (I was getting a little carried away at this point).

"And the electricity bill?" *Madame Admin* enquired.

"Quoi?"

I noticed that even Jean-Marie looked at me quizzically. To bring along the *facture d'electricité* was apparently so blindingly obvious he hadn't bothered to mention it. It would have been a bit like asking whether I'd remembered to put on my underpants.

"The electricity bill, *bien sur Monsieur!* " *Madame Admin* declared with a hint of triumph.

Please don't say *'il faut'* I thought to myself.

"Il f...," *Madame Admin* started victoriously.

"OK, OK, *je comprends!*" I interrupted, fearing I might shove my three proof-of-address documents where the sun doesn't shine if she uttered those two words.

"Ob-li-ga-toire!" Jean-Marie chipped in.

"Oh for crying out loud! Not you as well?!" I yelled in English.

"Quoi?" responded two Francophone voices.

"Oh never mind," I said, but I was desperate to avoid another fruitless journey. "I have a water bill if that's any use?"

Judging by *Madame Admin's* reaction, I might as well have offered her a rotten egg.

"Une facture d'eau! Trés amusant Monsieur Jones!"

I could see that Jean-Marie had covered his eyes in embarrassment.

"Please don't suggest a gas bill," he whispered.

An electricity bill is god-like in its status in the world of administration. Need to open a bank account? Get an electricity bill. Signing up for your local house taxes - the *taxe fonciere* and *taxe d'habitation?* Electricity bill. An electricity contract? Err… electricity bill. When you move to France, stop off at EDF on the way and beg them for an electricity bill. Trade in your wife and children if necessary, or even the very house you are intending to power with the said electricity. It's worth it.

Signing up for electricity presented a fresh realm of challenges. I telephoned EDF's call centre and a young lady, along with a colleague, openly laughed at my efforts to speak the language. I ended the call with no fruits to show for my considerable embarrassment and agitation. I stubbornly refused to call the English-speaking line as I wanted to behave like a seasoned local. Eventually, Jean-Marie helped me out. This time, a different assistant responded and was utterly charming. It's another example of how huge corporations can spend millions on projecting a punter-friendly image but, at the end of the day, it's all about the individual at the other end of the line.

After some weeks, we duly received our *Cartes Vitales*. This was a combined victory and miracle akin to me winning Olympic Gold in Figure Skating. When put into use, we experienced endless technical difficulties which, so it transpired, was due to the computer system having a meltdown because of our multiple-employment statuses. It seems that Kirsty and I were square pegs and the system desperately tried to force us into any available round hole. This sounds deeply frustrating and believe me, my refrigerator door carries multiple indentations due to my habitually bashing my head against it in exasperation. A genuine joy of French administration though is the fact that, for the most part, there will be an office available where you can actually speak to a human being face-to-face in the oft-encountered event of an administrative farce. For rural dwellers, the big government services open satellite branches once or twice a week. You can book an appointment with them online (before printing off the slip and popping it in the post).

Once, I needed to tell URSSAF about a change of job or some such triviality. I had been required to take Florence with me to the nearby satellite branch as Kirsty was otherwise occupied. Having gathered my ticket, I noticed one member of staff was a severe looking lady so I was trying my utmost to avoid her. As I watched the chillingly cold, efficient manner in which she dispatched the victims preceding me, I felt genuine terror in the very depths of my being. Suddenly, she became available. My number was next up so I pretended to have a nosebleed in the hope that somebody else would overtake me, leaving me with a direct line to the kindlier looking person at desk 7B. Unfortunately, when scrambling for another handful of unrequired tissues, I made eye-contact with *Madame Severe* and I was obliged to be served by her. Ob-li-ga-toire.

During that ten metre walk to her desk, I felt physically sick in the anticipation of being patronised, insulted and angered. I was stunned though by the change in persona that overcame her as her eyes drifted towards the nine-year-old girl at my side. She went from being a 1960's headmistress and hospital ward matron combined, to a sentimental, gooey granny in the bat of an eyelid. She, quite simply, couldn't help us enough.

As the interview progressed, we made breath-taking advances.

"My little dancer needs to be kept in good health," I said airily, gilding the lily somewhat.

This had the desired effect. That day, she corrected more administrative tangles for us in half an hour than the entire organisation had done in two years. At the end of our interaction, she gave me her direct line and said that if there was ever the teensiest of problems in the future, we were to contact her at once and she'd sort it out in an instant. Three months later, when applying for help paying our health insurance, I took Sam as well as the second line of attack. She nearly had a meltdown.

France has a reputation for both high taxation and National Insurance contributions. It's true that when we received our first payslips we thought that there had been an error, so lamentable was the figure at the bottom-right of the page. Further investigation revealed it to be quite correct and music teachers were indeed paid less than someone cleaning the public toilets in a park.

My main employment after 2013 involved running all music activities in a school. I got up at 5.45am to catch the train to Bordeaux and returned home at 7.00pm. I carried out all of the musical arrangements (for ages 4-18), made translations, wrote compositions as well as delivering the actual teaching. I enjoyed it but it was exhausting and, at times, stressful. I found myself researching the fact that I could have taken a job sweeping the roads in a nearby small town and earned considerably more. I'd have got up at 8.00am, enjoyed a two-hour lunch break, benefited from a wealth of strike-inducing employment protection rights, and been back home by 5.05pm ready for an evening *aperitif* whilst playing football with Sam, and being butted by my goats. My great friend Stéphane realised this as a young man. Despite being an excellent musician, he made the wise choice to earn himself an HGV licence and now makes his living by rising at 4.00am and driving bin lorries around the local villages with his jovial mates, before returning home for a substantial lunch and lengthy afternoon nap. He then wakes up in the early evening to participate in a number of wholesome and enriching musical activities which keep his soul intact. He enjoys all the employment benefits of the *fonctionnaire,* yet is able to live an active musical life as well.

It is because of this inequality of salary levels that rural areas of France experience a huge number of people carrying-out at least half of their activities 'on the black', that is to say, cash-in-hand and out-of-view of the taxman. This isn't an approval of such behaviour and morally-speaking, it is indefensible but I am routinely offered two prices for various jobs, one 'official' and the other 'in euros'. Such propositions are not made in a seedy or underhand manner; the practice being quite open and relaxed. I believe the threatening tone adopted by so much official correspondence, along with its complexity and the associated stress, contributes greatly towards black-market trading. Administrative letters, emblazoned with the *Tricolore* and the words *Liberté, Egalité, Fraternité,* contain dire warnings as to the consequences of failing to act upon their contents, the confrontational manner being topped off with one of the many ridiculous signing-off paragraphs which adorn every piece of official correspondence. 'I pray to you Sir/Madam the assurance of my distinguished regards' is one example. *Je vous prie de croire, Monsieur/Madame, à l'assurance de mes salutations distinguées.* What's wrong with 'Best wishes'? It's no wonder that people would rather take a grubby handful of used *euro* notes under the table than deal with this intimidating nonsense.

The flip side is that if you earn a pittance, there are extraordinary aids which can be claimed to help out. The French emphasise that the contributions which lighten your pay packet so dramatically each month should be seen as an insurance rather than a tax. Therefore, any families arriving in France must research their rights and claim their due. No-one will hand it to you on a plate. It is up to the household to approach CAF and make an application.

CAF give families an excellent helping hand a couple of weeks before the beginning of each school year. The *allocations de rentrée scolaire* are there to help you buy all the school paraphernalia required: pens, books, rucksacks, clothing, *Pelforth* (the last one is a joke). It is a substantial sum. Also, the splendid French administration believes that everyone who pays their weighty contributions deserves a holiday. *Cheques Vacances* allow you to phone a campsite or hotel from a huge list of scheme partners and enjoy a considerable price reduction. *Bonnes Vacances!*

There are also very impressive grants and interest-free loans available to improve the energy efficiency of your home. Most French houses built in the 20th Century didn't bother with costly extras, such as insulation or double glazing. At the time, huge, nationalised petroleum industries, such as *Total* and *Elf,* sold central heating oil for about one centime per litre. If it got too cold, one just cranked up the heating in the living room to full blast, opened the windows for ventilation and knocked back a *Ricard* wearing a pair of Bermuda shorts, and not much else. How things have changed.

Inconveniences such as global warming have kicked France hard in *les noisettes* and the country is responding admirably. We received a fantastic package to make our house 'greener', but I must admit, the administration required to apply for it nearly drove me over the edge. It took three years of repeated, mundane and pointless paperwork. I had telephone conversations, for example, when I was told that my bank account didn't exist.

"That account does not exist Sir," declared *Monsieur LeGrant. Ce compte n'existe pas.*

"But *Monsieur,* it *really, really* does," I'd implore.

"Try phoning again next week," he'd propose, for reasons unclear to me.

"But must I…. really," I'd plead, now openly sobbing.

"Oui, *ob-li-ga-toire!"*

"Nooooo!"

You must understand that these calls were made during working hours, so often took place in the school playground when I was on supervision duty. Following yet another pointless exchange with a *robo-fonctionnaire,* pupils witnessed the spectacle of me throwing my mobile phone in fury across the astroturf, passing through a window and breaking a gas tap in the science lab. I had to constantly renew quotes as they expired three months after being sent to me. The businesses employed to do the work started recognising my phone number but were immune to the ludicrous nature of it all. They seemed quite used to it and we ended up on first-name terms.

"Bonjour Dan," they would say. "You need another quote for your loft insulation? That's *numero dix-sept* I think. *Très bien, pas de problème.*"

Before we switched to heating with eco-friendly and renewable wood, our house relied on heating oil for both the radiators and hot water. The big companies would only deliver fuel if one ordered hundreds of euros worth at a time. This being impossible, I ended up driving each week to a diesel station with twenty-litre containers, filling up with financially-manageable amounts. This would have to be transferred to our oil tank via a siphon tube. I'd stand in our garden, come rain or shine, sucking my top-up of oil into the submerged tank, often enjoying a mouthful of diesel as a *digestif* to my evening meal.

A further administrative decision you will be required to make is whether to bring your car with you from the UK. There are pros and cons to this. A pro is that it appears to be considerably cheaper to buy a second-hand car in the UK than in France. The con is that there are weird and wonderful expenses attached to importing a motor vehicle.

In 2011, Kirsty decided to see if our Vauxhall Astra could smash a garden fence after driving through a ditch at 50mph. The conclusion was that it could. We were in pretty serious financial *merde* at that moment so her timing for such an experiment was questionable. Thankfully, my ever-generous In-laws gifted us their Vauxhall Vectra. I flew to the UK to collect it and proudly drove it back. We then needed to undergo the process of registering it.

Firstly, there was a 'certificate of conformity'. This is a document which confirms that a Vauxhall Vectra is, in fact, a Vauxhall Vectra. I phoned Vauxhall and requested the paperwork to which a kindly gentleman replied that there would be no problem. He then asked for £170. That was the most expensive piece of A4 paper I have ever purchased.

Next, I needed to ask for a document from the tax office. I have no idea what it was and didn't care. I just needed a form 2&BHZ in triplicate or something like that. Happily, in rural areas, you can just walk into a tax office and talk to real-life people (like you can with URSSAF). I can't abide those telephone systems which ask you loads of questions, none of which apply to you, and charge you for the privilege. In contrast, I saw a pleasant *Monsieur* in Ribérac tax office immediately. He took my paperwork and inspected it thoroughly.

"That is all in order *Monsieur Jones.* I just need a purchase receipt," he said.

"Ummm. I don't have one. The car was given to me by family," I replied tentatively.

"Mais Monsieur. Il faut."

I think something in my face suggested an impending nervous breakdown or maybe an act of extreme violence. *Monsieur Taxman* then did something I've never seen in an administrative office since.

"Mr Jones, here is a piece of paper and a pen. I am going to go away for one minute and when I return, you will have a purchase receipt."

I stood with my mouth hanging open in miscomprehension, like Dopey in *Snow White,* but then a sense of understanding dawned over me. I took the pen and created a fake receipt. I recall that, according to my document, 'Mickey Mouse' sold me the car.

"Excellent, that all appears to be in order," *Monsieur Taxman* said.

Casually pushing back my efforts to kiss him full on the lips, he gave me the piece of paper I had come for. My dossier, including the fraudulent receipt, made its way to a drawer and is probably now sitting in a Ribérac basement in a box marked 'destroy in 2082'.

You will also be required to line the pockets of the local *préfecture* - the amount to be handed over depending on the size and age of the car. I should note that there are companies online who offer to do all the paperwork for this part of the transaction for you - at a price of course. I decided to go for this when buying another car some years later. Once completed, I realised that all I had done was to complete exactly the same submission for the third-party company as I would have for the *préfecture.* It was a bit of a waste of money really.

My advice to potential purchasers would be to take every piece of documentation you own (not just that relating to vehicles) to your village *mairie* and go through it at a desk with a real person. *Definitely* photocopy your electricity bill. Many Brits fail to recognise that their *maire* is an elected person and will consequently fall over themselves to be of assistance, unless he/she represents the *Front National,* in which case you'd be wise to change your village of residence.

You will require a *controle technique* (MOT) which is only necessary every two years in France, and with older cars, you'll have to change the headlights and their casing. A tip: the originals are five times more expensive than imitations you buy on popular auction websites which work fine. Alternatively, I have friends who go to Spain to buy second-hand cars. They are apparently cheaper than in France and the headlights are already dealt with. French car insurance is pretty similar to that in the UK. The only notable differences are that the car tends to be insured rather than the driver(s) so, in most cases, friends and family can take the wheel when they come to visit, and breakdown cover is standard with the majority of policies.

Returning to the health-care jigsaw, the final piece required is a *Mutuelle* or 'top-up' health insurance. If you are unwell, the state will pay 80% of the associated medical costs. Your *Mutuelle* covers the rest, although critical illness is covered. You won't be left to die. When visiting a doctor in France, you will be required to hand over your *Carte Vitale* at the end of the appointment. This is swiftly followed by your bank card to pay for the visit. You will receive the partial reimbursement a few days later.

Mutuelle policies have been handed over to the free market and, predictably, there are masses to choose from. When, eventually, we were able to afford a *Mutuelle,* we were baffled by the claims of the various companies. Oft-seen statements will read along the lines of: 'Dental care, 200% reimbursement'. This is positively weird as it implies, in my eyes, that you can actually make a profit by having bad teeth. Imagine the advert: *'Your new denture may have cost 100€ but, as you have a policy with Super-Health, here's 200€ back!'* If this were the case, musicians all over France would be asking people to punch them in the mouth in order to earn a few quid. Having your wisdom teeth removed would be like winning the lottery.

Sadly, the reality is different. Basically, the state suggests an amount that a treatment *should* cost. A denture, for example, may have a theoretical cost of 100€. The reality is that it will always be much more. Spectacles are another example of where this happens. If the powers-that-be decide that my new glasses should cost 100€ but they, in fact, cost 500€, I'd need a policy with a 500% reimbursement in the 'glasses' section to make ends meet.

Therefore, choosing a *Mutuelle* can be as tedious as having teeth pulled out by a horse vet with no anaesthetic (maybe that would be a better solution). When I went to choose ours, I listened to the competent lady from the company for about five minutes before starting to daydream about important things such as whether adding garden peaches to my homebrew would be an interesting experiment, or pulling off a blistering guitar solo on stage during the following weekend's gig. I had been wearing a benign glassy look with a slightly insane half grin for some time when I noticed that there was a silence in the room. Her eyes were on me. This indicated that it was necessary for me to respond to a grown-up proposition.

"D'accord!" I said brightly.

This fooled no-one as I had been required to choose between one of three options offered to me by *Madame Mutuelle*. In the end, I decided that honesty was the best policy so I placed my hands on the table in an 'I'm-going-to-leave-the-room-in-the-very-near-future' gesture and proceeded to make a speech.

"Look, I understand that life has expenses. I imagine that if the children need braces or glasses, I'll have to pay. I would like to avoid nasty shocks in the form of enormous, unpredictable and unmanageable bills. Please, can you give me a policy that will do this? Let us terminate this discussion now, as I would rather place my own testicles into a coffee grinder than listen to any more *mutuelle* talk."

I didn't actually say the last sentence. I just thought it. As if reading my mind (hopefully not...) *Madame Mutuelle* responded.

"Tout à fait Monsieur!"

Minutes later we had a reasonable and affordable policy in place which did pretty much what we asked for. Years later, Sam needed glasses and Flo, braces. These blows hurt, but we were able to stand up on wobbly knees once the bills had been settled.

Paradoxically, whereas the French administration system can offer some ideas which make you want to unleash racking sobs of disbelief, it musters up others which can seem almost too good to be true. Many French *artistes,* including musicians and actors, benefit from a unique and extraordinary employment status known as being an *intermittent de spectacle.* In French, a *spectacle* means 'a performance' rather than the Anglophone sense of 'making a spectacle of oneself' although, in my experience, the two often go hand-in-hand.

The French *adore* a *spectacle.* Some of my more surreal teenage-French-holiday memories are those of *Son et Lumière* shows – reputedly the ultimate in *spectacles*. These were originally the brainchild of Paul Robert-Houdin, the one-time curator of the *Château de Chambord* in *la Vallée de la Loire.*

My father took my brother and me to see one such *spectacle* at a *château* (regrettably, I forget which one) during our camping trip in the Loire Valley. The event was, admirably, free. I recall sitting on the grass on a beautiful July evening as a crowd of thousands gathered. We, as one, admired the construction in front of us which was pleasantly illuminated to show off its Baroque curves and ornamentation. Suddenly, the serenity of the evening was gate-crashed by an explosion of 1980's *Europop* which came blasting through a PA system that appeared to have been dragged out of a local bingo hall. Any listener unfortunate enough to aurally experience 1980's French *Europop* will surely, like me, muse over the incomprehensible mystery of how a country capable of producing Debussy's *Préludes pour Piano,* Satie's *Gnoissiennes,* Ravel's Piano Concerto in G, and Messiaen's *Quator pour le Fin du Temps* can, in the same century, be the creator of a style of music that sounds like the fruits of a kindergarten class with a collection of Casio keyboards and a very camp teacher.

The *château* then underwent illumination with a series of wildly-oscillating spotlights of vibrant colour-choices which I suspect gave an accurate insight into the effects of heavy LSD misuse. The *spectacle* was fine but, like a Radio 4 poetry programme, intrigued for five minutes, yet thereafter became incomprehensible. One's attention was retained because of the apparent profundity of the performance and therefore we felt somewhat obliged to enjoy it. The programme alleged that the event told a story of some kind – probably involving a particularly deep and provocative piece of local history. To me, it looked as if the after-show party of Eurovision 1982 had been time-transported to the court of Louis XIV.

The *intermittent de spectacle* status is designed to avoid the 'boom-or-bust' lifestyle endured by those in artistic professions. In my own performing career, I may play around twenty gigs in July and August but probably none in January and February. An individual whose revenue is primarily driven by performance can become an *intermittent de spectacle* to earn a modest, yet consistent, income. It works like this: once a performer has played a gig, he/she receives about half of their fee, the other half being retained by the French employment service, *Pole Emploi.* If the performer completes forty-two of these events (known as a *cachet*) within one calendar year, he/she receives a monthly salary from the state the following year.

Many well-meaning musicians working as *Intermittents de Spectacle (IdS)* will do almost anything to play a gig with a *cachet*. Performers will also ask small businesses to create 'phantom' gigs where businesses state that they hired the *artiste* (when they haven't) and complete a declaration to process monies originally received cash-in-hand. This is, technically speaking, illegal, but it's tax fraud in reverse. The musician is actually looking for a way *to pay* the state rather than to conceal the income.

Similar schemes include workers under the title of *Saisonniers* or 'Seasonal Workers'. Maybe you like the sound of opening a pizza shack on the beaches of Arcachon. You would probably work 18-hour days for three months between mid-June and mid-September and declare these hours in a similar manner to the *IdS*. You'd be assured of a basic stable income rather than a boom-and-bust lifestyle.

***

Friend, Foe or *Fonctionnaire* – The Essential Tips

(1) Technology is met with fear and suspicion. Expect to send documents by carrier pigeon, smoke signals or drum-beating.

(2) A visit to an administration office may cause a trauma which will scar you for life. Make notes after the event so that you will have sufficient information for your therapist.

(3) Don't even try to argue with a *fonctionnaire* who says *'il faut'*. It's a non-starter.

(4) An electricity bill is a document which carries a status equal to a passport. If you do not have one, you do not exist.

(5) If you live and work in France, make sure you know your rights. The Family Allowance office (CAF) and your healthcare provider (varies by region) have all sorts of schemes to help you out. It's your right as the money is taken from your wage packet before you ever touch it. See it as a kind of financial merry-go-round which gives *fonctionnaires* jobs.

(6) Take children with you to an administrative meeting. Steal some if necessary. Dress them in cute clothing and make them give your interviewer a little flower or a box of chocolates.

(7) Importing a car is expensive and a bore. Budget the lion's share of £1000. It still may be cheaper than buying a car in France.

(8) A *Mutuelle* is important. Speak to friends. Think of it as buying car insurance in the UK; if you pay more, you have the right to a taxi to take you hospital as one would have a courtesy car in the event of a bump in your vehicle. If that interests you, then you'll *love* shopping for a *Mutuelle*.

(9) If it all gets too much, there are many individuals working in France helping out Anglophones trying to enter the system. Also, there is an abundance of internet forums where others who have lived the same experience will be only too willing to help you.

3. Finding Our Place

Connais-tu le pays où fleurit l'oranger?
Le pays des fruits d'or et des roses vermeilles,
Où la brise est plus douce et l'oiseau plus léger,
Où dans toute saison butinent les abeilles,
Où rayonne et sourit, comme un bienfait de Dieu,
Un éternel printemps sous un ciel toujours bleu!

Do you know the country where the orange flowers bloom?
The land of golden fruit and crimson roses,
Where the breeze is fresh and the birds fly in the light,
Where in any season bees are seen foraging,
Where radiant smiles are a blessing from God,
An eternal spring under a deep blue sky!

Thomas, Barbier & Carré – *Mignon's Aria* (19th-Century, France)

Upon arrival in France, we rented a house near the small town of Tocane-Saint-Apre in the Périgord Vert on the basis of the small amount of employment I had secured nearby. The owner was a gentle, kind and dignified lady of advancing years. She lived with her son who was about my age, unmarried, and showed no signs of producing offspring any time soon. I think we unwittingly took on the role of a surrogate family, Sam and Flo acting as replacement grandchildren. The house had been loving bedecked with soft pastels; home-made flower-themed artistic adornments, in a variety of media, were present on every available surface. The children's bedroom had also been freshly decorated, clearly with infantile preferences in mind. These were very generous gestures but we only intended to rent short-term so the effort, although appreciated, seemed rather excessive. Nests of *mésanges* (blue tits) were present in every bush and starlings would swoop down from the roof eaves, past the windows of our wonderstruck daughter's bedroom. It was a splendid welcome to the ambience of the French countryside.

A small music school had been set up in the picture-postcard village of *Montagrier* and I worked in a teaching room adjacent to a restaurant. To access it, I entered a courtyard covered with vines which had been grown horizontally over a wire trestle. In the summer, these provided abundant shade for diners, deep-purple grapes bursting with sweet juice dangling tantalisingly over their heads, as if to celebrate the months of abundance. I reached my little studio via a few weathered (and lethal) stone steps. It had a *Périgordine* peaked, red-tiled roof, beautifully discoloured by time. During my breaks, I regularly popped into the restaurant to enjoy a coffee while chatting with the friendly owners. After some evenings of teaching, I would stay on and play to diners under the grapes and snatches of twinkling stars to promote my CDs, and for the sheer joy of it. As I picked out the notes of the music I love in the fading light, I'd reflect on change from the daily routine of my former life when I'd weave my way home through thousands of commuters on a 125cc scooter, in the rain.

Having rented for over two years, we eventually found ourselves in a position to purchase a house in the village of Saint Cecilia des Dames. We had arrived with dreams of slashing our mortgage by about two thirds, but the recession in the property market soon put an end to that. The house which we eventually bought might not have been our first choice, but it was the only habitable lodging in our chosen village within budget.

We were blown away by the kindness and understanding demonstrated to us by the vendors. They desperately wanted a family with children to occupy the house and to breathe fresh life into the village. Despite having received many cash offers, some of which proposed more money than we could put up, the couple selling on behalf of their deceased parents held out until we were in a position to buy. I often wonder if I would take a serious financial hit for the benefit of my village.

In later years I witnessed this concern for community well-being daily. *La Boulangerie* would ring to the sounds of hearty *'Bonjours'* and pleasant chat as villagers happily purchased bread which was more than three times more expensive than the supermarket equivalent. Admittedly the quality was incomparable, but locals took a hit in the pocket to keep their baker in business. In a similar vein, there was great discontent when one shop proposed increasing its range of activities which would place it in direct competition with the much-valued bar. A chance to do some 'cherry picking' had been identified by the scheming owner of the establishment in question as during the summer months, foot traffic increases ten-times over. The devious plan was to sell drinks to tourists during the peak periods, but not to bother in January or February when it was just the locals who were thirsty. The bar operated on a shoestring and needed the summer trade to get through the lean winter months. The shop posing the threat received a barrage of vocal objections and eventually, backed down. People move to the countryside to live a certain lifestyle and will be very pro-active in preservsing this.

We said *au revoir* to the UK with our house sale a week away from completion. We had offered tremendous goodwill to the buyer and gave unrestrained access for her to take measurements and plan decorative schemes. Just after we'd arrived in France though, our estate agent informed us the buyer had decided to purchase elsewhere. It transpired she had been entering a number of homes, measuring to her heart's delight, discussing colour choices and sipping the vendors' tea with little or no sense of the moral conflict these actions suggest to my mind at least. To put it gently, she had acted entirely legally but thrown us deep into the *merde.*

In France, there is a house-purchasing system which I find entirely sensible and ethical. If you state that you intend to purchase a house, you have to hand over 10% of the asking price there and then. A *compromis de vente* is signed and the purchaser has ten days during which he or she can pull out with no consequence. If the deal is cancelled by the potential purchaser after this time, they lose the 10% which goes to the vendor for their troubles. That way, people only tend to say that they intend to buy if they really mean it.

Obtaining a mortgage was comparable to the process we experienced in South Wales; an unwelcome similarity being the difficulties we, as artists with incomes from several irregular sources, encountered when asking major banks to lend us sufficient capital to purchase a home.

After several unsuccessful applications, we were allocated a very pleasant, smiling and reassuringly-efficient lady by our regular bank to negotiate a mortgage with us. She seemed genuinely passionate about securing us a loan, partly because her daughter danced at the same ballet school as Flo. I'm certain had we arrived six months earlier, *Madame LaBanque* would have granted the loan 'on a hunch', skating over our fiscally-irregular lifestyle and acting on the basis of good old-fashioned gut feeling. Frustratingly though, French banks had just decided to follow the system employed by the rest of the civilised world some twenty years previously, and run applications through a computer-based credit-scoring system.

Kirsty, Flo, Sam and I attended the mortgage appointment as a family - maybe I was subliminally employing the technique with which I'd enjoyed so much success when sorting out our *Carte Vitales*. As *Madame LaBanque* was completing our application, she'd occasionally wince, or utter *'Oh là là!'* at our responses to questions such as the length of time in our current employment and the nature of our contracts.

"I think we're going to be homeless forever," I muttered to Kirsty, my morale wilting, as *Madame LaBanque* failed to conceal a mumbled *'Zut Alors!'* at my submitted response to the 'current salary' question. Our ally though had a heart of gold and will of steel; I'm sure she typed in a few figures which somewhat distorted the truth to our advantage, bless her.

The use of an actual real-life computer, with electricity and all, caused her considerable difficulty and agitation. The children had done really well in the office, but as the clock ticked by indicating that we'd been form-filling for forty-five minutes, they understandably became bored. My own mental attention had switched to modal improvisation after fifteen minutes for heaven's sake. A technological spanner was being thrown into the works by the fact that *Madame LaBanque* repeatedly deleted information she'd entered by using the 'previous screen' arrow without saving the original page first. Eventually, she called upon a senior colleague to help her out. *Monsieur LeBoss*, entered the office with a warm handshake and genial manner, but he seemed more accustomed to writing with a feather and quill than *Microsoft Office.* After a further five minutes, exactly the same issues arose once again.

"N'importe quoi! Where on earth has his employment history gone?!" yelled an exasperated *Monsieur LeBoss* as he pushed the dreaded 'next page' button in a hasty and speculative fashion, his actions based more on sheer hope rather than technological know-how.

As *Madame LaBanque* sat back in her chair with a smug 'told you so' expression, *la Famille Jones* collectively inched our wheelie office chairs up to the screen to offer the hapless pair an impromptu lesson in using the *'enregistrer'* (save) button in the most diplomatic manner possible. I took the opportunity to surreptitiously pop an extra zero onto the end of the figure in the 'applicant's salary' box. Things were going swimmingly at this point until an unwelcome guest gatecrashed the party.

"Praaaappp!" our toddler son vocalised anally - responding admirably to a boisterous yet indiscreet call of nature.

This opening bugle call-to-action was followed by strained expressions of intense concentration, all-too-familiar to parents of young offspring in public places. The pace of the interview quickened considerably thereafter. With six people in a small, windowless office, the atmosphere rapidly became conducive to getting the heck out of there as soon as possible.

I shouldn't have been surprised by these events, given my short experience of banking practices in the Dordogne. I was once given a cheque for a gig and attempted to pay it in at a branch of our own bank about one hour's drive away from *Chez Jones*. I handed it over to the cashier whose face soon adopted a startled expression.

"You'd like to pay in this cheque," she asked.

"Um, yes," I replied, surprised that, given the presence of a cheque and paying-in slip, further expansion upon the theme was necessary.

"Hold on a moment if you please," she replied while spinning her stool and ambling off into the bowels of the bank.

Some minutes later, I could see that at least half of the bank's staff had congregated over the two innocuous documents. I overheard snatches of their conversation.

"Pay it in, here!"

"It's impossible!"

"That's nearly fifty kilometres away!"

"Anglais?"

These were accompanied by smirks, chuckles and the odd tut. Eventually, a man in a suit, who could well have been a regional director, came over to the counter where a long queue had gathered behind me. He offered, as a one-off gesture of goodwill, to send my cheque to my own branch by post.

We had discovered the little village of Saint Cecilia des Dames soon after our arrival in France. Having originally rented about thirty kilometres away, my friend, Jean-Marie, had heard of an opening for both a piano and guitar teacher in the village's music school. On the same day, we tore through the forest in his little white van – the vehicle actually leaving the ground a handful of times due to the irregular road surface – to attend an informal interview. I remember mounting a dingy, crumbling flight of stairs which, unbeknownst to me at the time, would be the entrance to my office for the next seven years. Upon entering the interview room, a group of friendly faces greeted us with an *aperitif* and a smile. The president of the school looked at me, grinning ear-to-ear, and yelled triumphantly.

"Ah yes, it's him!" much to the noisy amusement of all present. *Ah oui, c'est lui!*

I had no idea as to the source of the joke but, to my surprise, he lifted up my CV and references which, inexplicably, he already had on his person. Then, after a little reflection, I remembered a day which had passed some months previously.

Having secured a small amount of employment online, *la Famille Jones* had made a job-seeking trip to the area in an attempt to augment my work portfolio. I had prepared a mountain of CVs and references, in French, and I somehow found a list of every music school in the Périgord. We spent days meandering our way around sleepy, picturesque villages, tracking down doorways of modest music schools, and popping CVs through letterboxes.

One mid-afternoon, we'd stopped at a bar for refreshment which was, unbeknownst to us, only 500 metres from the house which would be our home more than two years later.

"Where on earth *is* the music school in this place?" I asked of no-one in particular for the fourteenth time that day.

A retired British couple at the next table overheard my exasperated ramblings and kindly gave us sketchy directions to the president's home.

"Go over the bridge and you'll pass a line of trees. After fifty yards you'll see some bins. Next to this is an iron cross. Ignore Pierre's house and look for the one with blue shutters. There are usually chickens in his driveway."

Over the last seven years, I've skidded around muddy tracks looking for homes tucked away in forests or hamlets, guided by directions such as 'turn right at the oak tree' only to find myself driving through several kilometres of woodland. Homes nearly always have no house number (although there are moves being made to change this) and are identified by a gorse bush in the back garden or some similarly undistinguishing feature.

Undeterred, I left my family at the bar and zipped off on a quest to find the dwelling in question. Having become completely lost, I saw a guy coming out of a house and drawing on my O-level French from several decades previously, asked him directions.

"Bonjour monsieur, je m'appelle Dan. J'aime les guitares. Où est le président de l'école de musique s'il vous plaît?" I uttered, parrot-fashion, in partially-memorised phrases.

By a miracle of coincidence, it was the man himself. I tried my utmost to explain our situation but, due to my linguistic limitations, failed to clarify my intent. He looked a little nervous as if he believed I might be a hitman employed by someone who just couldn't master their scales on the piano. I handed him my CV and drove off feeling like a complete moron.

Bearing in mind that I had handed out hundreds of CVs, this encounter had slipped my mind, but for *Monsieur le Président* (now a dear friend, Michel)*,* it had been memorable, scary even. Therefore, when he heard a candidate coming to interview for the vacant guitar teacher post was a newcomer from Wales, he'd correctly put two and two together. I was impressed that he had kept the documents as most people would have put them to good use as a fire lighter. Maybe he was retaining them as potential police evidence should his house have been burned down at night.

We purchased our home in early autumn, 2012. The vendors had such confidence in us that they allowed us to access their garage to store our furniture, before completion. I made repeated trips to and from the barn where we were keeping our affairs, carrying van-loads of all the things which had, once upon a time, seemed so crucial, but which we'd managed without for two years. It was after one of these trips, on a beautiful summer's day, that we first met our future neighbours, André and Eliane. As we spoke over the fence, I could sense the warmth and goodness that radiated from these people. André was in his mid-80s and still as strong as an ox. He spent most of every day working in his garden, seemingly on a one-man mission to provide the entire community with their five-a-day. Immediately, we hit it off. I could see that Eliane particularly adored being around youngsters. After one delivery, André came over to the fence and, having exchanged the everyday pleasantries of life, spoke, looking me in the eye.

"Venez vite."

Which simply translates as 'come quickly' or 'hurry up'.

When purchasing a house in France, you are legally required to have certain tests carried out. These will be for electrical safety, the presence of asbestos, termites and sanitation amongst other things. The irony is that a structural survey - an absolute must in the UK - is never done as part of the process. The test results will serve as a warning to the potential purchaser as they will often be obliged to rectify certain highlighted problems. Upon glancing through our *diagnostiques* report, I noted the section dedicated to our septic tank was littered with red crosses, reminding me in an untimely and unwelcome fashion of both our delicate financial situation and my second-year Chemistry exam from the 1980's.

Septic tank technology has made great strides in recent decades. Today's tanks have ingenious biological and filtration systems which allow the majority of the unpleasant by-products to be released harmlessly into the garden. In direct contrast to this, the tank installed in our home was based firmly on 1960's technology. It was a concrete cube capable of holding four thousand litres of untreated foul waste underground, just outside our back door, and that was it. On a hot day, we were all-too-aware of its presence.

Our toilet used an essentially dry system. Without wishing to go into too much detail, the user's contribution would be initially stored on a tray. Upon flushing, the combination of a small jet of water, the kind of thing normally associated with Feng Shui *objets d'art,* and a trapdoor sent the offending materials at least partially out of sight, if not scent and mind. After a couple of days in our new home, Mrs Jones issued an ultimatum.

"We are replacing the toilet," she stated factually.

"But dear, it's really not so bad. It's like living in the wild. Did we not come here for the rustic life? It's like being on Ben Fogle!" I chanced ambitiously.

As if having temporarily lost her hearing, she reiterated the same ultimatum.

"We are replacing the toilet," this time with a marked increase in the level of assertiveness in her voice.

Hmm. I could see this conversation was getting us nowhere. I tried a fresh angle.

"But toilets are so *expensive!* Surely such an investment can wait a few years? It's just a question of getting used to it."

"We are replacing the toilet," stated my lovely spouse with a look in her eyes which told me that further interaction would be fruitless.

I know when I am a beaten man so, a few days later, a shiny, new modern WC took pride-of-place in the Smallest Room. This evacuated the usual several litres of water each flush, rather than relying upon a system which had all the efficacy of a leaky water pistol.

This approach contributed to an altogether more pleasing ambiance *Chez Jones,* but the down-side was that the septic tank filled up quickly. *Really* quickly. The first time I learned it was full, I was greeted with a sizeable backwash following an early-morning flush. A begging phone call to the local evacuation service thankfully led to the arrival of a huge lorry, kitted out with a maze of hoses and pumps, to relieve our system of its disagreeable contents - and our wallets of 10% of our monthly salary. Soon, the reality sunk in that the tank required emptying every two or three months, whereas a modern system is emptied about every five years.

When we had family and friends visiting in the summer, we would accommodate twelve people or more and consequently, the tank would fill at an alarming rate of knots. After a while, the guy who emptied tanks for his living, *Monsieur Bogevac*, became a friend. A broad and tall bloke, he was perpetually stressed with life. I'd have thought his primary complaint with his chosen career pathway would have been the extraordinary stench which accompanied his working days, but as he sipped an *espresso* whilst we completed the inevitable mountain of paperwork following each 'job', he would moan endlessly about his field of employment.

"Zut alors! The *préfecture,* is killing me with this paperwork! The truck needs new tyres… *500 euros apiece!* I can't claim that against *les impôts!* Profit margins barely allow us to eat! *Sacre bleu!"*

I did my utmost to utter appropriately-sympathetic words, simultaneously attempting to surreptitiously pinch my nose as I breathed in his presence before he'd eventually rise claiming to have to evacuate another twenty-seven tanks before clocking-off at midnight, if he was lucky. I only hope he fitted a shower into his schedule before slipping into bed with his beloved.

The plumbing system linking our loo to the tank was a rudimentary affair. The installation commenced with the loo itself, followed by three metres of piping and terminating with a drop of varying distance into the tank according to its fill-level. Forgive me if this is disgusting but, as time passed, I learned to tell how full the tank was by the tone of the splash having pulled the flush. I am a musician after all. With this simplicity, one would have anticipated a problem-free system. *Au contraire,* as the pipe linking loo to tank was too small for the task in hand, blockages became one of the regular challenges of life. This appeared to be a consistent design-fault in the village's dwellings, as the majority of my neighbours owned dyno-rods which I borrowed frequently. Clearing a pipe blockage initiated fervent discussion with neighbour André. On one particularly troublesome morning, I approached the garden fence frustrated, dripping wet and stinking like a sewage plant.

"Try adding several litres of boiling water, heavily laden with washing-up liquid, and then give a further hearty flush," advised André, simultaneously ducking to avoid the three-metre length of dyno-rod waving about erratically in my right hand.

Trusting of André, yet deeply reluctant to add more liquid to the already overflowing bowl, I evacuated the house and prepared myself both physically and psychologically to undergo the procedure. I half-considered donning face mask, snorkel and flippers - just in case - but eventually, with my family spectating from the safety of the vegetable patch some seventy metres away, I applied the soapy potion. I held my nose, uttered a prayer and, seriously doubting the wisdom of my actions, pulled the chain. I felt like doing a military salute, like a captain at the helm of a sinking ship but, against all the odds, it worked beautifully. Never did I think that the sound of raw sewage crashing three metres into a pit could be so beautiful. I ran into the garden whooping, and André felt it necessary to open a bottle to celebrate the occasion.

My biggest septic tank nightmare occurred following a period of particularly heavy traffic due to visitor numbers and a virulent gastric illness. I had arisen at sunrise to beat the early-morning loo rush, only to be confronted by the awful moment when, upon flushing, the water level in the bowl filled at a terrifying rate, swirling like a menacing (and particularly disagreeable) whirlpool, threatening to spill over onto the floor and my bare feet. I had taken my eye off the septic-tank ball and it had filled to bursting point. Flustered, I opened the loo door only to find my visiting Great-Aunt, resplendent in dressing gown and curlers, awaiting her turn to use the smallest room. What followed was certainly one of the most uncomfortable conversations of my life when I had to inform her that the facilities were out of order until *Mr Bogevac* was available to 'pay us a visit', to use an appropriate terminology.

"Errr... there is a little public loo in the village square where I could drive you," I offered, attempting to make a distinctly unappealing prospect sound like a pleasant holiday adventure – a kind of 'roughing it' safari experience.

Left with few remaining realistic options, we jumped into my little Renault Clio and I taxied her to the local facilities. It was a chilly morning and the Clio's heating had given up the ghost years before, only contributing to a frosty atmosphere, in more than one sense.

In 2016, our village wisely invested in a new mains drainage plant. We signed to be linked up, and a couple of weeks later, our relentless *fosse septique* challenges had been consigned to the vaults of history. In the ensuing weeks, I wasted a disproportionate amount of time, and water, flushing with freedom as a leisure activity rather than a necessity, marvelling at the sheer sophistication of it all. Our financial investment was returned within eighteen months at the expense of *Mr Bogevac*. The peace-of-mind which it brought was priceless.

Like so many homes purchased in the French countryside, a huge parcel of land came with the house which was rampant with years of unrestrained over-growth. Within days of having moved in, I glanced out of the window to see neighbours on our land commencing the clearing process on our behalf. It was a colossal task. We eventually found methods for the long-term management of our land which are discussed later, but the initial process was a question of applying sheer hard labour. We uncovered out-buildings, sheds, tools, building materials, net-covered birdhouses, multi-layered rabbit cages and much, much more. Our work was overseen by the ever-gracious and kindly André.

"You have a monstrous job to do!" he would declare with a chuckle. *Vous avez un travail monstre!*

One afternoon, after two or three months of labour, he called me to his fence and thanked me.

"This is the first time I've been able to see the church from my garden in ten years," André said.

I felt heartened and content.

***

Finding Our Place – The Essential Tips

(1) Villagers care about your contribution to the community. Repay their confidence in you.

(2) If you put in an offer on a house without really meaning it, you might find a €10,000 bill popping through your letterbox eight days later. Rightly so in my opinion.

(3) When completing a mortgage application, your bank manager will use Windows XP and require your assistance in saving a document.

(4) House numbers are an alien concept in rural France. Plant a vividly-coloured bush at the end of your driveway so that visitors, postal workers, delivery drivers, friends, and potential employees can easily track you down.

(5) Your *diagnostiques* are important. *Really* important. They flag up defects which you are legally obliged to rectify. Your *mairie* will give you a timescale within which you must act.

(6) When purchasing a house, you may find you unwittingly become a substantial landowner simultaneously.

(7) The necessity of land management means that you grow stronger, meet neighbours, share tools, exchange vegetables, make bonds and drink *aperitifs* with those who surround you.

Figure 2 My first 'office' where I taught guitar for several years.

4. Learning the Lingo

*Gros gras grand grain d'orge, tout gros-gras-grand-grain-
d'orgerisé, quand te dé-gros-gras-grand-grain-d'orgeriseras-
tu? Je me dé-gros-gras-grand-grain-d'orgeriserai quand tous
les gros gras grands grains d'orge se seront dé-gros-gras-
grand-grain-d'orgerisés.*

Big fat barley grain, all big fat tall barley grain that you are,
when will you un-big fat tall barley grain yourself? I shall un-
big fat tall barley grain myself when all of the other big fat tall
barley grains have un-big fat tall barley grain themselves.

Traditional French Tongue-Twister

Many of us are entranced by TV programmes which follow
couples considering emigration to European countries.
Predictably, rural areas of France feature heavily. The couples in
question are often shown ambling self-consciously into their
local *boulangerie* and requesting *'Une baguette s'il vous plaît'* in
an accent owing more to Doncaster than the Dordogne, before
walking away from the establishment with their prize.

The reality is that they should've called *'Bonjour Mesdames,
Messieurs'* the moment they entered the shop and, following their
request, the *boulanger* would have given a series of responses.

"Good morning! Traditional? Well-cooked? A bread?
Sarmentine?" and a wealth of further variations upon a
seemingly simple theme. *Bonjour! Tradition? Bien-cuit? Un
pain? Sarmentine?*

'A bread' suggests a thicker loaf and a *'sarmentine'* is a pair of
thin baguettes entwined like the stems of climbing plants. The
French word *'baguette'* actually means 'stick' rather than bread.

A drummer plays his/her kit with *'baguettes'*. The result of this bakery linguistic labyrinth is that many Brits quite understandably panic, run out of the establishment leaving their *baguette* wobbling on the counter, drive at speed to the local supermarket and buy a nice packet of Hovis sliced white for five euros from the 'foreign foods' section. Incidentally, Kirsty and I were approached, via an agent, to participate in such a television show but Mrs Jones was reluctant. It would have been pointless as our budget was so utterly frugal, and we knew exactly in which area we wished to live. Personally, I was right up for it and would have found countless opportunities to slip in the name of my latest CD release *(Les Cerisiers,* available from all major digital music platforms).

I have met hundreds of Brits living in France, and very few have got a real grip of the language. There is an enormous amount of goodwill shown and euros dispensed for this purpose, but there are traps placed everywhere for the Anglophone. After a few months in a French environment, Brits realise that a social life means more than going to a bar with French friends, successfully ordering a beer in French and then taking a conversational back seat. There is an abundance of internet forums run by ex-pats, for ex-pats in France and, consequently, it is easy to make British friends. One can soon find oneself speaking English 95% of the time and never really grasping the native tongue. It's true to say we've made some fantastic British, Anglophone friends in France, yet how easy it would be to fall into little groups of Brits, behaving like Brits, talking like Brits, but living overseas.

Immigrants to the UK are frequently criticised for failing to integrate with their newfound countrymen and women, mainly due to their lack of English. Well, the news is my friends that more often than not Brits are the worst offenders of all on this front. Personally, I see it as freedom of choice rather than a crime. People can talk to whoever they want in whatever language they wish. I am not The Social-Life Police.

A key to grasping the linguistic skills of your chosen country is developing the confidence to attempt them in the everyday world. There are barriers to this; more-often-than-not, they are psychological in nature. One of the most challenging is combatting the actions of *The Armchair Linguistic Intellectual.* This character will give you a wealth of advice (usually unsolicited) but never actually apply the knowledge they claim to possess in a real-life situation. When discussing one's progress in learning the language in the presence of *The Armchair Linguistic Intellectual,* a look will come over his face which suggests a challenge is in order. He will feign interest and then lean forward, stroking his chin with the tips of his fingers.

"Ah, but can you say *I ought not to have done?"*

A psychological trap is laid. Many Brits in this situation panic and lose confidence, believing that despite their best efforts, they are in fact pretty rubbish at French after all. They will sign up for Advanced-French Grammar classes and spend fruitless hours learning complex and easily-forgettable conjugations which *don't actually matter.* I've come to learn that language and communication are about pace, bonding and friendship. If one needed to say 'I ought not to have done' in a real-life situation, you'd just pop in 'I mustn't'. I agree this is technically incorrect, but my French pals have common sense and the context makes it obvious. It is much more desirable to keep the conversation flowing as one sips at an *apero* rather than to put the brakes on the banter as you dig out a phrase book to clarify some unimportant *minutiae* of dialogue. You hold everyone up as you give yourself a kind of spontaneous grammar test, forcing others to listen. I would rather spend my evening drinking Belgian beer and making fun of my mates than listening to a living version of *Countdown Français* in my own back garden. Consider this: when you go out with your friends in the UK, do you really think that everything which is said is grammatically accurate? What about all those wonderful regional variations? Here, in my new Scottish home, the term 'wee' is used routinely for 'little'; rather than 'live somewhere' you 'stay somewhere' and 'just now' refers to the future: 'I'll have a cup of tea just now'. In Wales, it is clearly the past tense: 'I had a cup of tea just now'.

When one arrives in France, there is fun to be had as you learn the language and try it out on your friends. Take care though as there is a risk that this becomes your entire identity. Before you can say *'Oh là là'*, all your conversations will be based on an everlasting joke about the limitations of your French alongside bumbling attempts to clarify your meaning. After three months or so, that wears thin and frankly, you run the risk of becoming a crashing bore.

So, how does one master the lingo? Here's the good news: the key to learning French is to indulge in a weekly regime of frivolous activities.

(1) Go to the bar; join a committee where *aperos* are dished out like jelly babies at a kids' party.

(2) Train with a football or rugby club. It's unimportant if, like me, you're hopeless at sport – just get used to hearing the banter. Be careful though. If the language is anything like that which I hear at our local matches, it's the kind of vocabulary that should not be tested when giving a concert in a local retirement home.

(3) Join a school fund-raising committee, an art club, a walking group. Anything. In our tiny village, there is even a philosophy discussion group which meets in the bar (surprise, surprise) once per month. I did laugh when I learned that due to highly-heated exchanges, the subjects of religion and politics are now banned. It makes one wonder what else there is to discuss at a *Café Philo*. Football?

Learn the language the way children do. I'm suspicious of statements such as 'It's SO easy for children, they're like little sponges'. It should read 'It's SO easy for children, they just dive in without self-analysis and get on with it'.

Of course, in my situation, learning the language was unavoidable. I had pretty ropey French when we left the UK, but was immediately thrown into about twenty-five hours per week of linguistic practice in my role as a guitar teacher. I had no choice as my pupils were French. Two weeks after our arrival, I had an intense job interview with a panel of three *fonctionnaires* which lasted well over an hour. There were several instances when I was half-sure I'd understood the question but less-than entirely convinced. I chose to say 'yes' to all of these and smile benignly. There was one moment when my interrogators looked surprised at this response. Maybe they'd asked 'Do you have a history of violent conduct towards your colleagues?' Happily, I got the job so I presume I hadn't made a complete ass of myself - there were plenty of other opportunities for that to come.

My day-to-day life ensured I acquired a rich and wide vocabulary; often the hard way. One particularly well-reinforced lesson came on the day when I was teaching a young boy whom I'll call Didier. He was a self-assured lad, about eleven years old and always a pleasure to work with, yet one week, when attempting a particularly tricky new technical concept, he appeared to lose confidence.

"J'ai mal a ventre," he said wearily, not for the first time.

Now, I understood this as *'J'ai du mal'* which can, in this context, mean that he was finding it challenging. I helped him reposition his left hand, offered reassurance and asked him to have another go.

"J'ai mal a ventre," he repeated yet again, this time with a degree of agitation.

I mentally congratulated myself on being such a patient and understanding teacher. I would not allow this feisty little lad's lack of self-belief stand in the way of our progress, so I continued to smile and identify areas for improvement, proudly employing my 'growth mindset' training.

Suddenly, completely out-of-the-blue, he lurched forward and spectacularly projectile-vomited across my teaching room, like a carrot-soup water-cannon. I sat there aghast. Believe me, since that experience, I am never going to forget the French for 'I'm going to throw up' which the poor boy was desperately trying to communicate to me. He'd been too polite to leave the room without my permission, bless him.

Some weeks later, the same lad marched into my room and came out with a statement I'd wholly failed to anticipate.

"Il y a une chauve-souris morte sous le réfrigérateur," he announced in a typically-functional manner.

"Good-day to you too," I replied.

Now, I knew enough French to understand that he was telling me that there was something dead underneath the fridge. *In* the fridge I'd have understood, but underneath? We went to the kitchen/waiting room together and, upon inspecting underneath the fridge, I saw the outline of a surprisingly large bat, complete with shiny, leathery wings, lying flat on its back. It was clearly one of those fake plastic things one buys at Hallowe'en so I gave Didier a wide-eyed comic glance and spoke in a moron one-syl-la-ble-at-a-time kind of voice.

"Oh non! What are we going to do with Mr Scary Dead Monster?!"

I pulled it out with a drumstick and when it entered the light of day, an awful realisation dawned upon me. It was no fake.

"Aaaagh! What the ****!" I screamed, this time adopting a voice which was anything but comic as I sprinted, retching towards the window. It would have been unwise, as well as wholly unnecessary to translate my response for Didier.

I'll spare you the details but the beast had evidently been there for quite some time. If I ever encounter another dead bat wedged under a kitchen appliance, I know that I will be able to forewarn French-speaking friends with confidence. Now I come to think of it, I should have told the drum teacher to wash that drumstick.

The way in which I have become comfortable speaking French resembles the instrumental teaching technique called The Suzuki Method. A second language, in its essential communicative form, can be acquired by the same method: through the imitation of peers. There are hundreds of little expressions which I've heard and copied over the years. I had no idea how they were written, or even where the words separated, but this is unimportant. Here are some great examples I use all the time – many of which I've had to look up now in order to write them down.

(1) *Tout à fait.* In conversation, say this to agree. It's like 'absolutely'. Imagine it's written 'tootafay'.

(2) *Mais non!* This is a sign of disagreement. You pronounce it 'maynor!'

(3) *Je ne sais pas.* We're taught that this is the expression for 'I don't know' but everyone says 'saypa'. Actually, you'll notice that the *'ne'* part of the negative is spoken less and less in real life - *'Je pense pas'* instead of *'Je ne pense pas'* (I don't think so).

(4) *N'importe quoi!* This is a great expression which can mean 'whatever', 'rubbish' or 'anything'. It is spoken rapidly as a single word 'namportakwa'. By means of example, I can effectively employ it if my friend Stéphane makes a rash statement.

"The French rugby team is much stronger than the Welsh."
L'équipe de rugby Français est beaucoup plus forte que les Gallois.

To which I can make the entirely appropriate response.
"N'importe quoi!"

(5) *Truc.* This fantastically-useful word, pronounced 'trook' as in 'book', is best translated as 'thingamajig'. Using a combination of mime, context and common-sense, *truc* can replace any noun for which you have yet to learn the correct French word.

When you *imitate* rather than *translate* you'll start to find a rhythm and consequently integrate yourself into conversations.

I'm somewhat embarrassed to confess this but, when I'm with French friends, I find that I imitate their *behaviour* as well as their words. During excitable conversations, I suddenly exclaim *'Maynor!'*, throw my bodyweight forwards at the person with whom I am disagreeing and make funny tree shapes with my arms, like a pre-school TV show presenter. I would *never* do that when speaking English. I also do that little side-mouth raspberry and shrug my shoulders to say 'I don't know' *(saypa)*. In later reflection I cringe at myself, but I can't help it.

We have witnessed this occurrence with our children and it makes us fall around laughing. Kirsty and I will never forget when Sam, at about four years of age, came out with a large *'Mais non!'* when told he needed to come in from the garden, or when participating in a conversation in English he exclaimed *'Oh là là!'* It was both wonderful and hilarious.

The French language is absolutely stuffed with words which it shares with English. I neither know nor care which came first - this is the kind of information divulged by *The Armchair Linguistic Intellectual* - but this is fantastically useful for us. It is said that pretty much any word ending with 'ion' will be shared between the languages: lion, condensation, improvisation, conclusion, delusion, erosion, illusion, solution, Eurovision… There are thousands of them so there you are - you're practically fluent already! You just need to learn to say them in a ridiculous mocking accent and you're away. I mean this last statement. If I'm ever stuck for a pronunciation (there's another one), I just stylise like crazy (usually with a bit of body language thrown in) and I'm more often than not congratulated for my accent when I half expect to be punched in the kidneys for taking the mick. This technique failed spectacularly once though when, in a supermarket, I was seeking red chillies. I stood in front of an assistant, arms flapping in a wealth of abstract shapes repeating *'sheellee, sheellee'* with no success. When I mentioned '*le curry*' as a further clue, she sighed and led me to what I'd been seeking: *piment.*

Be careful though. On many occasions (another 'ion') I have seen friends slip into 'Steve McClaren Syndrome' or 'Doing a Joey Barton'. If you are a follower of football, you will have seen the side-splittingly funny videos of the former England coach and the charming Mr Barton speaking, in English, to Dutch and French reporters respectively, unconsciously employing the accent of the region and furthermore, behaving *as if English was their second language*. It is gloriously surreal and I feel for these two guys who have been filmed and universally mocked for their antics. It is actually a very easy habit to fall into. Please, avoid it.

I have a wonderful friend called Huw, of whom you will hear more later, who became a pal after I gave him some guitar lessons. He is semi-retired and has a colossal amount of energy and a massive heart. He passionately believes in helping out others and, as he has been so generous to us, the best means I can think of to thank him is by mocking him in my book.

One day, Huw was helping me to build our cattery. This was a project we were setting up in the garden to earn a few extra *euros* and to satisfy my life-long fascination with felines. He had all the power tools, a wealth of expertise, and masses of timber so he made a great ally.

A wood burner was being installed *Chez Jones* the same afternoon and the gentleman employed for that task was called Raphael. He had installed Huw's wood burner so they were acquaintances. Having completed his job, Raphael came down to the cattery project with Kirsty to see the work in progress and say *'Bonjour!'* Now, you should know that Raphael is married to an English lady, and is pretty-much bilingual.

We started chatting away in French, sharing *un petit café*. Huw started his part of the interactions in French but, as the chat continued, Kirsty and I noticed that he had switched to English yet was employing a ridiculous French accent. He was blissfully unaware of his actions, and I believe that he thought he was *actually speaking French*. Huw is a pretty chatty kind-of-guy and was, somewhat unfortunately, dominating the conversation. I was trying *so* hard to intervene but to no avail.

"So, I eez comeeng to Dan and Kristee's 'ouse to bee 'elpeeng wiz zee… err. You know… cateree," Huw offered.

"Er, Huw," I interjected, squirming with embarrassment on his behalf.

"So, I ees comeeng as I 'ave zee *power tule!"* Huw continued, undeterred.

"Huw, please," I tried, visibly cringing.

"Dan! Pleese can you not bee… you know… (he paused as if searching for a word in his second language), interrupteeng! Oh là là! Eee is so… *rude!"* (with throaty 'r' and shrug of the shoulders).

"Huw, why are you doing this? You speak English for crying out loud," I uttered.

And so it went on, with Raphael staring at him in moderately-offended silence. Mortified, I locked myself in Unit 2, pretending to install a scratching post.

Aside from the 'ion' list mentioned above, there are hundreds of words which exist in the two languages but, over time, their strength and sense have subtlety changed. Of course, this makes them easy-peasy for the Brit to learn. Here are some of my favourites and most useful:

(1) *Deranger* is 'to derange' which in French means 'to disturb'. I was quite taken aback the first time somebody knocked at my front door and said what I understood as 'I hope I'm not deranging you'. *J'espére que je ne vous dérange pas.*

"If you're trying to sell me double glazing, you may well be," I replied to a blank look.

(2) *Une catastrophe* is 'a catastrophe' (the French pronounce it without the 'e'). In French, it is strong but commonly used for an everyday mess-up rather than, well, a catastrophe.

(3) *Terminer* is the verb 'to terminate' or 'to finish'. In a restaurant, you are far more likely to be asked if you've

'terminated' your meal rather than 'finished'. The waiter isn't asking whether you've blown it away with a sawn-off shotgun.

(4) *Grave* is obviously like the English 'grave', but it translates as 'serious' rather than 'deadly'. You'll hear *'c'est pas grave'* meaning 'it doesn't matter' as an everyday expression. It is casual and no-one is cheating death.

(5) *Proposer* is 'to suggest' and used far more commonly than the more-obvious *suggérer*. If someone 'proposes' to you in English, it's usually the case that your companion is offering his/her hand in marriage. In French, it's more likely to be suggesting a choice of wine for your dinner.

(6) *Arriver* translates as 'to arrive' but, as mentioned elsewhere, it is an important, multi-use word. It can mean 'to succeed', 'to complete', 'to pass' and 'to achieve'. It is also combined with other verbs for no good reason. *'J'arrive à gagner la loterie'* (I've arrived in winning the lottery). Logically it's just: 'I've won the lottery' which you could say in French but people tend to add the extra verb.

(7) *Accompagner* means 'to accompany' or to 'go along with'. In English, we tend to reserve this for a formal setting: 'I'll accompany you to the end-of-year ball'. In French you could use it in the context of 'I'll accompany you to take the bins out'.

(8) *Normale* is subtlely different from the English word 'normal'. If your French electrician announces that your system is *'normale'* it means that it is well up to the required standard rather than run-of-the-mill. That relates to the term 'norms' in English building regulations. The French also use this word to mean 'only to be expected or assumed'. If a friend feeds our animals when we're away, we'll say our 'thank yous' (too many times, being British) and he or she will reply *'c'est normale'*. By means of warning, the word *'normalement'* (normally) is

used by tradespeople as a kind of get-out clause when making appointments. If the same electrician says *'Normalement, je viendrai vendredi matin'* (normally, I will come on Friday morning) there is a sporting chance you'll be stood up. Insist that he/she removes the offending word from the statement and the appointment stands a far greater chance of being honoured.

(9) *Desolé* obviously has the same stem as our word 'desolate', but in French, it translates as a simple 'sorry'. 'Sorry, I forgot to put the *apero* in the fridge'. *Désolé, j'ai oublié de mettre l'apéro dans le frigo.*

(10) *Un chariot* is bizarrely 'a shopping trolley'. Every time I go to a supermarket, I fantasise about being *Ben Hur* charging down the aisles. This has got me into a spot of bother once or twice.

When children whose mother-tongue is English grow up in France, they unwittingly pick up verbs and nouns which are shared between the languages and end up speaking a kind of hybrid language. I attended a talk on bilingual children and was relieved to hear that this is absolutely *normale* and, in fact, shows intelligence and creativity as they are spontaneously making links. The resulting exchanges, such as those indulged in by my own marvellous offspring, can be surprising. By means of example, Florence may make a proposition to her brother.

"I say, Sam, I propose that I accompany you to the *Boulangerie* if that doesn't derange you."

To which he might respond.

"Yes Florence, I will command a *pain au chocolate*. It won't be grave if they are terminated but as it's late, it's normal."

They sound like an unlikely fusion between Jane Austen and Arnold Schwarznegger. It's strangely beautiful.

Our children will also routinely use certain French nouns in the context of an English sentence. They will still say *bibliothèque* instead of 'library'; similarly, Florence will frequently be heard asking whether anyone has seen her *casquette,* the French word meaning a 'baseball cap' for sun protection. Of course, the word is no longer required now we spend much of our time in Scotland.

It is such a joy to find obscure links between English and French. I'll bore anyone to tears when discussing this topic. If I wasn't a musician, I'd be the male Susie Dent. I honestly believe that learning French will make one's English richer and more interesting by reintroducing words which are fading away from the English language. Take the following wonderful French words which are shared within English but I never hear spoken by anyone under thirty years of age:

(1) *Se vexer,* 'to vex'.

(2) *Se cacher*, 'to cache' (to hide – strangely we use it for 'cached files' on our PC).

(3) *Un clavier,* 'a keyboard' which can be the musical instrument, like the old English 'clavichord' or the computer keyboard.

(4) *D'accord,* used for 'OK', related to being 'in accordance' with something. The English musical word 'chord' is linked as well as, one would hope, that the notes of the chord would go together and therefore be 'in accordance' with one another.

(5) *J'ai pris ombrage,* 'I took umbrage' or 'I clouded over'. The link in English is 'umbrella'. I overheard a pupil at a summer school in the Limousin using this lovely expression.

I find the English language is being watered-down by bland and mundane words. Wouldn't it be a joy if we used a passion for French to revitalise English? I worked in a bilingual school in Bordeaux and started a campaign to reintroduce old words. I even set up a Facebook group called 'Beautiful Words, Old and New' which has been a roaring success. All of the group's followers love it. Both of them. If you disagree with my view on the current state of English usage, I'd invite you to read literature for children from the 1950's such as *The Chronicles of Narnia* by C S Lewis. A lovely example is 'buskins'. This wonderful, sensual word means 'comfortable indoor shoes or slippers' and has now been adopted into the everyday vocabulary of the Jones household. The French have a number of gorgeous words for slippers, my favourite being *pantoufles.*

Worthy of special attention is *ami.* This is 'friend' as you will probably know, and the link is clearly our 'amicable'. I thought it prudent to highlight this word as one must be careful with its use. *Ami* can imply a friend *or* a romantic partner. The detail is in the little word which precedes it. If I, as a happily-married heterosexual man, introduce my burly-bricklayer pal Gavin as *'mon ami'* (my friend), the implication is that I am involved in a romantic relationship with him (as well as my wife I suppose). To clarify the situation, use *'un ami'* (a friend). In a similar vein, you may well, like us, be concerned about additives in your food. If you ask your delicatessen whether their sausages contain *preservatifs,* you'll be enquiring as to the presence of condoms. Just when you thought the barrel had been well-and-truly scraped, you may be alarmed to hear your children inform you they used 'tampons' in art class. No, it isn't a Tracey Emin retrospective; a *tampon* is an ink stamp. There's enough material there to fuel a 1970's retro comedy festival.

I also adore the weird and wonderful words invented by the French for modern-day items:

(1) *Un ordinateur* which is 'a computer'. To me, this sounds like something out of *Star Trek* (Beam me up with the quantum-particle-teleportation ordinateur Scotty).

(2) *Un aspirateur* is the word for 'a vacuum cleaner'. What a gem! You can hear the word sucking up the dirt as you say it.

(3) *Un robot* is pretty much any modern, automated device. In French, the vowel sounds are as you would use in the song 'Row, Row, Row your Boat'. A food processor? *Un robot de*

cuisine. I really hope an automated vacuum cleaner is *un aspirateur robot.*

(4) *Wifi* is the same as the English *wifi* for internet connection but pronounced *wee-fee.* This sounds like a name you'd give to a character from My Little Pony.

(5) *Un batterie* is the gloriously onomatopoeic-ish word for 'a drum kit'. Doesn't it illustrate the cacophony just beautifully? It is also the big electrical box you use to start a car. Weird. A little battery (like you put in your remote control) is a *'pile'*, pronounced 'peel'.

One final tip to develop your linguistic prowess: use *UPL.* This is *Universal Pointy Language.* The rural French are a gestural bunch and like to use their bodies in communication. Therefore, if a *Boulanger* says *'Bien-cuit?'* (well-cooked) and you think *'Quoi?',* hang in there. He will almost certainly point to various sticks of bread, some edible, others more cooked-up than a Volkswagen emissions report. Choose your bread, then research the language in the comfort of your home.

Finally, a French language joke for your amusement:

Q: What do you call a Frenchman in beach shoes?
A: Philippe Flop.

***

Learning the Lingo – The Essential Tips

(1) Make friends with fellow Brits but mix up your social groups.

(2) Avoid *The Armchair Linguistic Intellectual.* He's clever but acting like a bit of a dork actually.

(3) Avoid trying to be too accurate. Just dive in. Get your hands dirty.

(4) Go to the bar. A lot. In the interests of linguistic research and international cooperation, of course.

(5) Copy rather than translate. Be French. Buy a beret.

(6) When speaking French with friends, stop periodically and make sure that you are actually speaking the language rather than English with a ridiculous accent.

(7) Remember the amazing amount you already know.

(8) Be passionate about your language. Love it!

5. Le Tank

Mon papa me disait tantôt... QUOI?
Demain tu auras une auto... AH?!
Mais je n'en veux à aucun prix... OH!
Je préfère mon p'tit poney gris... NON!

My daddy told me not long ago... WHAT?
You will have a car tomorrow... AH?!
But I don't want one at any price... OH!
I prefer my grey pony, he's so nice... NO!

Traditional -*Le Poney Gris*
(The Grey Pony - France)

As already relayed, the failure of our house sale in the UK left us short of capital. Our plan had been to use a small amount of cash to purchase a car for my commutes to and from my workplaces. We are environmentally-aware people yet I am frustrated to confess that living and working as a one-car family in rural areas of France is near-impossible. The inter-city travel is good but, if you want to travel from Saint André de Double to La Tour Blanche on a bus, you may have one opportunity per week to make the trip and then it would be an all-day project. I took the train to work from St Astier to Coutras but my family were obliged to rise with me at the crack of dawn to drop me at the station. I would arrive at *l'École de Musique* at least an hour early due to the infrequency of the trains.

I had joined a chamber music ensemble and, during a break in rehearsal, I'd mentioned how we'd been struggling with one car. Later that evening I received a call from the violinist in the group. She told me, in a matter-of-fact kind of way, that she had an old car at home and we could use it, free of charge, for as long as we needed it. I was amazed and started to bumble a profusion of declarations of gratitude, as is the way with us Brits.

"But I couldn't possibly… Are you sure?... I must give you something," and continued in this vein until she more or less hung up the phone on me, mid-bumble.

A few days later, we arrived at the good lady's house *en famille* and encountered, for the first time, the vehicle which served me impeccably for two years. It was a massive Renault Espace – the first model. It sported a dark, murky green paint-job, the ascetic effect being enhanced by patches of swamp-brown corrosion dotted artistically across the bodywork. Flo turned to me.

"That looks like a tank!" she noted, with unerring accuracy.

From that moment onwards, the legend of *le Tank* was born.

Having scraped a layer of moss off the door handle, I clambered inside and turned the ignition key. There were a few laboured grunts and groans and then *le Tank* awoke in a cloud of diesel fumes and noisy exhaust explosions. With a feeling of doubt in the pit of my stomach, I took it to a local garage for a *controle technique* (MOT). It passed - who says miracles don't happen? The children begged to be allowed to travel back home in our exciting new acquisition. Obligingly, I gathered their child seats and searched for the seatbelts in the rear. Then the realisation struck that *le Tank* had sufficient years under its cam belt to have been constructed in the era before manufacturers felt that luxuries such as rear seatbelts were a necessity. I speculatively asked the garage man if it was possible to have rear seat belts installed in *le Tank* for my children.

"Monsieur," he said, looking at me darkly. "I would never take children in this car."

On that cheery note I drove off, releasing clouds of black pollution, spreading panic amongst fellow road users and causing pedestrians to dive into bushes in terror.

How I fell in love with that car. It had a rather flashy sunroof - the problem being when it rained, it became a built-in shower system. We're not talking a couple of drops here; the water absolutely poured in. I can only assume it gathered in the channels around the edge of the roof so when I took a corner at a certain angle and speed, it would positively gush into the cabin, drenching anyone unfortunate enough to be caught unawares. I soon learned the trajectories at which one would potentially be soaked. Consequently, I'd trundle through the lanes cutting corners in an unwise fashion, like a racing driver seeking out a slipstream, in order to avoid a cold torrent down the back of my collar.

Jean-Marie and I lift-shared every Wednesday. One cloudy day, when it was my turn to drive, I turned up at his house in *le Tank* wearing a raincoat and a dapper waterproof hat. He popped out of his front door sporting a rather *chic* collarless shirt and a pair of designer jeans, trotting across the garden to avoid the heavy drops of rain which were starting to fall from the blackened skies.

"Errr, Jean-Marie," I offered as he jumped into the passenger seat. "You may want to consider a raincoat, or maybe even an umbrella and wellingtons."

He looked at me with a confused expression and, upon my explanation that *le Tank* suffered from a leaky sunroof, he unwisely waved off my warnings laughing that 'it couldn't be that bad'. Half an hour later we arrived at work. He resembled a man who had driven out of a carwash, having entered it with the windows wide open. The problem was that I'd learned how to prevent the rush of icy-cold water from falling on *me* and, although I didn't do it deliberately, I somehow instinctively steered so that Jean-Marie was the repeated, unfortunate recipient of a good dousing every twenty seconds or so. He was not a *lapin content* (happy bunny).

The leaky sunroof was only one of the comfort-features which were faulty in *le Tank.* Since I had been using it, the blowers for the windscreen had been out of operation. I was perfectly relaxed with this state of affairs as the only thing that really mattered was that it carried me from A to B. If we had serious rain though, it became a problem.

I'd been enduring a period when I was particularly stressed about the failure of our house sale. On a dark, rainy Thursday night, I went out in my vehicle *de luxe* to teach. One venue was a private *château,* accessed via a mud track winding a path through dense forest. Upon departing after the lesson, the rain had become utterly torrential. I set off along the track and soon had my nose pressed inches from the windscreen, unable to see a thing. To make matters worse, *le Tank* lost grip and skidded amongst the trees sending wild boar and squirrels scattering in all directions. Soon, I had utterly lost my sense of direction and the chances of getting back on track, so to speak, were becoming increasingly slim. Tired, depressed and feeling somewhat on-edge, I found myself exclaiming out loud (although this quote has been edited somewhat for the sake of decency).

"For crying out loud, *give me a break!"*

As I sat there with rain dripping down my neck, close to whacking the bonnet with a stick John-Cleese style, there was a sudden eruption of sound. I presumed that *le Tank* had finally given up the ghost and there had been a catastrophic engine explosion, but in fact, the air blowers had burst into life and were blasting out hot, condensation-clearing and energy-reviving air for the first time in years. Within minutes, the windows had cleared and I was able to see the track beyond a few squashed bushes and hedgehogs. The blowers remained functional for the remainder of the journey but, after that evening, they never worked again. I came to see this incident as a spiritual one. It was as if I were being spoken to and I felt genuinely reassured. The following Sunday, I recounted this tale in church, making a change from The Book of Common Prayer. Strangely, that was the last time I was invited to lead prayer.

Le Tank also taught me lessons about neighbourly relationships. Upon turning the ignition key one late-winter Monday morning, I was met with a dull clicking sound. A neighbour came out to investigate and I stood alongside him under the raised bonnet, nodding knowledgeably and muttering things like 'yep, that's the engine alright' and 'it's probably the goggly pin' before he clapped his hands and announced that the battery was defunct. A mechanic-friend of his had taken the radical step of opening on a Monday - many small rural businesses still regard such innovations as too much like hard work - so he ran indoors to call him. Having confirmed a replacement battery was in stock, we started *le Tank* using jump leads. Within minutes, we had it rumbling away in its inimitable style. I thanked him profusely and nipped into the house to collect the wallet but upon my return, found him installed in the passenger seat.

"Um, what are you doing?" I asked sheepishly, fearing that he might be about to unleash his woes on me or have a mid-life nervous breakdown.

"We're going to the garage aren't we?" he replied.

I then understood that helping out a neighbour meant seeing a project through to its conclusion, this being an agreeable way to pass a Monday morning, catch up with a friend and to ensure I got a decent price for the battery.

"Oh really, I don't want to put you out... I never meant to intrude..."

My British submissive and over-polite instincts kicked in once again. When I look back, I cringe as I realise I thanked both him and the garage owner at least ten times. Far more than was appropriate. I also should have used the opportunity to propose a midday *aperitif* upon our return.

Driving in the French countryside is ideal for old, diesel cars. I am absolutely aware of the environmental issues surrounding such vehicles, but it is fair to say that these are of greater concern in urban centres. A diesel car, idling away, immobile in traffic, is very polluting. In our isolated corner of France, traffic was almost non-existent. My commute to Coutras filled my soul with peace. I would progress at a consistent, *gentil* pace, trundling through the villages of Ménesplet and Les Peintures, passing mysterious enterprises such as a second-hand boat salesperson in a front garden in Le Pizou, an accordion-repair workshop in Saint-Antoine-sur-l'Isle and sign for a *discothèque* in the middle of the forest. Who on earth are the clientele who patronise a disco in an area which hosts more livestock than humans? This is a genuine mystery to me. I bet it would make an amazing night out. I intend to visit this establishment for my next significant birthday celebration and you're all invited. In fact, maybe all the punters are folk from overseas who enjoy ironic humour.

The only hold-up we experienced on this road transpired *en route* to a food festival one Tuesday evening in mid-summer. We had my brother- and sister-in-law with us, along with their children, and upon rounding a corner encountered three escapee donkeys loose on the road. We stopped and duly gathered them up to the owner's eternal gratitude. One has to be genuinely careful of this kind of hazard. When driving at night, deer will leap out of nowhere at frequent intervals. Accidents involving collisions with deer are so common in our corner of France that most insurers exclude this risk from their policies. If you spot a deer, slow down. They tend to move about in groups so, if you miss deer number one, his buddy is likely to be right behind him. As a driver and deer number one eyeball one another thinking 'Whew! That was close', it's often deer number two who ends up flattened on the tarmac, like a fireside rug in a hunting lodge.

Wild boar also run the gauntlet with motorists. I saw them on several occasions, usually at night, but one afternoon a huge male lumbered across a field adjacent to a large supermarket as an enraptured *Famille Jones* watched from the sanctuary of our car. Some months later, a family of four – presumably a mother and three piglets (boarlets?) – memorably crossed the road in front of me as I returned from a gig. Other nocturnal drivers had similar encounters, not always with such positive outcomes for human and beast alike. Dottie, a jazz singer who fronted a group in which I played the guitar, unequivocally took out a luckless boar following a late-night return from a performance. Her car was damaged and, being stranded in the middle-of-nowhere, she called the local *gendarmes*. Once they'd checked over Dottie and her car, they looked at her, then at the ex-boar, and then at Dottie again.

"Errr... are you wanteeeng zis pigee?" they enquired.

Once Dottie confirmed she had no immediately apparent plans for a 100-kilo dead boar, the *gendarmes* hoisted the beast into their boot and went on their way. No doubt the creature was destined for the barbeque.

The fact is that such easy driving means a reasonably-serviced old diesel car will pretty much go on forever. I have friends who have done well over 500,000km in theirs (and are still counting). Consequently, such vehicles are highly-prized and desirable. *Le Tank* was viewed as a mighty warrior and trusty friend rolled in one rather than an embarrassing necessity. As I said, how I loved that car.

**

Le Tank – The Essential Tips

(1) If someone makes a generous offer, they mean it. If you make a generous offer, you will be held to it. Rightly so.

(2) Say 'thank you' just once. That suffices.

(3) There is no need to apologise for asking someone if they'd like a coffee in France.

(4) Leaky sunroofs can be repaired with silicone sealant. It is a hassle to do but necessary in order to maintain good relations with colleagues.

(5) Ancient diesel cars are capable of communicating spiritual messages.

(6) Look out for wandering beasts on minor roads; particularly at night. They are a frequently-encountered hazard.

(7) An old diesel car is a highly-prized commodity in rural areas of France. No-one is interested in a flashy modern vehicle with bells and whistles.

6. Bunnies and Bangers

At five in the morning as jolly as any,
The miner does rise to his work for to go.
He caresses his wife and his children so dearly
And bids them adieu before closing the door.
And goes down the deep shaft at the speed of an arrow,
His heart light and gay without fear or dread,
Has no thoughts of descending to danger and peril
But his life is depending on one single thread.

The Miner's Doom - Traditional (America)

I loved my job as a lecturer in music in South Wales, but the skip in my step became significantly laboured when the new-found practice of 'Health and Safety' became peculiarly *a la mode* in all major public institutions, particularly those in the field of education. As an employee, I am unable to recall feeling any healthier or indeed safer at work following the implementation of an abundance of improbable regulation, but I remember with painful clarity being required to attend training days where slightly hysterical gentlemen, who actually looked at ease wearing a combination of a shirt, tie and hard hat, would instruct us in meticulous detail as to the carrying out of everyday tasks. My fellow tutors and I had mistakenly believed these to be innocuous, but it seemed that lifting a box, tackling a staircase and drinking heated beverages were actions now placed on a par hazard-wise with swimming in shark-infested waters wearing a seal outfit padded with raw rump steaks. As our panting instructor stood in front of a mock package, knees bent, back straight, like a fellow suffering from a woeful bout of constipation, everyone in the room longed to put up a hand and

81

ask if they could go home, but no-one quite dared to do so. Minutes later, we were required to put what we'd learned into practice. Anyone entering our room might have thought they'd stumbled upon a new-age, multi-gender antenatal class.

Brilliant colleagues who'd made our own music degrees a breath-taking, white-knuckle ride of intellectual experiences were required to reel in their eccentric personalities and stifle their glorious, spontaneous teaching styles. The age of invites to supper with lecturers - followed by the singing of six-part madrigals as an aid to digestion - drifted away into a bygone era. Such evening experiences peppered the extra-curricular calendar of my own student years; we would also set off in minibuses with our inspired and motivated tutors to hear stirring concerts in wondrous, ancient churches, and receive invites to philosophise with some of the foremost musical thinkers of the twentieth century.

I'd felt uncommitted about the idea of emigration – no, actually I was absolutely terrified - but on the day I was obliged to sheepishly ask my class to switch off their laptop computers because they 'hadn't been tested for electrical safety' (or 'PAT tested'), my heart and soul made a shift towards a Monty-Python-esque *'run away!'* as being an attractive option. As we strolled through the cafeteria area where dozens of students had their untested computers and phones plugged into the mains, the manager instigating this decision explained that the policy was 'in the interests of pupil safety'. The straight face he managed to maintain when sharing this information with me was indeed, remarkable; I felt like suggesting he should take up poker. I understood the pressure senior staff must have felt to follow new laws and guidelines, but I would have appreciated being spoken to with sincerity. I believe most sane individuals are at ease with the concept of being healthy and safe at work, but it appeared that the restrictions were really about protecting organisations from the minuscule chance of litigation should anything go amiss. I accept that so-called 'ambulance-chasers' and their clients make up part of the problem, but I found such close control of my choices and lifestyle suffocating.

Over-excited H&S enthusiasts hit me in the pocket, as well as the soul. With worrying frequency, men wearing ill-fitting jeans and black T-shirts swearing allegiance to 1970's rock bands of the white, hairy and greasy type would turn up to band rehearsals in order to test our equipment for electrical safety. Such courtesy calls were a prerequisite to us entering many hotel venues in order to play a gig. Having relieved my wallet of a not-inconsequential sum of money, one sympathetic PAT tester gave me a pad of blank stickers so I could fill in the dates and attach them to my amplifiers as and when required. I understand that such stickers are now available on popular auction websites for musicians wishing to avoid the emotional and fiscal irritations associated with PAT testing. Ultimately, I came to feel that all my efforts to organise concerts, summer schools or short courses became complicated and expensive to an unmanageable degree by the requirements of a faceless and all-powerful body. It was actually rather depressing.

Of course, the disease of Health and Safety exists in France. Happily, it is blissfully ignored in rural areas. What a joy it is to be able to employ my own decision-making skills with reckless abandon in everyday life. What an equally great joy it is to work with people who, if things go wrong, shrug, do a side-mouth raspberry and say *'C'est la vie'*. I'd envisage that any serious attempt by the both invisible and unaccountable Ministry of Health & Safety to implement their fantastical rules in the French countryside would be met with the kind of strike action that would make Parisian air-traffic controllers look passive.

The moment that it dawned on me that our village existed in a world free from such fervent over-regulation came during our first Christmas holidays. One afternoon, we received an invite to bring our children along to *le bourg* (the village centre) to benefit from a visit from Santa and his reindeer. My expectations were not high and, sure enough, half-an-hour later than timetabled, 'Santa' came rolling up, smelling suspiciously of *eau de vie,* with his 'reindeer' and 'sleigh'. It was a local farmer with a less-than-convincing beard - made from sheep fur I believe, complete with flecks of dried dung - and a horse sporting a couple of twigs taped to its head. The obliging creature towed a trailer fitted with benches running along its sides. *Le Père Noël* pulled up alongside a now-substantial group of bouncing children, swung open the door and invited one-and-all to jump on board. I had no idea as to our destination - Lapland perhaps - but thereafter followed an afternoon of highly-memorable entertainment as children piled into the sleigh and 'Santa' paraded them up and down the street in the rain. Cars encountering this unexpected impediment to their progress pulled over and allowed Santa and his elated passengers to pass. What a pleasure to see motor vehicles being put in their rightful place - after family and fun - just for once. There was not a risk assessment in sight.

I am convinced that the urban obsession with Health and Safety leads children to more danger than they would otherwise be exposed to. This is because they rarely have the opportunity to understand limits and boundaries. Life is full of awful accidents and tragic events; I assure you that I know this from my own experience. It is impossible to avoid risk and we must protect our loved ones, but we must equally allow our children to learn common sense. It strikes me that the only truly effective way of acquiring this vital life-skill is through trial-and-error. Tragically, today's children are led to believe that the risk of a non-PAT-tested laptop computer spontaneously combusting in their faces is equal to that of holding a teddy bears' picnic in the fast lane of the Paris – Le Mans *autoroute*.

In rural areas of France, kids are invited, no, *expected* to participate in great pastimes such as the villages' communal eating festivals and for much of the evening are released to entertain themselves out of view of their guardians. These festivals are either held outdoors or in the local *Salle des Fêtes*, starting at around 8.00pm and sometimes finishing at dawn the following day. Rather than forcing children to sit down at a table and be bored out of their wits, they are allowed to run around outside *unsupervised* and have the time of their lives. I saw kids high up trees waving to their families at 1.00am, just as the main course arrived. Children are given the freedom to discover nature's gifts in a way which nourishes their minds, bodies and souls. Simultaneously, adults are given the freedom to discover nature's gifts in the form of *rouge, rosé* or *blanc*. Quite how much nourishment of mind, body and soul occurs in the latter is a matter for conjecture, but that's a debate for another chapter. How often have we seen some poor soul, on a zero-hours contract, wearing an ill-fitting fluorescent vest with the word 'security' scrawled on the back, employed with the express purpose of preventing children from having fun? Consequently, kids are denied the learning curves that are, sometimes painfully, of central importance to their development. What's more, when their needs to explore and discover are suppressed, they become a far greater source of irritation to the adults.

Even activities which one would be forced to grudgingly accept as being 'not without hazard' remain much-practised in rural areas of France, a fine example being wild-water swimming. A cursory flick through the old *Peter and Jane* children's books though proves that this was once the case in the green and pleasant countryside of the UK. I read these fine publications to my first son Matthew when he was a toddler, and recall being both delighted and astonished at the content of one particular story. Written in post-war Britain, the central brother-and-sister characters of the series popped out to swim in a river of considerable depth, accompanied only by their trusty dog, Pat. Their long summer days appeared to be disproportionately sun-filled in comparison to my experiences in South Wales but, having granted the authors this artistic licence, what followed is amazing. They made their way to their river of choice on a bus, with not an adult in sight. Once installed, they indulged in a wealth of wholesome aquatic activities. At one point, I recall Peter climbed a precarious-looking tree in order to gain sufficient height to effectively bomb his sister – the illustrator's depiction capturing the moment of her complete aquatic obliteration most competently. Next, the wacky pair settled on the grass for a picnic which had been stored at above the recommended refrigeration level for more than two hours. Their lunch was consumed with a brazen disregard for hand-hygiene; not a single disposable sanitation wipe was in sight. The crazy siblings, by some miracle of fortune, survived.

When I point out this story to supporters of the Health and Safety movement, the usual response is 'the world was a safer place then'. The truth is it wasn't. It was less populated, granted, but people enjoyed life without 24/7 access to the grisly news stories which fuel our lives with reasons to be fearful.

Road safety is a hot topic in rural areas. You will often hear Brits discussing the standard of French driving in derisive tones, with much shaking of the head and tutting. More often than not, these armchair critics will never have driven in the country in question. Having been at-the-wheel in France for seven years now, I must say I perceive no real difference between the standard of driving in the UK, and that across *la Manche*. The exception to this is the interpretation of certain road signs. Speed limits are adhered to as they are pretty strictly enforced (as you will later read). Flexibility exists though at the most surprising of moments, notably the 'Road Closed' sign. During our first years in France, I spent many pleasant hours trundling along winding roads, on my way to gigs, or to teach. What a joy it was to find road congestion a thing of the past. As I headed to a lesson or venue, the need for an hour's contingency for traffic became gloriously obsolete. Also, I could always park for free within five minutes of my destination.

It seemed the little country roads were often in need of maintenance. One would frequently come across a sign reading *'Route Barré'* (Road Closed), and be required to follow a *'Deviation'*. During one journey, I noticed the driver in front of me slip right past a *'Route Barré'* sign. In terms of Health and Safety, this struck me as a pretty crazy act so I was a little surprised, but upon reflection, I presumed he lived down the road in question. Weeks later, I was driving with the whole family through a sizeable town when we encountered a '*Route Barré*' sign blocking the main street. Despite this, I couldn't help but notice all the cars in front of us driving straight past the sign, heading right up the street in question. I looked at Kirsty and we decided 'when in France, do as the French do' so, presuming the sign was the last remaining evidence of a job now complete, we too slipped around it. Within moments, we reached a buttock-clenchingly deep hole in the road. This yawning chasm was surrounded by giant, noisy machines manned by a bare-chested, *Gitane*-smoking, sweaty workforce going about their obviously hazardous tasks. The men appeared oblivious to the everyday folk battling their way past their workspace in their cars. We, like the others, edged our vehicles along the crumbling perimeter of the muddy abyss which used to be the High Street. At one point, a large digger swung its bucket full of filth directly above our humble Astra, causing a shadow of foreboding doom to be cast over us. Our then-toddler Sam was going through the digger-obsession phase apparently shared by all boys of his age and found himself in paradise. As I gripped the steering wheel, pressing my nose against the windscreen in terror, Sam was crying out 'Bob the Builder, Bob the Builder!' in unrestrained glee. My caution in the execution of this task was unwelcome in the eyes of my fellow motorists, judging by the cacophony of horns which accompanied my modest progress around the gaping cavern inches to the right of my nearside front tyre. Once we reached the other side of the ordeal, I promised myself never to be so foolish again. This is a vow I have consistently failed to keep. To this day, I zip around *Route Barré* signs, recognising to not do so would be, well… just so well-behaved.

Another road symbol whose meaning is evidently open to a certain flexibility of interpretation is the zebra crossing. In French country towns, waiting at a zebra crossing is a pointless task. You may as well watch paint dry. The only way in which a driver will stop their vehicle is if you step out onto the crossing, thus obliging the majority of sane people at the wheel to apply their brakes and allow you safe passage. One would hope this would be the case at any given point on a public road so this renders a zebra crossing a kind of safari-inspired tarmac decoration. Maybe we'll have leopard-skin roundabouts next.

I'm also fond of a practice which sees members of the public seemingly spontaneously shutting public roads to suit their own purposes; on June 21st every year, the French host an event called *la Fête de la Musique.* In our disproportionately musically-active village, *la Famille Jones* and friends habitually give a performance in the church building followed by a programme from our village choir, *Polysons.* To finish the day off, the *Mozaic Jazz Band* – our twenty-piece jazz orchestra – will perform a programme in the street. Obviously, it makes sense to close the road in question (although it's hardly the M25) and for this part of the day, this is exactly what we do. *Monsieur le Maire* is present and he is normally asked if it's OK as a courtesy, but that's as far as the official application goes. On the odd occasion when someone passes the *Route Barré* sign (as is normal practice) the driver will encounter the unexpected sights and sounds of a jazz ensemble in full swing, blasting out a Duke Ellington number to a watching crowd of about 200 villagers. If someone really insists, we'll let them pass at the end of the song, although the far more-intelligent course of action would be to heed the advice of the friendly villagers and perform a 500-metre detour. Actually, the best advice would be to park up and enjoy the music. In 2017, a group of young scallywags tried to push their way through the installation before the piece of music being performed was finished. They were duly put in their place. The young driver got out of his vehicle to protest only to be met greeted by 200 men, women and children telling him to shut up. He then had a tantrum so everyone laughed at him. Boys will be boys. At the end of the concert, the *commune* always puts on an *apero.* Peach wine is shared, alongside quiche, pizza and *tarte aux pommes.* If you come across a scene like this on your adventures in France, slow down, park up and join *la Fête.*

Fêtes are a common occurrence in the French countryside. The big end-of-year event in French primary schools is the *Kermesse* or School Fete. Even these are being threatened in urban environments by the Health and Safety movement as so few volunteers wish to participate; this is due to the possible legal consequences should a child lightly scrape a kneecap whilst under their charge. In 2004, the UK's then-Cabinet Minister Stephen Byers, in a BBC interview, stated that claims against schools had left the country two hundred million pounds out-of-pocket in one year. That's enough to fund eight thousand teachers. In 2007, the NCVO (National Council for Voluntary Organisations) carried out a survey in response to declining numbers of volunteers. They discovered that 47% of those who responded cited litigation concerns as a reason for their withdrawal. Financial and time constraints were also major factors.

By all accounts, the overview of the *Kermesse* suggested much the same kind of thing as we'd experienced in our previous lives in South Wales: stalls, games, prizes to be won and the like. At the planning meeting for our first *Kermesse,* Kirsty and I were informed we would man the *Lapinodrome.* We had no idea what this would be but, as the word *Lapin* was present, we presumed it would involve stuffed toy rabbits. I had seen a stall at another event called 'Bash the Rat'; here, a bundle of rags was attached to a piece of elastic and fired down a section of drain pipe. The player had to whack the bundle (the rat) with a hammer as it flew out of the pipe at some speed.

When we turned up at the *Kermesse,* we were aghast to see our stall involved the use of *real live rabbits.* A large, wooden, open-topped playing zone had been constructed - like a sandpit - with a box at each corner. The boxes had an entrance hole facing into the pit. At the beginning of each round, we tentatively (and somewhat reluctantly) placed the rabbits into the game-zone and the players' objective was to lure their particular bunny into a designated box using a carrot suspended by fishing wire at the end of a bamboo stick. It goes without saying the rabbits weren't entirely in the mood for a leisurely nibble on a carrot. Some just stubbornly dug their feet into the ground; others bolted for the nearest box-hole and refused to come out. Much of our job consisted of preventing children from 'persuading' their rabbit into their designated box using the stick-end of the rod and brute force. To be fair, there was a pool of rabbits from which to choose, ensuring a fair degree of bunny-rotation. That also provided us with more meat when we barbecued them all at the end of the night (just kidding).

If we thought the *Lapinodrome* was unbelievable, then next year's stall was gob-smackingly astounding. On the big day, The Head Teacher talked Kirsty and me through the activity we'd be supervising.

"First, you give each child a bamboo fishing rod," explained the boss-lady.

"OK," I replied fearing the worst, whilst simultaneously seeking out the receptacle full of cute mammals which we'd be mistreating.

"Then you attach a firework on to the end of each line," she continued casually.

"Excuse me?" we gasped.

"Next, you light a candle," *Madame* continued unflinchingly.

"Ha!" I shrieked, a little too hysterically, "I suppose you're going to tell us the children dangle the fireworks into the naked flames next!"

"And then the children dangle the fireworks into the naked flames," she continued, seemingly oblivious to the fact that my jaw had dropped to ground level.

The winner was the first child to make their banger explode, causing women, children, rabbits and British dads to scatter in all directions. Kirsty and I had looked around, without high hopes, for some sort of protective panel for the children, but this was wholly conspicuous by its absence. Never have I experienced suspense as I did on that day as I watched the line of explosives swinging tantalisingly back and forth, with the flames licking up their sides.

Games at our annual *Kermesse* are free-of-charge with prizes donated by local shops. The serious money is generated at the bar. We're not talking orange squash here my friends, but a real bar, with beer, wine and, for the insane, *Ricard.* So, as the children tore around the playground soaking each other with giant water pistols, tripping over bunnies and avoiding shards of shrapnel, the adults took a *saucisson* from the *grillade* and a couple of beers from the bar and became pleasantly inebriated in the early-evening sun. The event finished well after midnight with everyone mucking in, cleaning up and packing away the stalls.

The school would make a packet, all of which went towards excursions for the following year. The attendees extended beyond the parents and kids from the school, all-comers turning up in droves for the food and drink. It was a good night out rather than an obligation.

During the week of writing, my family attended a 'Fun Day' held in Sam's new Scottish Primary School, organised as a fund-raiser. It lasted from 11.00am until 2.00pm. At the next PTA meeting, I'm going to suggest a paying bar with a 2.00am shutdown, a *Lapinodrome* and dangling live fireworks into naked flames. I bet those suggestions will be welcomed with open arms.

***

Bunnies and Bangers – The Essential Tips

(1) Dressing up as Santa and driving up and down the High Street in a rickety cart is appropriate.

(2) By removing the need to pay for warning signs ordering 'DO NOT DO THIS, THAT AND THE OTHER', community-building social events with heavily-subsidised wine provision can be organised by the *commune.*

(3) Recognise the choice is yours, as are the consequences.

(4) Ignore 'Road Closed' signs. Most of the time you'll be fine. Probably. Don't hold me to this.

(5) If you want to close a road, do so. Could be handy if you need to trim a tree or catch a rogue animal.

(6) Propose a fund-raising event which combines small children, light explosives and fluffy creatures. You'll be taken seriously.

(7) Propose a further fund-raising event for your school which involves the sale of fantastic amounts of food and intoxicating liquor. You'll be a hero.

7. Drink and Food

Le vigneron va planter sa vigne,
Vigni, vignez, vignons le vin
La voila jolie vigne où vin

The wine grower will plant his vine
Press, you press, we press the wine
The pretty vine or wine

Traditional – *Chanson à Boire*
(Drinking Song - France)

I have a distant recollection of an evening, in what must have been around 1974, when my Mum and Dad took my brother John and me out to a pub for dinner. I have no idea if it was in South Wales, or perhaps Devon where we had been on holiday a few times, but the events which unfolded remain etched on my memory.

On arrival, our car and its occupants were promptly relegated to the neutral zone of the car park; rather like being pulled over by the drugs squad at Dover Ferry Port. This could have been due to a tip-off, warning of infants in the vicinity of a public house. I remember my father having a lengthy and profound debate with the landlord which, as far as I could make out from my distant vantage point, involved a lot of nodding, finger pointing and gesturing. Eventually, after what seemed like half an hour, we were granted entry to the establishment and led to a table at least twenty-five metres away from any other human beings. You'd have thought we had the plague.

As we settled down John and I, being young boys, talked at young-boy volume which made our parents nervous.

"Sssssshhhhhhh!" came the repeated warnings.

Our table sounded like a bicycle puncture-repair shop.

Soon after drinks were brought over. John and I had cola. I doubt it was the 'Coca' type; probably being those 1970's imitations such as Panda Pops which tasted of sugar and, well… sugar. They came in small glasses with straws. As a child, whenever I was presented with a drink and a straw, the instinctive course of action was to blow hard and make those amusing bubbly sounds, like the noises made by quicksand, in B-movies. This behaviour must be genetic as my children do exactly the same thing. The bubbly-activity approached the edge of 'acceptable' in the given environment, so I was asked to stop. By now, the tension was palpable. Consequently, I went into idiot-mode - a characteristic happily not inherited by my children, much to the relief of Kirsty.

When no-one except John was looking, I placed both hands firmly at the sides of my body and picked up my glass with my teeth alone. I think I went cross-eyed to enhance the effect. John was suitably impressed so I did it again, making a more severe head-jerking gesture to really break new ground on the comedy front. Suddenly, I heard a resounding '*crack!*' This was followed by the smash of a glass, a sensation of cold Panda Pop in my lap, and an unmistakable awareness of broken glass fragments in my mouth.

My Dad went white. My Mum red. The landlord tore the considerable distance from the bar to the 'child-zone', like Usain Bolt having mistakenly taken Justin Gatlin's performance-enhancing drink. He demanded to know what had happened.

"I'm thorry thir, I dlopped my glath," I attempted to articulate through the remains of the glass shards and my mother's fingers.

After many apologies, promises of a replacement glass and much kissing of shoes, my father defused the situation and I was granted another Panda Pop.

Things calmed a little at this point and my parents engaged in a relatively relaxed conversation as we awaited delivery of our starters. John and I were bored. Using sign language, I suggested to my brother (who was older and consequently should have been wiser in my view) that he should slide his glass across the table which I would, in turn, attempt to catch. Always being one for a bit of sport, he obliged. The glass came my way at some speed, in fact much more rapidly than I had mentally and indeed physically anticipated. Unfortunately, I've never had great hand/eye coordination (although I'm always an enthusiastic participant in sporting activities). I missed the glass. An ear-piercing *'smash!'* filled the room as gravity took over and the glass hit the flagstones. This time, the landlord walked over slowly, yet purposefully. The writing was on the wall. My Dad settled up for five drinks (do the maths), two glasses and four unconsumed prawn cocktails. Subsequently, we did the 'walk of shame' to the exit door, having been advised we were unwelcome to return again until the end of the next decade.

1970's Britain strikes me as having been a confused and inconsistent place when it came to children and any institution which sold alcohol. Even the law seemed unclear on the matter and ultimately, it was often up to the landlord, or the more vocal drinker-clientele, to decide whether a family with offspring should be granted access to the hallowed turf of their establishment.

This continued into the 1980's. While on a rainy holiday in Devon with my mum, stepfather and some friends who also had teenage boys, we stopped for refreshment in a charming country pub. The proprietors denied us the opportunity of luxuriating on cushion-laden sofas next to an open fire and instead, swiftly and unashamedly directed us into a kind of leaky pre-fab shed to the rear of the building. As the adults sat on old beer crates, hoping the drips descending from the ceiling wouldn't fall into their Hofmeister lagers, we youths sought amusement in the broken Galaxians machine, so thoughtfully placed in the barn for younger guests.

I wonder if this attitude was a kind of Puritan hangover; the 'Just Say No' generation of the 1980's were taught if you were to even look at a glass of the most innocuous of intoxicating drink, you would instantly turn into a pale, red-eyed, mumbling zombie with no chance of any meaningful life ahead of you. Thank you Zammo. We were told drink was *'bad, bad, bad!'* but any teenager with an iota of common-sense noted this was inconsistent with what happened at weddings, family parties, on Saturday nights or at funerals even. The level of laughter, fun and banter increased proportionately with the amount of the evil fluid consumed. As far as I could see, it looked *'good, good, good!'* The messages failed to make any sense at all.

The predictable outcome was that as soon as young people were old enough, or at least looked old enough to obtain fake ID, they drank astonishing amounts of alcohol as if trying to make up for lost time. When I more-or-less reached the appropriate age, I immediately invested in home-brew making equipment and started producing ales on an industrial scale. What they lacked in flavour and quality was more than compensated for in terms of strength and, well, strength. Tolerant yeast extracts, triple fermentation, the addition of methylated spirits (just kidding) – I knew all the tricks.

This undesirable state of affairs is not one I have witnessed in France and I feel certain I understand the reasons why. Firstly, in our experience, cafés and bars *adore* having infants on their premises. In fact, any village bar barely deserves its status in the absence of small children being illicitly treated to iced-lollies by the owner. Kirsty frequented one such establishment weekly whilst Florence attended her dance class. Sam - at this time three or four years of age - was greeted by name, kissed, and his order *(menthe a l'eau)* correctly recalled week-to-week. Secondly, people tend not to drink alcohol in (a) massive quantities and (b) a short timescale. Consequently, their behaviour is unlikely to become so radically altered, that they become a threat to any child in their immediate vicinity.

My word, people certainly drink. For the vast majority I met, an *aperitif* alone consisted of more than the mythical 'daily two units'. To add to that, wine was drunk routinely with evening meals, if not at lunchtime as well. If you're going to have a tipple at midday and with your evening meal, why not go for the full house and do breakfast as well? One morning, I turned up at the station to catch my 6.25am train to Bordeaux only to learn it had been cancelled due to a strike. I believe the gripe may have been a proposition to reduce lunchbreaks to a mere two hours. Having forty minutes to kill, I rode my pushbike to a little *café-bar* in the town for a coffee. Upon arrival, a large number of working townsfolk were present, many drinking a *demi-pression* (a glass of draught beer) and several others, a small glass of *rosé*. This appeared to be the absolute norm.

Similarly, when I worked for *l'École Municipale de Musique* in Coutras on a Saturday morning, one of my greatest pleasures was to take mid-morning coffee in the covered section of the market. The far corner hosted what might be diplomatically called a 'working man's bar'. I would order a heart-palpitation-inducing *double-espresso* and the young barman routinely offered me a large slosh of *eau-de-vie* to liven it up. Knowing its properties as an excellent substitute to firelighters, I would decline. How I loved that little bar. Market traders would come along for mid-morning refreshment and, alongside their *demi-grenadine, demi pêche* or the much-loved *Ricard*, they would share banter and chit-chat. Many of the men were tough, 120-kilo beasts, and looked incongruous with their *petite* glasses of their chosen tipple. I was the only Brit in the company and, coupled with my guitar case, I drew attention. I became the target of warm leg-pulling which I received with pleasure. At some point, a drinker would inevitably stroll over to the fishmonger and return with a large bag full of oysters or cooked prawns; these were crashed down on the bar. Without missing a beat of the conversation, all present would pull out a knife and dive in. I was expected to be a participant in this too, my puny pen-knife always being a source of further good-natured banter. I think our corner of France is the only area where I've witnessed a teenage boy being berated for *not* carrying a knife.

I can still envisage the little sign the bar had posted above the cash register. It read:

*Le Christ n'a pas transformé le vin a l'eau
Mais l'eau aux vin.*

(Christ didn't change wine into water
But water into wine).

The *aperitif* is an essential part of the daily ritual in rural-French life. One needs to understand that having a drink before eating is not about the alcohol content of the drink; it is a stimulant, a kind of delicious anticipation and elongation of the meal to follow. Our wonderful neighbours André and Eliane would invite us, whenever eye-contact was made, to share an *apero* at any pre-meal opportunity.

One sunny summer's morning, my brother-in-law, Ian, was helping me to put up a fence for our chickens – tough work in thirty degrees heat. At about 11.30am, I needed to return a shovel to André. When I showed up, a cool *Leffe* with my name on it appeared. Not wishing to disappoint this good man who always enjoyed hearing the latest news in our lives over an *apero*, I reluctantly obliged in sharing a convivial moment with him. Soon after, Eliane joined us. Twenty minutes later, Ian glanced over the fence to see what had become of me (I like to imagine I had left him holding one end of a beam or something). The *Anglais* was immediately summoned to partake in the ritual with us.

I loved spending time with André and Eliane, but there were days when I had to exercise extreme caution when passing *Chez Eux*. If I had any kind of intellectual obligation to fulfil in the afternoon, it was a dangerous game to pop next door. One morning, I ran a trivial errand for them and, before I could say 'I really shouldn't't', André had fetched four glasses and a bottle of *Porto*. Kirsty was called in order to share the moment and, as we chatted to Eliane, I noticed a noise like a running tap coming from behind me. I was alarmed to see André casually slug about half a pint of the rich, deep and rather potent liquid into each glass. I'm not really much of a drinker and Kirsty less so, yet, having a motto of 'waste not, want not', I set about my task of consuming the offering. Once I'd drained my glass, Kirsty exercised a beautiful sleight-of-hand movement with which she swapped my empty vessel for her still half-full one, and I heroically dispatched hers too. The walk back to *Chez Jones* is about twenty metres but upon our return, my somewhat scenic route would have been at least three times this distance. I slept all afternoon.

The Art of the Aperitif

This following section is of such critical importance if you are intending to live in France, it deserves its own little sub-chapter. Upon arrival, you are very likely to be invited for an *apero* by neighbours or acquaintances, unless your dog murders their chickens or something. Therefore, you simply *must, must, must* know what is expected of you, and how to behave. What's more, we can't have you, Dear Reader, hosting such an event and letting the Anglophone world down.

Here are seven golden rules you should keep in your bedside cabinet and read every morning and night until you have them memorised word-for-word.

(1) Never, ever outstay your welcome when invited for an apero. To do this is a social gaffe akin to belching loudly at a funeral service. It is not an all-nighter, despite what the early indicators may suggest. If you are hosting, your guests will probably arrive at about 6.30pm and should be on their way not long after 8.00pm. The apero is a fantastic way to sound them out without risking being stuck for an entire evening - and possibly some of the night - if they turn out to be crashing bores. If someone asks whether you'd like to hear about their model train collection, you can declare that nothing would give you greater pleasure in the safe knowledge you'll only have to endure the ensuing tedious monologue for an hour or so at

worst. If your guests look like they are staying later than 8.30pm, you are well within your rights to start crashing around pots and pans and saying things like 'Oh dear, the dinner is burning' or 'Do you not have homes to go to?'

(2) Choose a designated driver. This is because you are likely to receive refills of potent beverages, whether you ask for them or not. You must avoid appearing drunk as a consequence; good conversation is pre-requisite.

(3) Have something interesting to say. Please see the end of point (2).

(4) You will be offered a variety of beverages but not necessarily ones you'll enjoy. The French have a taste for very sweet or rather sickly-flavoured drinks. Ricard and Pernod are both hugely-loved pastis drinks. I find them pretty disgusting but have been obliged to drink many in the past seven years. Belgian beers are also popular. They are characterised by their richness and sweetness as well as being so strong, drinking a pint would be frankly, irresponsible. If you ask for a Tango in France (pronounced Tongo, with a nasal kind of 'o' sound), you will receive neither an Argentinian dance nor a can of carbonated fizzy drink claiming to bear some distant relationship to oranges. You will, in fact, receive a small beer with a dash of grenadine sirop (a thick fruit squash) resulting in a bright-red gassy solution which could pass as a dessert in another setting. I'm actually rather fond of a Tango. You can add any sirop you wish but grenadine and peach (pêche) are the most common. After one summer of partaking in many a Tango, I became more concerned about my teeth than my liver.

(5) You will enjoy a delightful variety of nibbles at an apero. It is important to prevent your children from devouring them all at high speed before anyone else has had a look-in. I know this

from bitter experience. Sometimes you can get away with providing crisps, nuts and little biscuits. On other occasions, our hosts have created a delightful array of miniature nibbles – hand prepared with love and effort. I often returned home having eaten my fill (far too much so socially-speaking) and struggled to finish dinner as a result. This is a major faux-pas on all fronts and I apologise. Incidentally, the delightful word 'biscuit' comes from the French bi-cuit meaning 'twice cooked'. The French will refer to a biscuit as a gateau as in 'a cake'.

(6) When hosting an apero it is civil to make an effort. Yes, I have friends who are just in it for the beer and a handful of peanuts, but if you're inviting classier folk, such as André and Eliane, then one should push the boat out. I must confess the best apero ever seen Chez Jones was due to the work and creative imagination of my afore-mentioned brother-in-law, Ian. I tried my best to take the credit but fooled no-one.

(7) An apero is best enjoyed in groups of about seven or eight participants. Fewer makes you Mr No-Mates. Any more and it is a party rather than an apero.

The French also enjoy a *digestif*. This is a blatant and lame excuse to further elongate a good evening. I fall around laughing when intelligent, even brilliant people claim they take one for 'health reasons'. In 2016, I played a gig with a jazz quartet at the home of a truly exceptional and highly successful man. I say 'home' but I mean *'château'*. Having performed and subsequently indulged in an extraordinary meal, the host offered me a *digestif* just as we were packing up. I thanked him but pointed out I had to drive. He looked concerned.

"You must have one as you have eaten such a large meal," he said.

Upon further interrogation he explained, with a perfectly straight face, the French take a *digestif* to dissolve the fat in the food they have consumed. This allegedly eliminates the potential weight gain and other negative effects resulting from the consumption of an eight-course meal. The implication is that one could have pork scratchings for ten, followed by a family pack of Mars Bar ice creams and, as long as you polish off a little *cognac* before the end of the night, it's pretty much like tucking into a light salad.

It will sound as if your average French meal will finish up with the participants staggering around like three-legged giraffes on a pirate ship. This is untrue. I have been on many a night out with my French friends and I cannot ever recall seeing anyone truly plastered to use a British terminology. I accept some of this might be due to tolerance levels rising due to the regularity with which alcohol is imbibed, but I believe it is more to do with the *way* in which alcohol is consumed and, perhaps more importantly, its much-revered association with food. This last point is endorsed by the experts inhabiting the legendary wine village of Saint Emilion. We lived not far from this wonderful and picturesque place which is associated with some of the greatest wines in the world. Visitors – especially Chinese in this day and age – come from afar to taste, enjoy and purchase fine vintages with their unique, rich earthy tones (the wine, not the Chinese).

Proprietors offer tours of their *caves* and the experience is always both fascinating and enlightening. One guide told me words which rang with profound truthfulness. He said there is no such thing as 'bad wine' but there are wines for different occasions. Therefore, if you were having a spontaneous barbecue with your buddies, or maybe a curry, it would be madness to open a 2009 Saint Emilion at the peak of its perfection.

"Save this for special family days with fine food," emphasised our guide.

You see, the wine is connected to food, like a perfect partnership: Torvill and Dean; bread and butter; Saint Emilion and Camembert. The experience of seeing, swirling, sniffing, sipping and savouring acts in harmony with the accompanying food to create a single experience. Consequently, the French are not snobby about wine. They will happily put ice into a cheap red; of course, they know to do so will disguise the finer notes of the flavour (if they were ever present) but if it's a hot day, go for it.

Alcohol is also an integral part of the French working day. If you are employed, you may like me, have to attend staff meetings. I can almost hear you moan under your breath. I can think of very few things more agonising than a badly-run staff meeting, particularly if the chairperson is unassertive. Over the years of my career, I have attended such gatherings where 150 busy, professional people are kept waiting by colleagues using the occasion to have a public whinge and moan. Even worse is when someone asks a question which need not be aired at that moment.

"When do the exam entries need to be completed?" a voice from the rear of the hall will ask.

There is silence but you can telepathically hear 149 pained responses.

"Look it up on the website for crying out loud… later… at home… out of my presence."

Painful.

Staff meetings in our French village are not like this. We have get-togethers to organise events such as concerts for visiting artists. When putting on a *soirée* there are many things to consider: tariffs, seating, keys, the get-in, the get-out, chairs, lighting, heating, and legal authorisation amongst others. I kid you not but I sat through one such meeting, called to finalise a last-minute event, and the committee spent an hour arguing whether *rosé* or *rouge* would be appropriate during the interval. I stared, completely mute in bewildered amazement, as normally-reasonable people got in a real flap over Bergerac or Bordeaux. Anyway, a decision was eventually made (on a split vote) and we all put the real concert organisation on to 'Any Other Business' for the next meeting. Then, out came the *aperos*. I'd like to suggest to any reader in charge of a body of staff that if you were to offer them a beer at the end of a meeting, you would be revered and loved by all. I suspect your staff-retention rates would go through-the-roof as well.

Such attitudes towards drink, so typical in French rural areas, are utterly alien to other cultures. In 2015, I was working for a well-known school in Bordeaux. As the school's sole music teacher, I often received requests from agencies representing musical groups from all over the world seeking venues where their clients could perform. On one such occasion, an Austrian agency contacted me as they had a youth choir from Wisconsin, USA, touring Europe. They were seeking a venue in the Bordeaux area where they could offer a concert. Sadly, my school was closed on the proposed day (it was one of the innumerable public holidays enjoyed by the French each year), but I wrote back suggesting perhaps the choir would like to sing in our village church.

On paper, the proposition must have looked unappealing to the agency. The glamour and *chic* of Bordeaux exchanged for a concert in a village with more bovine inhabitants than humans should have been a worrying trade-off. Anyway, the contact was a fine and open-minded young lady, and she had a mysteriously-deep faith in my ability to avoid creating a car-crash out of her career. The Music School Committee was instantly put into action, like a crack SWAT unit, to organise a major event in just five weeks. In the first meeting, the essentials were laid down; we arranged for the village bar to set up a tent outside the church for interval refreshments, and it was decided there should be beer served on draught. The second meeting ensured there would be ample *rouge* and *rosé* present at the post-concert party, sourced at a preferable rate, albeit with some compromise in the quality department. During the *rendezvous* held the day before the event, I tentatively proposed that we should venture into the organisation of music stands, benches, toilet facilities, a printed programme and other such trivialities. My suggestions were ignored with a shrug and stifled *'Namportakwa!'* but thankfully, a consensus was finally met upon the thorny question of 'the *digestif*' which had caused tantrums and resignations within the *cognac* and *whisky* camps. All-the-while though, the necessary effort had been invested into organising and publicising the event in the villagers' own time. Posters were placed at the side of the local *route nationale,* papers ran articles about our unusual visitors and local online forums were overloaded. Friends knew what needed to be done and just did it; a smooth and seamless machine having been organically developed through the provision of numerous concerts over the preceding years. This allowed more time to quaff an *apero* in meeting time which was an altogether more agreeable way to pass an evening than filing risk assessments.

Late in the afternoon of the big day, the choir pulled up in their touring coach. They were overwhelmed by the energy and industry this little village had put into promoting their performance. I have to say they were the most polite, gracious and lovely young people I've met in many years - a true credit to their state. When they took to the stage a few hours later, the church was bursting at the seams. More than 250 people crammed themselves into the building; many seated on hastily-arranged benches and others standing two or three deep to the rear. Our village choir *Polysons* sang first. They were inspired and motivated and did a fantastic job. Then the American youngsters put their heart and souls into one of the most exquisite, heartfelt and profoundly beautiful evenings of music making I have heard in many-a-year. At the end of the event, the two choirs sang together. They walked offstage, still singing the final chorus of an African song they had learned in the late afternoon, to the sight and sound of hundreds of locals standing, stamping and whooping in their ears. That will remain etched on my heart and soul forever.

We had proposed a little after-event party and the tour organisers had agreed as long as it didn't go on for too long. Fat chance. We forayed over *en masse* to the local *Salle des Fêtes* and the eating, and yes, drinking commenced. Anyone who has lived in the States will be aware of the super-conservative laws in place relating to alcohol. Whereas the sale of a firearm to a twenty-year-old is legitimate in Wisconsin, offering a half of lager to the same client is illegal. If our shopper fancied purchasing a small chocolate egg containing a plastic toy alongside his double-barrelled pump-action shotgun, his request would be denied as the latter item is regarded as too hazardous for sale. Well, I'm sure there's good reasoning there somewhere, but while I scratch my befuddled head, let us return to our tale. Many of the village choir were enjoying a glass or two of wine, and our charming American friends, sipping their orange juices, courteously respected their right to do so. All was going swimmingly until I spotted one French choir member, a larger-than-life jovial fellow, strolling across the room towards our guests. He was wearing a broad, beaming, wine-induced smile, and in his hands was a large tray balancing many glasses of *rosé,* just the right number in fact to quench the thirst of an under-aged, super-conservative American youth choir. I watched, transfixed, unable to decide what to do. I half thought of rugby tackling him in slow-motion but, in the end thought 'Oh stuff it, *que sera sera'*. The drinks could have been some kind of blackcurrant squash or something similarly non-fermented, and the young singers from across the Atlantic each took a glass, thanking him profusely. Moments later I heard a voice with a strong North-American accent crying out.

"Oh, my word! It's *alcohol!"*

Twenty young pairs of hands dropped those glasses as if they were hot potatoes (metaphorically rather than literally). There was astonishment amongst our guests and their parent representatives; the gentleman who had handed out the beverage looked genuinely hurt and confused.

"Mais, c'est rosé!" he kept saying, implying he would have understood the problem had he handed out large whiskies (as he may well have done) but *rosé*...

I must admit, I couldn't help but agree with him.

Anyway, once one-and-all had recovered from the shock, and I had gently explained to *Monsieur DeRosé* that Americans have yet to put rum punch into their babies' bottles, the incident blew over. A wonderful evening exchanging folk songs, dances and good humour ensued. My daughter Florence remembers the party with hilarity as, when a village tenor brought out a fine, local circular cheese, a young American asked without a hint of irony whether 'it was a donut'.

I was deeply moved upon receiving a message from an American parent some weeks later. She said the choir had sung in Bilbao, Madrid, across France and Germany, but it was their evening in Saint Cecilia des Dames which had endured in everyone's hearts. On that night, despite our noteworthy cultural differences, the youngsters from Wisconsin had seen the soul of a country.

I think the difference between France and other cultures is that I have rarely noted *les Français*, youthful or otherwise, going for a night-on-the-town *with the express purpose of becoming inebriated*. Just as Eskimos have twenty words for 'snow', the wealth of expressions extant in English to communicate the action of deliberately allowing the effects of alcohol to take hold of mind and body for the purposes of recreation suggests it is all-too-common a practice in the Anglophone world: we're going out for a session; fancy a bit of a sesh? (diminutive of 'session'); let's go out on the razz; we're going on a pub crawl; I'm organising a Leo Sayer (all-dayer); I intend to get wrecked; Jeff got sh*t faced, and other such charming idioms of the language to name just a few. The Health and Safety Police have not permitted this tendency to escape their notice and have reacted accordingly. Recently, a British friend of mine attended a conference in a large UK city; at the end of the week, delegates were invited to partake in a night-on-the-tiles. To my friend's amazement (and vast amusement) attendees were required to sign a disclaimer, absolving the organisers of responsibility should a participant find him/herself dressed in a gorilla suit, placed on the train to Edinburgh and nailed into a timber container with the words 'To The Zoo' roughly scrawled across the side. One might suggest to the conference directors that they relieve their H&S staff of their responsibilities (to use the modern, cosy synonym for 'sack') and use the budget to employ fine local chefs, purchase scrumptious, fresh food and gift guests a case of 2009 Bordeaux *Médoc* at the pinnacle of its perfection.

British pubs exist primarily to sell intoxicating liquor. Consequently, the United Kingdom can rightfully claim to be the home to some of the world's finest real ales. Amen to that I say. In the French countryside, you will truly struggle to find such a venue as nearly every bar will prioritise food over booze. The exception to this rule is the ever-increasing number of British-style pubs opening to cater for the demand created by ex-pats wanting to do a 'Leo Sayer'. The vast majority of bars in the countryside keep hours unsuitable for a pub crawl. They will open doors at a very early hour – 6.00am typically – to cater for the aforementioned pre-breakfast *apero* market. Most will serve lunch, yet propose dinner only once or twice a week. These evening meals are usually pre-advertised *soirées* where just one fixed-price dish, such as the ever-popular *moules frites* is available. Many a traveller has arrived on holiday in a picturesque French village fancying 'a bit of a sesh' after an 8-hour drive. Upon ambling down to the local bar at 8.30pm in delicious anticipation of a cool beer, they're astonished to find it on the verge of closing for the night, with the owner perhaps reluctantly prepared to offer them a quick *digestif.*

You'd have thought a bar owner in an area hosting plenty of ex-pats could be on to a good thing financially, particularly if he/she encouraged groups of *les Etrangers* to frequent his/her establishment every weekend to 'get leathered'. Indeed, this did occur in a charming village south of Angoulême where friends of ours lived, but the events which unfolded should serve as a cautionary tale to all.

The little bar in the central square of the village had been a regular haunt of a couple of immigrant British builders for a few months. One evening, they asked *Monsieur le Landlord* if they could watch a Premier League football match on his modest TV. The landlord agreed and before you could say 'Zinadine Zidane', his bar had become the local haunt of choice for viewing British football. Initially, *Monsieur le Landlord* was overjoyed – as was his accountant – due to the fact many of the clientele seemed to require the accompaniment of seven pints of fizzy lager in order to enjoy *le match.* Multiply this by thirty lads (and it was lads, no lasses) 'on the razz' and it was '*Ch-ching! Euros-in!*' As time went by, *Monsieur le Landlord* couldn't help but note the consumption of generous quantities of *Stella Artois* did coincide with less-than-desirable behaviour and the use of language which he was unable to recall from his primary school English lessons. He decided to turn a blind eye though, as his foray into this hitherto unexplored market sector was making early retirement an increasingly-realistic proposition. Inevitably though, a group of retired gentlemen who had lived in the village all of their lives were finding these changes undesirable. They had seen the Nazi occupation, toiled over the land and raised their families in the area. They felt, quite reasonably, they were entitled to go to their local bar at 6.30pm for an *apero* and to watch life trickle by in pleasant reflection. Instead, they watched a plaster-dust and tattoo-covered bloke called Wayne falling out of the bar door and vomiting in the gutter each time West Ham conceded a goal. Admittedly, they would have enjoyed the *spectacle* the first time but, as with a visit to URSSAF, more than once was too much. Soon after this practice commenced, the local elections were called. Noting his opportunity, the local representative of the lamentable extreme-right *Front National* realised the goings-on in the local bar were the perfect weapon of manipulation in his campaign for power. Needless to say, within weeks, the village found itself with an FN *maire*. No doubt the footie-crew whinged as to the injustice of it all. Gentlemen of a certain persuasion will take every opportunity to moan about immigrants to their homeland 'not behaving like the locals' but it has to work both ways. As immigrants, those moving to France must surely avoid turning their village bar into Blackpool promenade with an agreeable climate.

The little house we eventually bought in France included a wonderful garden; the wise person who designed it obviously understood the rhythms of nature. We benefited from an abundance of fruit trees which gave mountains of sweet-tasting, fresh, chemical-free produce every year, yet the yield was staggered - each tree producing fruit at a slightly different moment from the others. In May or June, we harvested deep-red, succulent cherries. We were lucky enough to have three massive cherry trees; the first to fruit standing next to our goat field about halfway down our land. We hardly saw any of this tree's crop as its plump fruit was devoured annually by flocks of starlings. They made an incredible noise – a kind of continuous screeching like an army of schoolboys scraping a thousand fingernails down a huge blackboard. The first year I noticed their presence, I took to running down the garden clapping my hands and shrieking to scare them off. It was a pointless activity, serving only to amuse the neighbours and terrify the hens. Friends with a similar challenge tried techniques such as hanging old CDs in the tree. The idea is that the flashes of reflected sunlight as they spin startle the birds. I suspect many of mine are up there, covered in starling droppings. Other methods included hanging transistor radios from branches playing music and chat twenty-four hours per day. Programmes dedicated to 1980's synth-pop are said to be particularly successful at scaring off the starlings. The problem is they cause the fruit to go bad as well.

In August we gathered a wealth of plums and greengages. In the late summer, the harvest was peaches and quince. We made jams, chutneys, pies and pretty much any other fruit-based concoction you care to name. One of the most satisfying ways to start my summer days was to go down to the garden early in the morning when the light was beautiful and all was quiet and, having attended to my animal-related chores, to place sheets around the plum trees before giving each of them a gentle shake. The resulting fall would fill two baskets of fruit every day. I loved giving the children fresh chopped plums for their breakfast.

One afternoon, we were invited to Sunday lunch by friends and our hosts handed us a home-made fruit liqueur as an *apero*. It was, as always, sweet and potent. I enquired how it was made and found their efforts were a tad fraudulent. It was simply fruit added to a low-quality alcoholic drink which would be left to mature for a few months. This 'fruit alcohol' base is available off-the-shelf at supermarkets, such is the popularity of creating hooch with minimal effort. That evening, I spent a few hours online and found many people worldwide were turning their excess fruit into alcoholic beverages. My eyes widened in crazed excitement. There were even recipes for courgette wine - tempting, but I do have limits. We had made enough jam to last until 2028, I was beginning to resemble a fruit pie and the goats were practically bleating out loud 'Not more plums!' Here was the opportunity to use our excess fruit to provide ourselves, and the whole *department,* with sufficient sweet *apero* fodder for the entire winter.

A little more research on the ever-reliable Google yielded a recipe entitled 'Easy Plum Wine'. I liked the sound of this - particularly the 'easy' bit - as we had sufficient plums to sink a small ship. Having recently re-entered the world of home-beer making, I had all the kit and, within a few weeks, there were three gallons of plum wine bubbling away next to our boiler. For many months I doted upon my concoction lovingly. In the depths of winter, I placed hot water bottles under the barrel as my children shivered in bed. As spring approached, I gently syphoned it into bottles with a little priming sugar to aid clarification. For a further six weeks, I tenderly rotated each bottle of fruity joy, kissing it gently on the neck as I sung it a *petite berceuse.* Eventually, the day arrived for the *degustation.* We decided to video-call my brother and stepmother; de-corking a bottle in their cyber-presence, to mark the birthday of my late dad. I had noticed the *vin* was different in colour from the alleged 'finished result' modelled by the smiling lady on the website which had provided me with the recipe. Whereas hers resembled a cheeky light *Cabernet Sauvignon,* mine was not dissimilar to Coca-Cola with a splash of milk. Still, the proof of the pudding was in the eating (or drinking) as they say so, watched closely by my family and friends in real life and online, we pulled the *bouchon.* I recall a loud explosion which sent chickens flying in terror and small children diving under their beds. Once I'd cleaned the sticky liquid off my face, computer screen and kitchen ceiling, I decanted the remaining 'wine' into two glasses and handed one to Kirsty who, suddenly, seemed to be unsure as to the wisdom of the whole enterprise.

"When I said plum *wine,*" I lied to the onlookers, "I of course meant *champagne.*"

The stuff had a pleasant-enough nose, but when we put the glasses to our lips, neither Kirsty nor I could restrain an audible *'yeeurk!'* much to the amusement of our watching family. I was forced to acknowledge a temporary setback and poured the remainder of the bottle down the sink.

I clung to the hope it might improve, given more time to clarify, but when I attempted a second explosive *degustation* many months later, I was forced to admit defeat. I opened fifteen bottles of the stuff in the garden and poured it all away. It sounded as if we were holding a clay-pigeon shooting competition. The patch of ground where I disposed of it has failed to yield any plant life since. Ah well. Some you win…

Eating in France is like a religion, a *raison d'etre,* a *mode de vie.* Children, as a rule, eat far later than their British counterparts. When children come home from school at around 4.30pm, they invariably devour a *goûter* (snack) which carries them over until the family dinner. This is normally served after 8.00pm so consequently, French kids tend to go to bed late. This is why younger children have a *sieste* in school which can last for several hours.

I loved the fact that on Monday morning, youngsters, including my own offspring, gathered around a noticeboard outside the school gate in a deep conference. The notice on display was the lunchtime menu for the week. Parents and carers also craned their heads to study the propositions of *la cantine* and discussed them earnestly with their infants. It was a healthy and reverential attitude towards food. Our children enjoyed two hours for lunch, the majority of the time being spent in the dining room rather than the playground. There were always three courses on offer, and *baguette a volonté.*

The evening meal is of enormous importance in a French household. This will start with an *aperitif* which I imagine as the grown-up equivalent of the *goûter*. At about 8.00pm, cries of *'A table!'* will ring out across the fields of sunflowers. There will be an *entrée* followed by a *plat* and *dessert*. Eating will last until around 10.00pm when all will retire for the night. What you will deduce is *eating the meal is the primary activity of the evening*. I cannot recall a single French friend asking me if I had watched a soap opera the previous day. Conversely, if I had a quid for every time one of them asked what we'd eaten, I'd be a rich man. If you're going to have a passion for something, to give it time and effort, there are certainly worse things you could choose than the foodstuffs you prepare for the nutrition of yourself and your family.

When living in other countries, I've noticed that comparatively speaking mealtimes are treated as a necessary inconvenience, unless celebrating a special occasion. When picking up our children from their friends' houses they will often have been 'given tea', referring to the evening meal, thus saving us the supposed trouble. This is generous and thoughtful, but if you live in a French village, never, I mean *never* do this without prior arrangement. It would be rather like obtaining tickets for a big international football match on Friday night for you and your son, and coming home only to find your neighbour 'took him for you'.

If my friends go on holiday, I naturally ask upon their return whether they had an agreeable time.

"Ah yes! We ate very well," they reply if it was a successful vacation. *Ah oui! Nous avons bien mangé.*

They may have endured relentless rain for a fortnight and had their wallets nicked from their hotel room but, the only criterion which appears to count as far as I can discern is whether they ate well. This mentality expands to their holidays to the UK. Anyone who has read *Asterix in Britain* will know how the French mercilessly mock British *cuisine*. A couple of years ago, our village big band travelled to Norfolk to play some gigs. There is a *photo-memoire* board in our music school with various snaps of the band members enjoying their activities. At least 90% of them feature trumpet players smiling over full-English breakfasts, fish and chips, and pints of bitter. I'm unable to recall any pictures of them actually playing their instruments.

The importance of eating can be beautifully illustrated by our visit, along with my afore-mentioned brother- and sister-in-law, to a pleasant fun-fair and water-park complex called *Parc Jacquou*. It is tucked away in the woods of the Perigord Noir and makes a most agreeable family day out. It had been a mere fifteen minutes since our arrival when a noisy horn sounded. To the utter incredulity of everyone from outside of France (many of whom had been queuing for some time), those operating the rides switched off the power and closed their booths. Roller coaster, big wheel, carousel, tea-cups, the whole lot, were shut-up for an hour-and-a-half as everyone descended upon the restaurant. Subsequently, one-and-all were obliged to enjoy a leisurely lunch, complete with wine and *digestif.* I would love to see the reaction of everyday folk if that happened at Chessington World of Adventures, Alton Towers or Disneyland.

Inevitably, food has crept on to the agenda of our music school meetings and causes nearly as much of a heated debate as the question of wine choices. One year, someone had the bright idea of giving the children a little sachet of chocolates for Christmas. Immediately, committee members loudly extolled the virtues of a wealth of confectionary options, from strawberry creams to *ganache au chocolat blanc*. After an hour of this, I glanced down to discover a puddle of drool on the table where I'd been dribbling while listening to this *bonbon fantasie*. The need to include everyone's *bonbon préferé* resulted in each and every child receiving a colossal bag of tooth-enamel-dissolving goodies, presented in a transparent sack with gold ribbon, making both parents and their offspring gasp in disbelief. The music-school kitchen resembled Willy Wonka's dispatch centre.

The *Mozaic Jazz Band* – a twenty-piece big band linked to the music school rehearse in the *Salle des Fêtes* every Thursday evening. Each week, different musicians are responsible for preparing a *casse croûte* (literally meaning 'breaking a crust') for the end of the practice. Quiche, *baguette,* salads, fruit tarts, home-made beer, ciders and wine are served up as a matter of course which is a pleasing change from the pint of bitter and a bag of crisps I used to snatch during breaks in rehearsal with an equivalent band in Wales.

In the Perigord region, there is a local *cuisine* with a proud tradition. It is extremely carnivorous and some items served up are, to put it diplomatically, a bit of an acquired taste. Now, I should point out I am not a fussy man. My children refer to me as *la Poubelle* – The Dustbin. We are, for the most part, vegetarian and we support the organic cause with a passion. When offered food though, I'll tackle pretty much anything if necessary. As mentioned in Chapter One, I consumed a jellyfish mountain in Japan out of respect for our hosts. While on tour in Hungary, I also picked away at sufficient boiled cabbage in pickle to last me a lifetime for similar reasons. I think this is known as 'taking one for the team'.

Below are the items on the rural French menu which are somewhat specialist. You may love them, but I think it's only fair to be forewarned about what you'll be letting yourself in for.

(1) *Boeuf Tartare.* In 2015, we undertook a family day trip to Bordeaux and stopped for lunch at a café near the lovely *Gambetta* area. I ordered a simple omelette and Florence unsuspectingly chose a *boeuf tartare.* Once the *plats* had arrived, I could see she was struggling so we swapped plates. *Boeuf tartare* is basically raw minced beef, with seasoning, and a raw egg on top. Many of my friends adore it but I found it a bit of a challenge, to say the least. I'm not saying 'don't eat it', but I am making you aware you won't be getting a steak and ale pie which you could well be led to believe. Incidentally, if you

order a *steak tartare,* there's a sporting chance you'll be eating a horse (or part of one). Just saying. Once, I was eating a piece of meat in Normandy and it suddenly crossed my mind that I might be consuming Shergar. I was so disconcerted with this possibility, I checked with the waiter who was leaning against the bar with a group of his mates. I was met with a look that could only be described as 'nonplussed' followed by a series of sniggers which were echoed, rather unfairly in my humble opinion, by those sharing my own table. If you want to have a go at preparing a *steak tartare* yourself, take a beef burger out of the freezer before you go to work, cover it with salt and pepper and, upon your return in the evening, crack an egg over it and *presto!* You'll have prepared a classic. You can impress all of your friends and possibly poison them at the same time. Incidentally, Florence tells me the omelette was excellent.

(2) *Foie Gras.* This is one to stir the emotions. *Foie gras* literally translates as 'fat liver'. French duck and goose farmers have traditionally used the technique of *gavage* (forced overfeeding) in order to fatten up the liver of their birds. It is this action which supposedly creates the rich, fat *paté* which is *foie gras.* Needless to say, there are loud and passionate objections to this practice from those concerned with animal welfare. I hear and understand this, but it irritates me when I see people protesting against small, specialist producers in rural areas when a certain large burger chain with a seriously-creepy clown as a mascot allegedly uses about 67,000 cows *per day* to supply its outlets. Similarly, a chicken outlet with an elderly military character as its figurehead is said to kill around 65,000 chickens per day. These live indoors for just thirty-five days. That is just two brands out of hundreds. You can then tack on the problem of how to feed these pitiful creatures; great swathes of land are put aside to grow miles upon miles of crops which will act as animal feed. The lack of biodiversity encourages

parasites – an inconvenience resolved by sloshing thousands of litres of pesticide onto the exhausted soil; the over-farmed earth will then be chemically re-fertilised to grow animal feed... and so the merry-go-round continues. As for the 'food' itself, well, the lack of any discernible flavour can be resolved with a few sacks of refined sugar and salt. Job done. I can't help but think protest efforts ought to be focused upon these giants, rather than some old fellow with fifty or so birds enjoying a free-range life. I did have the opportunity to talk to a duck farmer who produces birds for the *foie gras* market and he explained his ducks are just plain greedy. According to him, he simply puts out too much food and the ducks will eat it. Anyway, whatever the rights or wrongs, *foie gras,* to my palate, is a kind of posh sandwich spread. I have friends who would strike me a severe blow for that statement.

(3) Oysters *(huitres).* I just don't understand oysters. People rave about them, and there are specialist oyster outlets on corners in most villages. To me, the experience of eating an oyster is like swimming in the sea with your mouth forced open by a super bouncy ball. I know you're meant to swallow an oyster whole, but that fails to change the experience in my book. Each to their own.

(4) *Gesièrs* (Gizzards). You will see *Salade de Gesièrs* on many a lunch menu. It is a rich, dark meat with a deep flavour. Thin slices are usually served within a salad, with plenty of dressing. You won't need much meat as it is so intense. So what's the problem? Gizzards, in case you are unaware, are stomach lining. Many people eat this in rapturous appreciation until they find out what it is. Best to tell a white lie to fussy relatives.

(5) *Andouille.* Some foods are challenging and others, in my view, deserve to be categorised elsewhere. Grass is edible, but should it be defined as food? The same could be said for the

sausage known as *andouille.* In the US, *andouille* is a renowned speciality with rich, dark meat, rather like a *chorizo*. In France, it is very intestine-rich, fatty and stinks to high heaven. I once consumed some (yet another food exchange – this time with Kirsty) and the experience could be best described as 'grim'. Years later, when recounting this tale to a French friend who is an *andouille* fan, I offered the opinion that it tasted like stale meat. Without batting an eyelid he explained this must have been a good *andouille* as it 'should taste of the animal's last meal'. *Bon appetit.*

(6) Vegetarians are placed in the same category as people who believe the Earth is flat or that their next-door neighbour is a spy from the planet Zargon. Upon a visit to the cosmopolitan and well-to-do tourist town of Arcachon, I asked a waiter if his menu had a vegetarian option. His reply was as abrupt as it was monosyllabic, being a conclusive *'Non'*. Although the gentleman omitted to look up from the table he was clearing, his body language suggested thoughts along the lines of 'Why don't you just eat a slab of bleeding flesh like everybody else you great big wimpy *Britannique*'. My dad enjoyed telling a story of how one evening, he'd enjoyed an exceptionally tasty late-evening plate of chips in a hotel in Brittany, only to suffer terrible indigestion for the entire duration of the night. It transpired that the chips had been cooked in pure goose fat.

(7) If you order a steak without conferring with your waiter, it will arrive in such a rare state that it will moo as you chase it around your plate.

I am amazed and amused by the astonishing amount of butter and salt which the French consume – especially the older generations. André would pop over with a range of vegetables on a near daily basis in the summer and, having consumed a cheeky beer, would advise us on how to prepare them.

"It is necessary to add butter and salt," he would proclaim, index finger raised in wizened fashion. *Il faut du beurre et du sel.*

If he was giving us cauliflower, I would suggest *le curry* at which André would pause and tilt his head slightly.

"Mais non!" he would say in a bemused fashion as if I'd just suggested serving it with a dollop of used engine oil and iron filings.

The French in the countryside just don't get curry. It was near-impossible to find in our little *department* in its takeaway form. On one occasion, I performed a concert in Perigueux, the administrative capital of the Dordogne. After the event, we were treated to a takeaway curry from an exotic new restaurant which had just opened in one of the more trendy areas.

The events which followed illustrated to me only too clearly the sheer dearth of curry-education suffered by my colleagues. Firstly, they spent ages scrambling around in the bag trying to identify the *entrée.* How could one explain to these people that there was no real starter? It was as perplexing to them as the concept of *Ricard* tasting like ditch water. Next, the poppadums were eyed with suspicion; I think at least one of my fellow diners thought they were table mats and the naan bread a face flannel. Following this came the luminous-green mint sauce. All self-respecting curry *connoisseurs* know this exists solely for the purpose of dunking poppadums. I heard one lady say it was *'une sauce pour le riz.'* I was forced to hurl myself across the table and knock it out of her hand before she upturned the whole lot onto the *pilau rice,* leaving nothing for dunkage. Philistine. As for the curry itself? Well, it was a chicken tikka masala-type affair, but a better title may have been a 'moderately-perfumed chicken casserole'. Pleasant yes, but not quite hitting the right notes; a bit like receiving a *Grifter* for Christmas when your heart was set on a *Chopper.* The heat levels were laughable, but my co-eaters were running around the room, frantically flapping their hands in front of their mouths like demented penguins, and getting into fist fights over a bottle of *Evian.* French country-dwellers don't do spice.

The final warning I should deliver is of the all-night meal. These are marvellous but require serious staying power. We have an annual neighbours' meal in our little hamlet. It is great fun and I'd wholeheartedly recommend it to any community. We make it a bring-and-share affair, so everyone is out to impress; the competition becomes quite fierce which is good for the standard of *plats* on offer. One year, Kirsty provided a hummus with garlic and lemon juice, served with pitta bread. It was a bit of a hit amongst the diners and consequently, I couldn't help but notice some other *plat*-providers gave her the cold shoulder for the rest of the evening. They had been well-and-truly out-*plated*. When someone turned up with a less-popular offering, I found myself slipping into my oft-employed 'eat-for-everyone mode', grotesquely overcompensating out of sympathy. The dish in question would usually be a pasta salad (the standard fare for skinflints at bring-and-share events) and I'd take a humungous portion, followed by seconds, and then thirds until the contents of the bowl looked sufficiently dented to save both hurt feelings and neighbourly relations.

Our event would start mid-afternoon with a *boules* tournament; here I routinely let down Team UK. As the evening drew in, a rum punch was handed out, alongside lots of tasty things such as quiches, melon-balls, olives and the like. For our first neighbours' meal, I made the schoolboy error of 'going too early' and stuffed myself with these offerings; frankly, I became rather merry on the misleadingly-sweet and fruity-tasting rum punch. A note on this beverage: it is taken very seriously in our corner of France and is prepared many days in advance of the event. This allows the rum time to infuse all of the fruit and juices. It appears to merge most effectively if stored in a cool, dark environment; some of my friends have dug a hole in their lawn to act as a kind of rum-punch maturation-zone. In the unlikely event of it not being drunk on the first evening, it apparently improves with age, so *pas de problème*. It is insufficient to chuck it all together half-an-hour beforehand.

Anyway, to return to the meal. By 11.30pm, one neighbour was standing on a table, solemnly extolling the virtues of the *brie* which he had made a 250km round-trip to collect from a little farm in the *Auvergne*. At this point, I was trying really hard not to vomit due to the combination of too much food and *way* too much rum punch. By midnight, the young chap who lived directly opposite offered me a mint liqueur. As always its principal features were strength, sugar-content and obscurity, but it was game over for me. I staggered back across the road to the gastronomical respite-zone that was my bed. It was a poor show scoring *la Famille Jones nul points*. My elderly friends were still going at 4.00am, not raucously pissed I hasten to add, but just consuming slowly, anticipating the *digestif* which would render the whole affair equal to half a cucumber and a carrot stick.

Lastly, our village is one of many which has an *association* – a group of volunteers with a publically-funded budget – responsible for arranging pleasant events for the community. Much of their effort is dedicated to organising school excursions, cultural trips for the retired and other similar and worthy endeavours. Considerable resources of finance and energy are also directed towards the provision of locally-produced drink and food in order to guarantee fun, cohesion and fond memories for all.

I love this country.

***

Drink and Food – The Essential Tips

(1) Enjoying a beer with mates at 6.30am is acceptable practice.

(2) Having an *aperitif* twice-daily is the norm. Any ill-effects will be eradicated if following meal is finished off with a cheeky *digestif* chaser.

(3) Hosting an *aperitif* has a strict set of rules. Follow them.

(4) Expect to enjoy a drink at staff meetings.

(5) If you unwittingly create a 'Brits' bar', respect and include the locals.

(6) Excess fruit can be used to create alcoholic beverages. If you succeed in achieving this, I'd be most grateful if you'd send me your method.

(7) Eating is the central activity of a day. Respect this.

(8) Never feed your kid's friends without prior arrangement (preferably in writing).

(9) Purchase butter and salt in bulk.

(10) The rural French struggle with curry. If you plan to prepare one for friends and neighbours, the spice level should be sub-*korma*.

(11) Neighbours' meals are dangerous. Very dangerous. Pace yourself. Be patient. It is a marathon rather than a sprint.

8. Making a Splash

Wade in the water
Wade in the water
Children wade, in the water
God's gonna trouble the water

Wade in the Water - Traditional Spiritual (America)

As you will have learned from my courtship with the French Atlantic coast as a teenager, placing myself at the mercy of bodies of wild water, or indeed jumping into them from great heights are actions which remain central to my wellbeing. I'd go as far as to say that the abundance of opportunities for such behaviour offered by the French countryside, and the accompanying climate, played a significant part in our decision to change our country of residence. The seeds of this eccentricity were sown when I was of seven or eight years of age. Every Sunday, as Mum prepared a vast lunch, Dad took my brother and me swimming. The pool which we frequented was Cardiff's much-lamented Wales Empire Pool. This colossus of a building, with 1700 seats for spectators, was constructed in 1958 to host the swimming competition of the British Empire and Commonwealth Games. It was originally a gargantuan fifty-five yards long, but in 1970 lorry-loads of concrete were presumably pumped into the deep end to comply with shorter international competitive distances, measured in metres.

I was already a confident and competent swimmer and was drawn to the otherworldliness of deep water where life seemed to pass in slow-motion. A favourite pastime of mine was to float on the surface, face down, gazing at the floor tiles of the basin way below me, imagining I was some kind of aquatic bird.

123

Unfortunately, when lying prostrate and immobile, I developed the ability to hold my breath for a good two minutes. Upon one particularly-lengthy aquatic-bird-fantasy session, I rose for breath only to note that a lifeguard, who resembled JPR Williams at his hairiest, had leapt down from his throne and was making his way with some haste towards the deep end. Believing me to be floating unconscious face-down on the surface, he was on the verge of hurling himself into the water in order to effect a rescue. When I popped up, grinning gormlessly, still half in my aqua-bird *reverie,* he skidded to a stop. For a moment, he balanced precariously at the edge of the pool, rotating his arms reverse-windmill style, like Scooby-Doo and Shaggy escaping a ghoul. Thankfully, he *just* managed to avert the indignity of falling face-first into the water. A shrill blast of a whistle exploded in the swimming public's collective ears and Mr Lifeguard threatened me with a sound wet towel whipping were I to ever imitate horizontal and inert marine-based bird life for more than five seconds again.

The Empire Pool featured the classic Rules and Regulations signs of the era, including the legendary cartoon of a highly-excited young man pursing his lips towards an improbably buxom, coy female companion (wearing a spotty bikini if my memory serves me correctly) accompanied by the warning 'No Petting' - a word describing an amorous embrace of a lover in a public place only ever used by county councillors in the UK.

The *pièce de résistance* of the Empire Pool was its set of five diving boards which dwarfed the swimmers below them like oaks over pond skaters. The first two were springboards whereas the third, fourth and fifth boards were platforms. 'The Top Board' required oxygen assistance if one were to scale its lofty peaks and it enjoyed legendary status amongst the young menfolk of South Wales. Once or twice every session, a brave soul would make his way up to the top board (it was always a man – this was the 70's after all) and the whole pool would fall into a reverential silence. Once up there, a fellow's credibility was on the line - to descend via the slippery, steep metal steps once again was indeed a walk of shame (and probably more dangerous than diving off the top board). I would watch in awe, and some considerable envy, as the lunatic swallow-dived through the air and landed in the pool with a pleasing *'Kersploosh!'*

There was always a real risk of substantial damage to the diver which, needless to say, made each plunge all the more fascinating to watch. Teenage boys would nod gravely and knowingly while describing consequences such as 'a ruptured spleen' and 'ripped stomach muscles' – fates which the ever-reliable urban grapevine informed us had met some of the unluckier, yet incontestably heroic high-divers. I recall one chap's legs rotating beyond the prerequisite vertical entry position creating an almighty smack, like a large trout being slapped onto bare buttocks, as his calf muscles hit the surface. He emerged with a grimace resembling a man sucking a whole clutch of lemons. Upon being dragged from the pool, his lower legs looked as if they had been soaked in raspberry juice for a week.

All-comers were permitted to jump feet-first off the one-metre board, but rules dictated any height beyond this required a head-first dive, on pain of a decade-long ban for a feet-first bandit. As we developed into teenagers, my friends and I became foolhardy enough to attempt this at three-metre level, encountering sore heads, red stomachs and slapped legs *en route*. The journey from three-metre to five-metre board though was a torturous one. There was a distinct lack of playfulness in that platform, which refused to give any kind of friendly *'be-doing!'* as one jumped.

I vividly recall the day I first dived from the third board. It was a kind of pre-destined moment; the mental decision to take the plunge having been made during double physics the previous Thursday. Firstly, I made sure all my mates were watching. I then proudly made my way up the three flights of steps to the damp, lonely platform, feeling strangely calm - like a condemned man recognising the inevitability of his fate stepping up to the gallows. At the edge of the precipice, I ducked my head between my arms and toppled my body weight forward, face-first, with very little in the way of forethought and technical consideration.

I seemed to be falling through the air for at least half an hour before hitting the water - head first at least. The pain was moderate (about a seven-out-of-ten) but so, *so* worth it. I was a hero and, being pretty crap at sport, this was a notable feather in my cap.

I practised this manoeuvre week-in, week-out, so when the school took all fourteen-year-olds to the Empire Pool for swimming instruction, I was able to impress the entire year group and earn considerable credibility. This was only matched when I mastered the introduction to *Paranoid* on the electric guitar some months later.

The Empire Pool was eventually closed down and 'redeveloped' into one of those faceless, soulless 'cinema and leisure' complexes introduced into every British town centre during the 2000's. I went to see Marillion there, accompanying a friend who is a Marillion nut (they were quite good to be fair). I wondered whether the stage they occupied was the remnants of the top board.

So began my love affair with placing myself at the mercy of, and jumping from great heights into bodies of water.

Three decades later, my family and I were enjoying our first full summer in St Méard de Dronne when friends advised us to visit Ribérac *piscine,* located, not entirely unexpectedly, in the small market town of Ribérac. It is an outdoor pool, open for the summer season. Upon arrival, I found myself leaping up and down on the spot with joy and excitement, like a puppy having an *andouille* sausage dangled above its nose. This fine pool of distinction and class, to my joy and delight, sported three diving boards (one, three and five metres) in their own independent, purpose-built basin.

We entered the reception area to be asked our home address by the less-than-joyous lady behind the desk. Even at this early stage in our French adventure, I'd learned not to question the administrative requirements of anyone in authority, particularly if they had the power to deny one a diving experience, so I kept my mouth shut. You may be asked your address when taking a dip because, in France, there are often two pricing policies for leisure activities. If you live in the *commune* you pay less than if you are an outsider. As a local family, we paid a pittance to enter this aquatic wonderland.

Newcomers to France often express shock at their local tax bills *(taxe fonciere* and *tax d'habitation)* which are basically your rates. Part of these will chip in towards the maintenance of your local *piscine* so you really are getting what you pay for. One of the keys to appreciating life in a rural *commune* is to take advantage of what is being offered for your *euros*. Many incomers take residence in these areas, pay through the nose, yet fail to benefit as they miss out on heavily-subsidised local delights. It is often the same people who complain 'there is nothing to do'.

We paid our entrance fee to *Madame Piscined-Off* at the desk, who then sternly pointed at a sign on the wall which read '*SHORTS INTERDIT!*' Swimming shorts are absolutely forbidden in French swimming pools, upon risk of death-by-guillotine. If you are intending to live in the French countryside, you simply must invest in a minimum of three pairs of Tom Daley-esque Speedos. Don't worry, no-one will laugh at you (except for your family and friends). Such attire is unequivocally *ob-li-ga-toire* in French swimming establishments. After a few visits, entering the basin area looking like the tail-end of a spoof Chippendales show will feel quite natural. Of course, if you are a local, this is second nature and you keep your Speedos in your man-drawer - alongside that cheap watch needing a new strap and all those foreign coins which should come in useful someday. It's the tourists and newcomers who are caught unawares by the system.

Although the Dordogne enjoys beautiful, hot summers, it is not wall-to-wall sunshine. One will always have a week or two when the weather is miserable. In July 2011, following a particularly grim period of drizzly days, *la Famille Jones* awoke to a glorious sunny morning. The only logical course of action was to pack our

Speedos, carrying the confidence of a family in-the-know, and spend the day at Ribérac *piscine.*

Having enjoyed a couple of hours of water-based frivolity, I spotted the oft-witnessed spectacle of a young British tourist running through the footbath, grinning ear-to-ear, thinking he was about to hurl his pale body into the welcoming waters of the pool. In Bermuda shorts. Not a chance laddie. In a millisecond, shrill whistles from all four corners of the pool screamed out in protest. Lifeguards leapt down from their chairs and tore towards the boy, ready to rugby tackle him to the ground should this insolent Anglo-Youth have got anywhere near the clear, blue and welcoming waters.

This poor lad, about twelve years of age, had endured a disappointing week of rough weather; he'd clearly been eyeing up the pool for days. He had got to within inches of his prize before having it snatched away from him by the inexplicable French concern for appropriate pool attire. As he was being pinned against the wall in an arm-lock, he looked utterly bemused. What was his crime? Maybe he'd run a little exuberantly; he hadn't shouted boisterously and certainly hadn't been involved in any petting. I felt so sorry for him, I approached his Mum and promised her my Speedos (once I'd got changed of course) so the lad could have a swim. After their dip, the family left them at the front desk for me to collect from a bemused-looking *Madame Piscined-Off* the following day.

It soon became apparent that lifeguards in rural French swimming pools are, in fact, clothing police. On one occasion, I witnessed a group of them practically beat up a German tourist who had the audacity to enter the poolside area wearing *sandals* for heaven's sake. At the same moment, a group of young French boys were doing a three-man shoulder ride on the five-metre platform (teetering towards the edge, where they would have missed the water had they fallen) before being pushed off by their mates into the pool. They landed on a mother-and-baby swimming session below. This was allowed to pass as mere good-natured banter, whereas the German tourist was banned from the pool until 2025 and had his sandals thrown under a passing articulated lorry.

The fact that French children are used to fooling around on the platforms meant my high-diving antics were met with indifference. French toddlers are habitually chucked off the top board before they can put together a couple of steps or cry out *'Papa?!.. NON!!!'* The result is they are diving forwards, backwards, somersaulting and doing all sorts of things to make me jealous before they hit puberty. I still took great joy in reliving the sensations of my youth some thirty-plus years later and being the only Brit to even consider diving off the top platform.

So what is the reasoning behind the requirement for sparse swimwear in French pools? Upon questioning, *Madame Piscined-Off* at the desk informed me it was for hygiene purposes. The implication is Bermuda shorts carry more dirt than budgie-smugglers manufactured from the same amount of material as a dolly's handkerchief; thus rendering the latter a superior prospect sanitation-wise. A little mathematics renders this argument nothing short of *merde*. Such pools contain several million litres of chlorinated water. What difference does a little extra cloth make? *Rien*. The real reason, although no-one would ever confess it, is the rural French like to look good. To be fair, I noticed many French do carry off the look with confidence and style. I purchased a pair of body-hugging Speedo shorts (these passed the test – just) in an attempt to emulate Daniel Craig emerging from the sea as *007* in *Casino Royale*. Sadly, those who saw me were shaken, not stirred.

Some people push the Speedo-length boundaries, causing lifeguards agonising and long-lasting mental trauma. In 2015, I'm sure I spotted one lifeguard/clothing policeman pinning a youth to the ground as his colleague measured the length of his daring Speedo/Short hybrid number, using a purpose-built ruler. In the summer of 2017, *la Famille Jones* stayed at a campsite in Arcachon, on the coast, south of Bordeaux. The *Speedo-Gendarmes* were out in force. One glorious afternoon, a tall, distinguished-looking Dutch gentleman entered the pool area wearing swim shorts which were just a little loose around the crotch. They could hardly have been described as Bermuda shorts, having more in common with the kind of thing sported by Gary Lineker in *Italia 90* than present-day surf-wear. The man had a presence and confidence about him. He was over six feet tall, around sixty years of age, and wore designer glasses and a kindly smile. It wouldn't have surprised me in the slightest to have learned he was a Nobel-Prize winner in the field of cancer research. As he ambled amiably towards the pool steps, it soon became apparent he was intending to enter the water in *those shorts*. I found my eyes shifting towards the young lifeguard in morbid fascination, as did those of the fifty other Speedo-clad bathers present. The lifeguard in question had spotted his adversary but was understandably reluctant to blow the whistle on this man. Beads of sweat broke out upon his forehead and the whistle trembled between his lips. Outrageously, he bottled it. The gentleman entered the water unmolested and enjoyed a predictably efficient and stylish swim before retiring to read an academic journal on his sunbed. I later learned he regarded his success in beating the Speedo-trap a more extraordinary achievement than his entire life's research, and that of his colleagues, combined.

I confess I exaggerate when I state that lifeguards are merely clothing police. They are in fact required to possess a range of skills and talents. Only days after the Dutch scientist incident, our afternoon swim was interrupted by an *animateur* or *animatrice* (gender identification was impossible) invading the pool area in a full cuddly dinosaur costume. These holiday-camp hosts carry a wealth of responsibilities, from running activities for children to leading noisy bar games. The creature didn't enter the water (it was not wearing Speedos) but instead, a colleague initiated a recording of some truly abominable *Europop* to which the dinosaur started a somewhat rigid dance sequence. The lifeguards on duty were obliged to descend from their thrones and flank the dancing dino, busting the same moves as their prehistoric buddy. To say their faces looked strained and their smiles forced would be the understatements of the century. The poor chap who'd failed to arrest the scientist found himself alone at the wrong end of the pool, dancing a solo which reminded me of a drunk uncle at a wedding trying to do the *Macarena* with his nieces. The poor fellow had watched *Baywatch* as a boy and had dreamed of cruising the Atlantic beaches in a sand buggy, surfboard slung over his shoulder, wearing red shorts and mirror shades only to find himself doing the Jurassic Jig and learning the phrase 'I'm sorry but they're too long and baggy' in seven European languages.

A further phenomenon is French ladies almost always wear bikinis which are indubitably frugal in the fabric dispensed for their manufacture. This goes for everyone: from children to teenage girls, housewives to retirees – the latter carrying the normal quota of excessive pounds to be expected of persons of a certain age. You can spot a British family from 500 yards as the 'mum' figure will always be wearing a swimsuit which is either 'sensible' or 'sporty', even if the last time the wearer participated in aerobic activity was two decades previously. Their children will also be equipped with those ridiculous bodysuits and hats which look more suited for a lunar landing than a Sunday-afternoon dip. Initially, I found myself being rather sniffy at this excessive display of French female skin, finding it tasteless and inappropriate. As time went on though, my perception changed. I realised this attire is not donned for the benefit of menfolk. It strikes me French ladies wear bikinis for the sheer joy of feeling the sun and water on their skin rather than to show off their bodies – a kind of freedom-asserting, positive feminism. The female body, whatever its size or shape, is put out there with pride and joy, regardless of the contemporary opinion of how it *should* look, which is sadly, so destructively central to the modern mentality.

Upon my return to the UK, I went to an indoor swimming pool (as it would be in Scotland) with my family. I was aghast by the amount of clothing on display. There now a fashion for wearing T-Shirts over swimwear which I find bizarre. Of course, it is up to everyone to wear whatever makes them comfortable (I am not a *Speedo-gendarme*) but it struck me as rather joyless. I had left my own Speedos, slightly damp and now probably mould-ridden, in the bottom of a bag somewhere in our French house so was obliged to purchase new swimwear from a local supermarket. Needless to say, only shorts-style were available, so for the first time in years, I entered a pool feeling as if I'd just parachuted, rather than jumped, into the water.

The final difference you'll notice when swimming in a French public pool is the much-codified behaviour of young people. Boys are *absolutely* expected to throw their female friends in at the deep end. It is all part of the swimming experience. Teenagers will line up at the poolside and before you can say '*Oh là là!*' four lads will be man-handling a girl, each grasping a limb, dragging her towards the water. She will inevitably be screaming *'Non, non!'*, but will appear curiously cooperative in her endeavour to resist. Female friends, rather than running back to the changing rooms, or fetching weapons, remain inexplicably inert and watch on coyly.

"Oh no, I hope it's not me next!" they mutter. *Non, j'espere que c'est pas moi après!*

Of course, everyone knows if they weren't to be unceremoniously chucked in, they would be deeply hurt and it would probably all end in tears. In another setting, such actions would result in legal proceedings and prolonged psychotherapy. Once the females have been dispatched, the boys will retire to the deep end and indulge in noisy bombing and undoubtedly some 'petting' with their previously-lobbed-in victims. Having had their aquatic fill, they will play football and frisbee on the grass. During this entire pantomime, the lifeguards will be eyeing an awkward middle-class family from Kent, like tigers stalking an injured gazelle, as they reveal their swimwear of choice lest they unleash the curse of cloth-excess on an unsuspecting public.

This being France, all ages will bring a little picnic or *goûter* which is consumed away from the pool, in a leafy area set aside for that purpose. Foodstuffs of choice will be the expected *baguette* and *fromage,* maybe with a little bottle of red tucked amongst the damp towels. In cities, I've observed part of the swimming experience is to stuff one's face with junk food after a swim, thus counteracting any health benefits gained from the previous hours' dunk.

If your commune has yet to construct a *piscine,* then have no fear. An equally-joyous pastime is to experience river swimming. Kirsty and I first discovered the wonders of France's hidden river-swimming culture on our honeymoon. It was 2003 and France was enduring one of its most severe heatwaves on record. We had hired a small canal boat and were meandering our sweltering way along the Canal de Nivernais in Eastern France. This magnificent waterway was constructed in 1784 in order to carry timber and stone through the region, but now primarily exists as a playground for *vacanciers*. It is stunningly beautiful, peaceful, and picturesque, wandering through a whole range of scenic *tableaux*, from chocolate-box villages to deep, cliff-lined valleys. Much of the time, it runs alongside the river Yonne which feeds the canal its water supply. Sections of the canal are adjoined by locks which can be in close proximity for steeper gradients. As the water levels were dangerously low in the upper river in 2003, a rule was put in place that boats had to descend the locks in groups of two or three. The result was that there could be a considerable wait at each lock until a few boats arrived together, thus authorising the descent. This was fine with the majority of navigators as it gave an excuse to moor up, enjoy an amiable chat and drink chilled white wine.

One day, we found ourselves chugging pleasantly along behind a rather intense German gentleman and his long-suffering wife. They were the owners of a super-boat – an enormous machine with all mod cons including satellites, fridges, freezers and TV. This permitted them to pass their entire holiday without having to engage with, or invest in financially, the community whose waterways they were benefiting from. *Monsieur Bateau* was clearly in some haste and expressed considerable agitation at having to wait for us before descending each lock. Even though it was our pleasant ambling which was the source of his frustration, he appeared to vent his fury on *Madame Bateau* at every opportunity. Despite this, I refused to rush on his behalf. I would not be a victim of canal-rage. The driver's station of his cruise liner was sheltered by a large parasol and at one moment, his irritated arm-waving caught a necessary mechanism on the shaft. It collapsed on his head, consuming him with a pleasing *'whoomph!'* At this point, he appeared to approach the point of a nervous breakdown so we decided to pull over for a couple of hours and let him go ahead.

We moored up at a picturesque hillside village whose name we have inevitably forgotten. Riding our pushbikes up to the local bar, we quaffed a leisurely beer, purchased a few necessary supplies (more beer) and then, fortified, made our way back down to our boat. It was about 3.00pm which is the time when those living in the French countryside tend to come out for their afternoon leisure activities as a necessary respite from their two-hour lunch break.

We noticed some families making their way down a lane with towels in hand so, on a whim, followed them. Soon after, in a little clearing next to the feeder river, we stumbled upon an aquatic paradise. Laughing toddlers paddled, older folk swam breast-stroke serenely, teenagers jumped off rocks bombing each other noisily, and families relaxed in the shade nibbling at picnics. There was a labyrinth of deep pools, shallow pools, waterfalls and rushing streams. Nature had provided the ultimate water park for all generations to enjoy together. For me, it was an image of Heaven.

When we settled in the Dordogne some years later, we found many of these wondrous places hidden away alongside its three beautiful rivers: la Dordogne, la Dronne and L'Isle. They became known by the names with which the children described them: *The River Beach, The Current Beach* and, just a stone's throw from our front door, *The Weir,* or as I know it, *Saint Cecilia International Casino and Leisure Resort.* This last hidden gem gave us some of our happiest memories of our time in the village.

The Weir is found by walking down a farmer's dirt track. As one progresses, the distant sound of cascading water is heard, gradually strengthening in its intensity. When the track ends at a cornfield, there is a little gap in the bushes on the right. Upon descending a steep, slippery mud bank, a *petite* pebble beach is revealed and opposite is an elevated, cascading weir which spans hundreds of metres across L'Isle.

I have little doubt in most urban areas this would be shielded from the public by iron railings, barbed wire, and signs warning of dire consequences should anyone ever consider approaching it with the intention of having fun. Here though, children swim on-the-spot against the current, trying to reach the raging descent, encouraged and pulled along by their parents; fishermen in shorts and flip-flops wobble precariously on the slippery stones, pulling catch upon catch from the deeper pools gouged out of the river bed by the cascade - from minnows to mind-bogglingly huge catfish resembling extras from *Jaws* - and teenagers stand at the top of the precipice, showing off to their girlfriends, falling backwards into the deeper waters which precede the tipping point. *La Famille Jones* would take an inflatable tyre, lilo or boat and pilot it, in foolhardy fashion, over the edge of the weir. Habitually, we'd end up capsized, but just occasionally we'd succeed in navigating the rapids into the calmer waters below. It was bliss. No-one telling us what to do, everyone respecting the space of others and each participant looking out for the more vulnerable.

One might have thought those in authority would have frowned upon such actions, but on one afternoon in July, I spotted *Monsieur le Maire* at the weir with his grandson and their dog taking in their aquatic fill. They were enjoying the experience as much as anyone else until he ended up neck-deep in the river after his grandson's glasses fell off into the rocks. Everyone searched for them in the swirling pools but to no avail. The lad was also in deep water when he got home.

Finally, one can find a wealth of man-made lakes with artificial beaches in the French countryside. There is a beautiful spot about

20 minutes' drive from *Chez Jones*. A substantial lake, with a purpose-created beach, *le Grand Etang de la Jemaye* is a little corner of France where *la Famille Jones* can be found at least three times per week in the summer months. All-day shaded parking and access to the facilities, including showers and toilets, are completely free of charge. There are bars, ice-cream stalls and of course, a variety of restaurants. One of these hosts live music evenings and, when I perform at this venue staring out at the water twinkling under the stars, I shake my head in disbelief knowing that I am being paid for passing my evening in such an agreeable fashion.

When swimming in lakes or rivers, bathers are at liberty to select the swimwear of their choice. I knew I had changed fundamentally when I realised I would reach for my Speedos over a pair of baggy shorts.

***

Making a Splash – The Essential Tips

(1) Buy Speedos in bulk.

(2) Use the facilities. You're paying for them after all.

(3) Be body-proud. No-one's judging.

(4) Behave poorly. It's OK, as long as you respect the space of other pool users and wear frugal swimwear.

(5) Find the secret river-swimming spots in your area. Your children will enjoy the greatest days of their lives.

Figure 3 La Famille Jones and friends messing about in a river.

Dan Jones

9. Mathematics, Mushrooms and Turkey Management

Bonhomme, bonhomme, que savez-vous faire?
Savez-vous jouer de la mist'en laire?
L'aire, l'aire, laire
De la mist' en laire?

Good man, good man, what can you do?
Do you know how to play the mist'en laire?
The air, the air, the air
The mist'en laire?

La Mist'en Laire - Traditional (France)

The education system in France, as with government administration, has been resistant to new practices within the field. I caught the tail-end of Britain's 'old school' teaching style, and was tutored by some genuinely eccentric and fantastically inappropriate teachers. I recall a day when a member of our class was struck in the face by an irate teacher for a moment of mild insolence. Having completed his assault on the boy, he returned to the front of the class and continued to make us recite verb conjugations as if nothing remarkable had passed. In a similar vein, a very good friend was introduced to The Word of God through a good smiting over the head with a leather-bound family Bible and I, amongst many of my peers, coughed up chalk dust for days following a direct hit from a board rubber, hurled with unerring accuracy by a teacher who'd reached the end of his patience. Going hand-in-hand with this unimaginable behaviour was the worrying fact that at least one teacher had a relationship with a pupil. The teacher in question possessed sufficient confidence in his actions to drive her to school in his rather fancy open-topped car for all to see, like a human certificate of achievement. The school pretended not to notice.

So, when in the 1990's and 2000's Matthew took the same school route as I had followed, I was deeply curious to see developments in twenty-first-century schooling for myself. Although there was much to be praised (notably an absence of aggravated assault in the classroom), ideas which had been devised to protect the vulnerable and promote equality had been given the derogatory title of 'Political Correctness' due to a somewhat overzealous application of certain principles from some quarters. Sports' Day became an event where no-one was allowed to win or lose to avoid the possibility of feelings being hurt. Participation prizes were awarded to all. I found this rather bothersome as the children who were good at sport were often weak in the classroom; consequently, their opportunity to impress within their sphere of excellence was snatched from their hands. My discontent was maybe, in some small way, fuelled by the fact that I won the dad's race and felt I justly deserved an enormous, glittering medal; I was frankly robbed of my sole chance to shine in the sporting arena. Please understand me correctly. I champion positivity, energy, inclusion and encouragement within our schools, but to follow the line of thought applied on Sports' Day, wouldn't it have been logical for schools to have given everyone the same grade at maths or physics in order to protect the feelings of the less academically-inclined? New vocabulary was invented almost weekly to define children of all races, needs, shapes and sizes. Should someone use an out-of-fashion term in ignorance, he or she could be dragged in front of a disciplinary hearing faster than you could utter 'deferred success'.

The lessons which all school children of my era reflect upon with tones of idyllic nostalgia are those which were either gruesome or dangerous. Unforgettable was a class spent dissecting organs which we had been required to collect from the local butcher. One pupil fainted, another vomited, and a lab technician slipped in the puddle created by the latter incident before landing smartly on her backside with a splendid or sickening *'splat!'* depending on your personal perspective. It may have been a farce but my word, I recall every detail of how a pig's eyeball lens changes an image when it is squashed. Incidentally, my school friends and I had been pleasantly surprised by the ease in which the local butcher had unquestioningly handed over a rich and exciting range of vital organs for 'educational purposes'. For weeks following dissection lessons, illicitly-gained pigs' eyeballs, cows' hearts and sheep lungs became the basis of a range of bad-taste pranks undertaken by my social group. I also recall the explosive qualities of custard powder when a science teacher created a significant scorch mark on the ceiling using an improvised armoury of a coffee tin, a candle, a bicycle pump and a generous scoop of Bird's finest.

By Matthew's time, these magnificent lessons had been tragically relegated to being shown on video to protect a sensitive minority. I should point out that Florence is a sensitive individual and as a schoolchild in France, she was forewarned of potentially problematic classes and given the option to study the topic from a book in an adjacent room. To this day, French pupils continue to dissect offal in science classes. I suspect they fry up the fruits of their research with butter, salt and garlic in double cookery, just before lunch.

It is so very difficult to judge France's entire education system from one's own experiences but much of what is positive in a more individualistic and old-school approach remains present in day-to-day life *a l'école*. Naturally, some of the less-desirable elements have slipped through the net and remain omnipresent for each child and parent to deal with as they see fit. My main observation is, as with so many other things in life, success or failure boils down to the actions of individuals on the front line rather than the system itself. For her primary education in France, Florence enjoyed the same teacher for four consecutive years. This was due to the tiny class sizes necessitating mixing the year-groups – Florence's year hosted a mere three pupils. I'm deeply grateful this was the case as happily for her and us, the teacher was creative, dynamic and assertive. The kids adored her. By a strange coincidence, it transpired that the house we bought had been her grandparents' years before. André and Eliane, our neighbours, recalled the teacher as a child, calling to them over the fence, just as our Florence did decades later.

Joyfully, the teacher was at liberty to run her class as she saw appropriate. Unshackled by the constraints of the more ridiculous elements of the PC movement, she was able to apply consequences as she saw necessary, and the kids knew it. She was no bully - all the children fulfilled their genuine potential. Sporty kids were praised. Flo danced solo at the end-of-year show. Mathematicians were accelerated to a higher level. Critically, no-one was ridiculed and all gifts were respected. The teacher left the school at the same time as Flo in order to pursue a new opportunity. The tears shed on both sides showed the depth of the relationship which had been forged and the genuine love and gratitude that existed.

Conversely, I saw evidence of a lack of flexibility and creativity in teaching practice. On my very first day in my new job as a guitar teacher, I was approached by an agitated parent who complained she hadn't been told which *'cahier'* (textbook) had been set for the year. Bewildered by this statement, I tried my best to explain I would set work according to many factors such as the preferred learning method of the pupil (visual, aural, kinaesthetic…), the style of music to be played and the tastes of the guitarist him/herself. There would therefore be no set textbook. She was apparently deeply dissatisfied at this response and her body language failed to conceal it as she huffed her way out of the door with a generous shoulder-shrug and a barely-stifled *'N'importe quoi!'*

As the weeks passed, I noted every pupil in their second year or beyond turned up with the same previously-prescribed *cahier,* regardless of age, culture, preferences or anything else for that matter. Perhaps my predecessor had regarded this rather dry children's book as the sole route to musical success. Setting a seven-year-old girl *Au Clair de la Lune* to play for her granny may have been a winner, but as for the same lesson delivered to a spotty 15-year old mad about Metallica... For him, the *cahier* was about as motivating as a three-day Health and Safety seminar in a cardboard-box factory.

There was a belief that in order to advance as a musician, the only thing which would be effective was hours of mundane suffering and drudgery, with the question of musical satisfaction relegated firmly to the back seat. Happily, today there is a wealth of brilliant, creative and thoughtful teaching material which can suit all types of learner.

For many years I taught a lovely boy called Louis who was to become our neighbour when we bought our house. It was clear the guitar was unlikely to become his life's work, but that was unimportant. He did his best, and we advanced together. I loved working with him. One week, his mum turned up at his lesson to inform me he would be absent. I asked if he was OK, hoping he wasn't *malade,* but she sheepishly informed me he had to stay back in school to attend a meeting with the head teacher and herself as he had *fait l'âne* ('done the donkey' or 'played the fool') at school. I was amazed. I couldn't imagine anyone less likely to indulge in horseplay, or indeed donkeyplay than Louis. I soon learned this was a recurring problem in his school life. As the months passed, I recognised he was no academic but he was undoubtedly a very brilliant young man, alongside being both modest and courteous. It's just the values upon which he was being judged were all wrong.

One early autumn evening, there was a tap at our door. Louis was there with a bag of wild mushrooms which he had gathered himself and brought to share with us. I expressed my thanks and later, revealed our gift to Kirsty. Naturally, we were moderately concerned; no, if the truth be told we were utterly terrified, as wild mushrooms have the potential not only to make an excellent *Rogon Josh* but to drop you stone dead if selected by the untrained eye. After much contemplation and staring at innumerable inconclusive images on Google, I took them to André next door for his expert verification. Having fed me a couple bottles of *Leffe Blonde,* he confirmed they were good for eating *avec du beurre et du sel* and seemed bewildered as to why I would ever question their suitability for a good meal. It was as if I'd brought a pizza over and asked, 'Is this really a pizza André, or do you think it may be an enormous, fresh steaming cow-pat?'

Having enjoyed that evening's meal, albeit with a nagging doubt that we may have been consuming our last supper as we masticated, I asked Louis if he would teach me how to find wild mushrooms or *cèpes.* He willingly agreed. That weekend, Louis, Sam, Flo and I set off to the woods on our bikes, baskets at the ready, like an oddly-mismatched *Famous Five,* only with no dog. After an invigorating ride, we arrived in a dense patch of woodland miles from civilisation, although many would argue our village itself is miles from civilisation.

"This is perfect!" Louis said, looking around with a satisfied countenance.

To my untrained eye, it looked exactly the same as the three miles of woodland which preceded it, but I kept my views to myself. We were instructed to scan the forest floor for mushrooms, and to my pleasant surprise, I soon found myself spotting them everywhere. The problem was they were all kinds of different shapes, sizes and colours, so I could only assume a good proportion of them were lethal. As he hunted, Louis nonchalantly pulled a sizeable knife from his pocket. I withdrew my own tiny but practical knife and felt, not for the first time, I had been out-knifed. It was particularly galling to receive this treatment from a 10-year old boy who was my pupil.

Soon after, Louis coolly said *'voila'* and with an effortless swipe at a clump of fungi, half-filled my basket with that evening's dinner. Being a novice, they looked pretty much like all the others to me, but upon closer inspection with my mentor, Louis pointed out the colour beneath the cup, the formation within the stem and a range of other identifying factors. Inspired and motivated, Flo, Sam and I got our heads down, walking in random formations staring downwards, like commuters with their smartphones on a Monday morning.

We started to make a few finds and celebrated wildly when our judge confirmed the bounty was edible. Every now and then I'd take a *cèpe* to Louis and he would frown and shake his head.

"Poisonous?" I asked.

"No," replied Louis. "It just tastes like shit."

At one point I found an interesting-looking, rather tiny mushroom so I swiped at it with my knife and, at the third attempt, managed to detach it from its roots. I carried it over to Louis wearing a quizzical look. The mushroom-guru's eyes opened like saucers and he froze on the spot.

"That is the certain-cruel-lingering-agonising-death mushroom," he said with a tone one normally reserves for infants caught playing with matches.

Before continuing, he advised I sterilised my knife and avoided contact with foodstuffs for the next forty-eight hours.

The search continued and I grew increasingly fascinated and impressed with the relationship this young boy had with the land. He belonged there. He was part of it. When we heard a sudden explosion of sound made by invisible animals in a heavily-bushed area nearby, Louis explained, due to the rhythm with which the feet hit the ground and the weight of the contact, they would have been a couple of wild boars. These are abundant in the forests around our village but very tricky to spot, unlike the deer which you practically trip over as you amble through the woodland.

Feeling like Bear Grylls, we returned home with our feast. I filled two freezer drawers with foraged goodies, and had plenty to give André and Eliane. It should be noted that I took the precaution of photographing our bounty to show a doctor in the event of the whole family keeling over. It was a memorable afternoon and I'm itching to enjoy this activity with Louis once again when we return to our beloved home.

Incidentally, you may be aware that in France, you can take mushrooms into any *pharmacie* and the assistants therein will be able to confirm whether they are good for eating or good for murder. I am yet to have the opportunity to try this (take mushrooms to the *pharmacie,* not murder) but I am assured it is still the case. Unhappily though, I've heard rumours that some of the larger chemists have stopped providing this service. I fear they may have cottoned on to a theoretical possibility that, if a customer were to become ill following false advice, the *pharmacie* could be sued. I pray The Health and Safety Brigade is keeping its predatory claws out of the area I've come to love, and the local chemists will continue to encourage the traditional practices of gathering what the land so freely gives.

Louis is undoubtedly a bright, strong and dynamic lad with masses of good sense and intuition. He understands his environment, knows the value of good manners and is a heck of a rugby player to boot. His difficulty within French schooling is that, to coin a phrase used elsewhere in this book, he is a square peg which the system is twisting and turning at a whole range of angles in a desperate yet foredoomed attempt to force into a round hole.

Kirsty had a violin pupil who was an energetic and engaging young man of about thirteen years of age. His family were organic farmers and encouraged their children to learn the crafts of the land. There were many days when I encountered him settled in the kitchen/waiting room with a huge knife, cutting and weaving baskets out of willow. Where are such fine and worthy practices assessed? This young chap also gave Kirsty the most original-ever excuse for having done a limited amount of practice the preceding week.

"I'm very sorry," he said. "I hurt my shoulder."

"I'm sorry to hear that," replied Kirsty. "What happened?"

Without batting an eyelid he gave a response which was as startling as it was unprecedented.

"I was attacked by my turkey."

His house is absolutely the kind of environment where one may expect to be ambushed by a turkey. Judging by the deep gouges in his shoulder, these beasts are quite capable of fowl play.

The result of this rather strict and inflexible system is if you have children who are academically strong, they are likely to excel in the French system. If your child is creative and artistic, you could be fine if your school has a teacher who is open-minded and imaginative, as we were fortunate enough to experience. If this is not the case, well, *bon courage* to one and all.

I have witnessed many instances when adults working in the real world appeared to have had their whole *modus operandi* moulded by schooling which allowed no room for on-the-spot thinking and imagination. An example is when, only a few months after we had arrived in France, I had reason to call the car breakdown service. At this time, my French was still rather weak but I was determined to make the call myself and practice. I had not learned the expression *'en panne'* which is what one says in France when referring to the fact your vehicle has broken down. Drawing upon my deepest reserves of courage, I phoned the breakdown line and did my best to communicate the problem.

"My car does not work," I offered. *Ma voiture ne marche pas.*

"Sorry sir, I don't understand," came the reply. *Pardon monsieur, je ne comprends pas.*

"Ma voiture ne marche pas," I tried again.

"Desolé monsieur, je ne comprends pas," she responded.

Hmmm. I tried another tack.

"Madam, my car does not start," I proposed to my linguistically-challenged correspondent. *Madame, ma voiture ne commence pas.*

"Desolé monsieur, je ne comprends pas," came the disheartening but none-to-surprising response.

And so it went on for some minutes. Soon I felt flustered and rather desperate.

"Is your car *en panne?"* the operator eventually asked in a scarce moment of improvisation. *Ést-ce que votre voiture est en panne?*

I wearily enquired as to whether that meant it didn't work.

"Oui monsieur," came the reply.

Therefore we were able to progress.

Now, maybe I am assuming too much, but if I was a telephonist in a call centre specialising in responding to calls from motorists with broken-down vehicles, I'd speculate that if a client with an overseas accent called and said something like 'My car will not move' or 'My car is not rolling', I would have a pretty clear idea the car in question was out of operation and breakdown assistance was required. In the case of *Madame En Panne* who had answered my call, there was absolutely zero possibility of matters advancing until I'd used the expression which would have got her that little red tick in her *cahier* at school. I really believe this manner of working is a direct result of the narrow and single-minded education pathway she most likely would have followed.

As already mentioned, Florence's primary school experience was simply wonderful thanks to a very special teacher and the magic and innocence of such a rural setting. Flo, Sam and I would go to school on pushbikes, passing a field with miniature horses and cows e*n route* and waving to those taking an early *aperitif* at the bar. In France, Primary classes finish at midday on Wednesdays. Children are encouraged to use the afternoon to attend sports or arts classes – many of which are supplied by *associations* for ridiculously low fees. Flo used this opportunity to develop her dance skills with a wonderful, albeit strict ballet teacher, *Madame Danseuse,* who had attended the world-renowned *Opera de Paris.* This legendary professional ballet company and its associated boarding school has a fearsome reputation for absolute discipline and not suffering those who fail to make-the-grade. *Madame Danseuse* had then enjoyed a lengthy career in performance and choreography before setting up her ballet school in the Dordogne. As a teacher, she was certainly tough – many parents were terrified of her – and her classes were run military-style, but the children absolutely adored her. She pushed them very hard and strove for excellence, but combined this with a heart of gold and an obvious deep-rooted love for her charges.

Sadly, she had former colleagues who had allowed their success to dangerously augment their sense of self-importance. One summer, *Madame Danseuse* organised a week-long summer school for her advanced pupils, and a gentleman who was a former soloist with the *Opera de Paris* was invited to come and teach. *Monsieur L'Arsole* appeared to enjoy using his position of power to torment children. He would select individuals and try to humiliate them in front of the class, bringing them to the verge of tears at which point he would aggressively interrogate them.

"Why are you crying… what is the matter? This would not be tolerated in the *Opera de Paris!*" he would bark in their faces.

I noticed he felt the need to mention his auspicious CV at least fifteen times per class. One day, Florence was the victim of his pathological desire to psychologically abuse young girls. When I collected her from class, she was calm, philosophical and obviously trying her best to understand *Monsieur L'Arsole's* motives. That's Florence in a nutshell. She seeks the good in everyone she encounters and will always reflect on her experiences with compassion. Unfortunately, I am a lesser individual. Upon hearing the afternoon's events, I gently enlightened her to the fact that the gentleman was a complete dickhead who used far too much hair product. I speculated that he was jealous of his pupils as they were young, fit and strong and he had rather let himself go - the only part of his being which had swelled to the same degree as his ego was his girth. To conclude, I explained that this once-fine *artiste* had been reduced to a podgy, boring and irrelevant bully who raised his self-esteem by making sure those around him had theirs flattened. I believe it is always good to be honest with children.

When she was due to go to *college* (secondary school) we were faced with a dilemma as she was already showing clear signs of wanting to be a dancer at a serious level. We attended the parent/teacher meeting for the school which she was destined to attend where I asked a number of tricky and unusual questions of the head of lower school.

"Would there be flexibility in terms of her choice of second language study as she was already fluent in English?"

"Non," replied *Monsieur LeHead* who appeared to find both eye contact and clarity of speech beyond his remit.

"Would there be time for her to study dance in arts lessons?"

"Non," came the all-too-predictable response from a gentleman who was evidently a committed disciple of the *il faut* way-of-life.

It was in this laborious fashion our dialogue ensued for a full forty-five minutes.

This made for a depressing outlook but, just before the beginning of term, she was offered a place in a private school in Bordeaux which shared a project with a dance academy. In France, this commendable option is known as *Sport-Études*. As the title suggests, there are schools which develop a specialism outside of the regular scheme of work in an attempt to encourage excellence in the arts and, most commonly, sports. This was an amazing opportunity but the daily commute would have been too much for us so, with heavy hearts, we felt obliged to decline. Then, one of the dance teachers spoke.

"Florence can live with me. There will be no fee," she said as if it were the most simple and obvious thing in the world.

So, in the bat of an eyelid, Florence was obliged to master city bus timetables whereas, in Saint Cecilia des Dames, the mode of transport of choice was the pushbike. She was required to negotiate the *boulevards* of the urban centre, with its 24/7 nose-to-tail traffic - in our village, the principal objective was to avoid tractors. Rural life suddenly seemed so innocent, so safe - although Sam did once end up riding his bike into a three-metre deep, nettle-filled drainage ditch when distracted by a donkey, so it had its unique hazards. The teacher who offered to act as hostess to Florence demonstrated a spirit of generosity, kindness and trust which blew us away and will always remain something special in our hearts.

Immense commitment is required of *Sport-Études* participants; missed academic classes being the responsibility of the children to catch up in their own time, using their own initiative. These lessons were to be sent to us online. Some teachers responded to the initiative admirably, the geography teacher being especially flexible saying to us privately that she was not obliged to complete all of her homework as she needed rest and family time. If only such an attitude were the case with all subjects. Regrettably, the French teacher, *Madame Dinosaur,* seemed to belong to another era. I never had the pleasure of meeting her, but I sense she disapproved of the *Sport-Études* scheme as a principle and therefore stubbornly refused to cooperate. Consequently, she failed to send Florence the necessary lesson notes each week and was mule-like in her refusal to communicate using the new-fangled twenty-first-century invention called email. For her first French test, despite having revised diligently, Florence was confronted with topics she'd never encountered upon opening the question paper. Dissatisfied with this, I made an appointment to see the Head-of-Year, little realising that this would be the first of a painful and prolonged series of encounters I would endure with this affable chap.

The first meeting was pleasant enough and one could not help but like *Monsieur LeProf.* A smiling and warm young man, he promised to revise her mark to take into account the work she had not received. The next test, the same happened, then again, and again. *Monsieur LeProf* and I were soon on first-name terms. I sensed this well-meaning fellow was faced with a formidable foe who probably harboured a *Minitel* machine in her bedside cabinet which she took out the last thing at night, kissed lovingly, and hugged as slumber took over her body.

As the year progressed, *Madame Dinosaur* appeared to concoct policies to create the greatest number of barriers to Florence's well-being and progress. For example, she berated Florence for having handed in perfectly good homework one week early to a replacement teacher. My daughter had anticipated missing a class due to an audition and *Madame Dinosaur* had been away when she submitted her work in advance of the due date. According to *Madame Dinosaur*, this was an absolute no-go. I became furious.

Bearing my best warrior-face, I paid a visit to the weary *Monsieur LeProf* for the eighteenth time. I violently burst into his office (well, actually, I knocked and waited until he said I could come in, but you get my drift) and demanded sight of the sacred, stone-carved policy documents of which *Madame Dinosaur* had spoken. Of course, he couldn't produce them. All the poor man could do after each unjust incident was to call Florence to his office and apologise.

Towards the end of the year, I was concerned. Flo, who has always been the most hard-working and carefree of children, had lost her mojo. When she was set French homework, she would complete it half-heartedly saying there was no point in trying hard as *Madame Dinosaur* would only give her a bad mark anyway. How could I argue with that? She was correct. The straw which broke the camel's back came in the final examination of the year. This was based on a book which the class had been set to read. Florence is an avid reader and will devour books in either English or French with the same gusto as our goats devoured our raspberry bush one year. She approached the exam with renewed confidence yet when she turned over the paper in the exam room the first question read the following:

What is the first word in the book?

Astonishing. Needless to say, no-one in the class knew the answer. Therefore, *Madame Dinosaur* was able to satisfy her failure-lust with a pleasing line of red crosses in perfect symmetry on the answer papers of the entire year-group. I was aghast. I undertook yet another after-work bike ride to Flo's school and visited my now-bosom-buddy *Monsieur LeProf.* We participated in a kind of bewildered exchange through the medium of body language where I pointed at the question and then raised my eyebrows. He opened his hands, showing his empty palms, shrugged his shoulders and did the side-mouth raspberry. *N'importe Quoi!*

Dissatisfied with this response, I wrote again to *Madame Dinosaur* (she had never answered the fifteen or so previous polite emails I had sent, and we had no *Minitel* machine). My note read:

Dear *Madame Dinosaur,*

Please, can you inform me what you are hoping to achieve by asking a child to remember the first word of a book?

Cordialement

D. Jones

She never answered.

Monsieur LeProf resigned at the end of the year to take up a post in another school. I hope it wasn't I who drove him away. I've no idea what has become of *Madame Dinosaur* but I'm relieved she has nothing more to do with my child.

I am painting a somewhat mixed picture of education in France. I must highlight factors which I thoroughly approve of, mainly because they fly directly in the face of The Health and Safety Police who appear to have become the deciding body behind everyone's pursuits elsewhere. At break time, children are allowed to run and jump, skip and play. And fall over. Part of growing up is the act of taking a tumble in the playground. Although undesirable, I do believe little legs and feet learn the limits of balance through trial and error.

As mentioned, I worked in a school in Bordeaux as well as the music school in our village. I became progressively more and more depressed at the sight of kids tearing over to the teacher with the tiniest of scratches, screaming the place down. They would demand an entire pharmacy of ointments, creams, sprays, plasters and bandages for their non-existent wounds. This wasn't their fault. The problem lay in the fact they had experienced teachers, parents and carers supporting this drama, all of whom were either obliged or hypnotised by a culture which bypassed any iota of good sense and individual judgement. Treatment parallel to that employed by intensive-care paramedics in war zones became the norm in the playground. One wonders if the massive pharmaceutical industry encourages this behaviour to inflate consumption.

I was also amazed at the way in which at least three children appeared to break limbs every weekend. A gaggle of infants with crutches would be hobbling around the place every Monday morning. The playground looked like a scene from *Saving Private Ryan*. Teachers had to carry them upstairs and classmates were allocated as the invalids' helping 'buddies', yet upon being offered an enticing treat from afar, they would become curiously pain-free and mobile. Whenever I enquired as to what had happened, I would receive a conveniently ambiguous explanation along the lines of 'I was running in the park and twisted it very badly'. Two or three days later, once the novelty had worn off, they would discard their crutches and tear around the place like all the others. The reality is that there was never any significant injury in the first place.

It must be said that the French appear to have a deep passion for prescribed medicines and treatments. A visit to the doctor's surgery and subsequent stop at the *pharmacie* for a relatively minor ailment would yield two large sacks of products, many of which would require refrigerated storage, taking up space which could have been more fruitfully surrendered for the noble purpose of chilling beer and wine. I found it disconcerting that if one of our children required a vaccination, we'd be obliged to collect the vaccine from the pharmacy and then take it to our doctor for the inoculation when a mutually-convenient appointment could be made. During the interim period it would be stored in our fridge and consequently, I nearly distributed diphtheria or polio serum on to my stir fry on at least two occasions having mistaken them for sachets of soy sauce.

To go back to our village's school, staff were allocated to be helpers in the playground. When a child fell over, they were expected to pick them up, sit them on their knee, give them a cuddle and within minutes all would be fine. In the UK, we witnessed a phase where if a child hurt him/herself, adults would be forbidden even to touch them. The 'thinking' (and I use that word reluctantly) behind this policy was children would be protected from potential abuse. Has anyone ever considered that a genuinely-injured child being ignored by every adult in the vicinity, until eventually, a designated person ambles back from lunch, is grotesque psychological abuse? What sort of lesson does this deliver? One where compassion and care are ignored in the interest of some fictional protection strategy?

The village school had a pre- and after-school club called *la garderie*. It was free of charge and there was a glorious flexibility as to its use. If Sam was having a ball with his buddies in the playground after school, we just went home and collected him later. When the light began to fade, the declining group would retire indoors, huddle over a piece of artwork, play a board game or just read a book together. The children would hug the carers like grandmothers. There were no computer games or screens of any kind. Just good, soul-enriching life experience.

If you are seeking out-of-school extra-curricular activities for your children, the opportunities are abundant. The French system of *associations* is particularly popular in isolated areas. An individual or group of people can set up an *association* to deliver activities such as music, sports or dance lessons. These are often managed by volunteers who want to put something back into their area. Our village's music school is an *association* and it is incredibly well-run. If the service being provided will deliver opportunity and quality of life to the local inhabitants, incentives are offered to the organising bodies such as premises, grants and help with overheads. Many sports and music teachers work part-time for a network of *associations* in order to provide some stability in their employment.

As a music teacher giving one-to-one lessons, I noted that older folk expected an authoritarian style of teaching. They often failed to comprehend the progressive techniques modern teachers employ to encourage their kids along. I use a method known as 'question-led teaching' when working with teenagers. This is because they often become strangely mute, almost overnight, and are thus obliged to interact but, more importantly, the fact they unfold the solutions to their own challenges (with my guidance) builds confidence, which seems to be so painfully absent at this stage of life.

One young lad, whom I'll call Jean-Paul, typically attended his lessons alone, but one week he was brought along by his grandmother. Usually, parents waited in a room next door during the lesson but *Mamie* (the French for Granny) decided to listen in which was fine by me. The lesson started and Jean-Paul played through his piece making a few errors along the way, as one would expect. Using question-led teaching I spoke gently to my pupil.

"OK, Jean-Paul, what can you improve in bar twenty-seven?"

"But it's *wrong!*" burst out a loud, distinctly feminine and mature voice from the other side of the room. *Mais c'est faux!*

Jean-Paul and I jumped out of our seats at the explosion of sound. *Mamie* had offered her wizened judgement, and with some gusto.

"Merci," I mumbled awkwardly and tried to regather my thoughts.

Having given some pointers, we had another go.

"OK, let's try the same bar with the new fingering."

Jean-Paul composed himself. The melody was played with a fluffed note mid-phrase.

"What *are* you doing?!" enquired *Mamie,* her intervention and enquiry being unsolicited in my recollection. *Quest-ce que tu fais?!*

I mustered the warmest smile I could manage in the given circumstances and attempted to continue with at least some remote semblance of normality.

"Try it with finger three here Jean-Paul," I uttered, feeling helpless, and more than a little sorry for my pupil. Jean-Paul looked nervous. I heard him grind his teeth ever-so-slightly.

'Twang!' went the near-inevitable wrong note.

"C'est faux!" yelled *Mamie* – as if we needed telling.

Jean-Paul looked at me pleadingly for support. I noticed little beads of sweat had appeared on his forehead, and this was only three minutes into a thirty-minute lesson.

Had this dialogue been in English, I would have had the confidence to have smiled at *Mamie* and suggested Jean-Paul should have a stab at working out the solution for himself. The difficulty was, being diplomatic in a second language is hard. It only takes one wrong word or a misplaced nuance for words to be construed as impolite. The next twenty-seven minutes were some of the longest of my life, and I suspect Jean-Paul's as well. Every error was met with cries of disapproval.

"Mais Non!", "N'importe quoi!", "Oh là là!" and the like.

Mamie also edged closer and closer, inch by inch as the lesson progressed until she was practically hovering over him like a very vocal vulture, advancing upon a dying beast. Predictably, Jean-Paul's playing went to pieces. Of course, *Mamie* believed she was helping. She had been educated in an era where results were ground out of children through repeated, agitated correction. I think Jean-Paul appreciated my more gentle and interactive approach more fully after that day. Incidentally, *Mamie* and I are friends now. I'm also aware that, despite her warm and generous volunteering of expertise, she has never touched a guitar in her life.

I noticed many adult learners were very nervous when they came for a one-to-one guitar lesson. I'm sure this was due to the *je n'arrive pas* mentality installed in their heads as schoolchildren. They seemed to presume they wouldn't be able to play the instrument and the lesson was anticipated as a thirty-minute confirmation of this. I spent most of my time battling to free them from such a mindset. One adult pupil, whom I'll call *Monsieur Techno,* would always turn up late, in a fluster, because of his supposedly incredibly busy life. He had a Bluetooth earpiece permanently fixed to his head and I sometimes questioned whether it had been surgically attached there. He would enter the room and unpack an immaculate array of kit: smart guitar, capo, digital tuner, digital metronome, plectrums of every shape and size, a *cahier* (aaagh!), pencils, manuscript paper, the list goes on. Once we got round to playing some actual notes his mobile would inevitably ring with a gloriously-polyphonic blaze of tinny sound. He would apologise, reach into his pocket and look at the screen.

"I'm sorry, I must take this," he'd declare.

Then a dialogue would ensue.

"Allo... Yes, it's me.... I'm in my guitar lesson... *guitar lesson!...* Yeah.... I'll call you later."

This would happen, on average, three times per session. I am at a loss to understand why this conversation needed to be undertaken with such urgency at exactly that moment - I'd propose it could have waited another ten minutes. Actually, I think I do understand. I believe he was so anxious, he was stalling to waste time, perhaps without even realising it himself.

But let's finish on a positive. The school calendar features many splendid events which are renowned in French country life as being unmissable for young and old alike. One of these is *Carnaval*. This takes place in early spring, preceding Lent. It forms part of the *Mardi-Gras* (literally 'Fat Tuesday') series of celebrations. The word is obviously shared with the English 'carnival' and they both relate to meat, like 'carnivore'. It is because meat and fatty foods would be eaten in abundance before the fasting season of Lent.

Nothing prepared us for our first *Carnaval* in our little rural village for which preparations had been underway for some weeks. We understood the children would go to school in fancy-dress on the big day and parents were welcome to do likewise. Kirsty and I did show up to join in the festivities but felt too British to don fancy-dress. We soon regretted it as we were the only parents present in everyday clothes. One 'Mum' in particular pushed the boat out to the extreme by turning up in a full-length all-encapsulating penguin suit, thus completely concealing her identity. Even though it was late February it was a warm day and the poor woman must have been sweltering inside.

Firstly, there were group photos taken in the playground and then confetti handed to each child. Following this, the procession around the village commenced. The older teachers led the children in traditional *Carnaval* songs and percussion instruments were passed around and bashed with vigour. The procession continued for a good half an hour by which time the penguin was visibly drooping. The older folk of the village stood at their gates, beaming with pleasure to see the old traditions being maintained and pretending to object when showered with confetti.

Upon returning to the school we witnessed the spectacle of the trial of the *Pétassou*. For many months, the children had been building an enormous figure from recyclable materials (to match the school's annual theme) and stuffing it with paper and straw – rather like a Guy on Guy Fawkes Night in the UK. A line of final-year pupils lined up on the steps in front of the school where a PA system had been set up. Silence fell, and the drama began. Each pupil took it in turns to read an accusation against the *Pétassou*. These ranged from the trivial to the deadly serious. The first speaker told of the severe winter which had just passed. Uncharacteristically, we had experienced temperatures as low as minus fifteen degrees and, as a result, the taps in the playground had frozen and burst. At the end of her speech, a young boy playing 'the judge' turned to face the now considerable crowd.

"How do you find the accused?" he asked.

"Guilty!" cried about 100 voices causing me and Kirsty to jump out of our skins.

"What shall we do with him?" asked the judge.

At this point, I noticed the *Pétassou* was absent from its usual place in the shelter at the end of the playground. My eyes wandered to the adjacent field and I suddenly spotted it on top of an enormous pile of kindling and wood. The penny dropped.

"Burn him!" screamed one hundred men, women and children (and one dehydrated penguin).

The next prosecutor stood. He spoke of serious world affairs, including terrorist attacks which had recently rocked France. The judge asked the question of the crowd - the answer was somewhat predictable.

"Guilty! Burn him!"

And so it went on until each child had spoken and the *Pétassou* could be seen mouthing 'It's a fair cop'. A chant of '*Au Feu Pétassou!*' rang out across the playground, and the crowd was mobilised to the adjacent field led by *Monsieur le Maire.* Once the mob was assembled, he took a flaming rag and chucked it into the kindling. The loud explosion which followed suggested his deputy had been liberal with his use of an accelerant and, just to spice things up a bit, some wag had popped a few noisy fireworks into the pyre. As the flames reached to the clouds, accompanied by a concerto of whizzes and pops, *le Maire* staggered away from the inferno, face blackened except for white eyes where his glasses had been blown off, but no matter, the crowd were cheering wildly and had gone into a kind of animalistic pagan frenzy, crying out a rich and vocabulary-broadening range of obscenities at the shell of the *Pétassou.* It became so crazy I became concerned that in the passion of the moment, someone might choose to chuck the village Welshman on the fire as well but happily, I was left unmolested. Then everyone ambled amicably back to the school and shared an *aperitif.* The penguin had a fish.

A few days later the school where I worked in the heart of the city of Bordeaux held their *Carnaval.* The differences were more than evident. The kids turned up in fancy dress, but one could only feel deflated at the sight of so many wearing the outfits of the current Disney characters. The procession was fenced by teachers, all obsessed with the secure crossing of a tiny side street which hosted about three moving vehicles a day. Once they'd walked 100 yards, they did a U-turn and went back to school where the music was the year's manufactured pop hits rather than anything reflecting the culture or heritage of the country.

The highlight of the day was provided by a young boy who had persuaded his parents to purchase him a Rastafarian outfit. It had the usual clichés: a red, gold and green hat, a dreadlock wig and

Bob Marley T-shirt but, to his considerable surprise (and that of the teachers) the pack included a massive fake spliff. He'd been 'toking' on it for about fifty yards along the street before the Head of Primary spotted him and ripped it out of his mouth with unnecessary vigour. There were no mums disguised as Arctic bird-life.

***

Mathematics, Mushrooms and Turkey Management – The Essential Tips

(1) If your children are academic, they will love schooling in France.

(2) Like so many other things in life, the system is only as good as the individuals which deliver it.

(3) If you have an artistic or sporty child, research the Sports-Études option.

(4) Ask a small boy to teach you how to pick mushrooms. He'll know more than any book.

(5) Your kids will be allowed to run around and hurt themselves.

(6) You'll have access to music and dance lessons at ridiculously-low prices.

(7) Elderly ladies are really scary in music lessons.

(8) Wear fancy dress to Carnaval. You'll look like an idiot if you don't.

Figure 4 The Pétassou, guilty as always, burns.

Figure 5 A selection of the mushrooms I picked with Louis.

Figure 6 The penguin mum is finally unmasked!

Dan Jones

10. *Bonjour,* What's Your Emergency?

I know you're a Pat by the cut of your hair
But you all turn to Scotchmen as soon as you're here
You have left your own country for breaking the law
We are seizing all strangers from Erin-go-Bragh

Erin-go-Bragh – Traditional (Scotland)

In the French countryside, you will encounter both *la Police* and *les Gendarmes* with regularity. They are different animals and need to be treated accordingly. *Les Gendarmes* (the word deriving from *'gens d'armes'* or 'armed people') carry the demeanour and attitude of the military rather than a friendly local bobby on the beat. They are, quite frankly, scary. The *Police Municipale,* although tooled up to the hilt, are the kind of coppers you'd feel happy to stop to ask for directions.

Carrying weaponry is the norm for the most modest members of the law and order enforcement representatives, particularly since the horrors of the *Charlie Hebdo* attacks in 2015. At times it seems wholly inappropriate. Three times weekly, I took the Bordeaux-Perigueux train to and from a school where I was teaching. French trains are, on the whole, excellent when the staff are working rather than going on strike. Frustratingly, the latter occurs much of the time. In order to travel on a train, you must enter into an archaic and complex ticket purchase and validation system which, if you get wrong, leaves you open to a variety of fiscally-painful consequences. Upon successfully purchasing your ticket, you sometimes (not always) need to 'compost' it using a post-box sized, temperamental yellow machine of which there are many peppered around the station concourse.

When I first started using the train, I honestly believed that SNCF had put a used-ticket recycling scheme into place and these yellow machines would shred your ticket to transform them into soil nutrients. I sagely applauded SNCF and nodded approvingly as commuters queued patiently in order to ensure their environmental responsibilities were fulfilled. In fact, one must *compost* a ticket (the French verb is *composter),* which means it must be inserted into a stamping machine to validate it before entering a train.

The first time I presented a fully paid-up yet conspicuously uncomposted ticket to a guard, he unsmilingly thrust it back into my face.

"Sir, it is not composted," the guard said. *Monsieur, il n'est pas composté.*

"Well, I'm still using it," I mumbled, bemused at this kind of pre-emptive eco-intervention proposed by *le controlleur.*

SNCF trains are often patrolled by security staff. These are usually lumbering, bored men, armed to the teeth with weaponry which looks better suited to a week's holiday in Kabul rather than a train trip through the sleepy villages of the Dordogne. The consequence is, in the event of the mildest hint of aggro, these brutes, desperate for action, become involved.

I recall seeing three teenagers slipping onto the train without purchasing, and consequently composting, tickets and then witnessed the entire spectacle of their being caught by the French equivalent of the SAS. Teenagers are so funny when they try to be inconspicuous. As the ticket inspector entered the carriage, they stood up *en masse* to go to the toilet all at the same time, looking downwards at the floor, hands in pockets, shuffling awkwardly, resembling a line of emperor penguins. They might as well have tattooed 'no ticket, no compost' on their foreheads. Minutes later they were cornered by a guard, supported by three fully-armed military police who I thought were going to pin them to the floor, handcuff them and throw them into the path of the oncoming Paris-Angoulême TGV. French nationals are required to carry ID (although I never did) so I could hear the offences

163

racking up as the lads were aggressively and intimidatingly interrogated by their bully-boy captors (no ID, no proof of age, no proof of address, no ticket and no compost to name but a few).

Sadly, some of the *controlleurs* on French trains appear to have attended the same course of study as their friends working in government administration. During many commutes, I found myself cringing in discomfort as I overheard pointless and fruitless conversations between rookie travellers and control-freak, robot-like *controlleurs*. Such exchanges involve the *controlleur* repeatedly maintaining that the ticket in question needs to be composted, like a recording stuck on loop, whereas the traveller obviously fails to comprehend the system. It's so frustrating when the staff member refuses to show any flexibility or goodwill to the hapless passenger.

Three times I have intervened, twice translating for awkwardly-smiling tourists, and once offering a simple explanation as to the root of the problem to a perplexed French traveller – a seemingly straightforward task which the *controlleur* was evidently incapable of executing. I once overheard an exchange between a *controlleur* and a stern-faced lady, whom I can only assume was a full-time *fonctionnaire,* where they engaged in a kind of verbal stand-off. Each party doggedly repeated their lines *ad nauseum,* not dissimilar to five-year-old children arguing over a preferred teddy bear at recreation. Rather than being linguistic, the barrier existed because neither party would compromise on his/her fixed position. The exchange lasted for at least thirty minutes and was continuing when I descended from the train, gnashing my teeth and ripping out clumps of hair at the frustration of it all.

French road traffic is controlled by both police and *gendarmes.* If you drive on French minor roads, and cars coming in the opposite direction flash their lights at you, it means *gendarmes* are ahead carrying out checks. In France, police can stop cars as and when they wish, unlike their British counterparts who must justify their actions with a reason. Just months after we arrived in France, Kirsty was driving along an open road when she spotted, way in the distance, a crouched figure in the road pointing what looked like - to all intents and purposes - a gun directly at her. It was a *gendarme*. She had Sam in the back who was just six months old and making a racket. The *gendarme* in question approached the driver's window, stopped, approached the other side because it was an English right-hand drive car and, unsmilingly speaking in monosyllables, showed her the speed gun. The instrument confirmed she'd been going too fast. All the indicators suggested the chances of a gentle warning were limited. Indeed, we were obliged to pay a hefty fine. You can pay these on the spot in France which at least grants you a reduction.

In the UK, the police are obliged to warn you they are carrying out speed checks. Of course, the result is everyone slows down when they see the camera sign which is, I suppose, the desired effect. Not in the French countryside though. *Les Gendarmes* choose the most obscure places to literally catch people out. A plumber friend of mine once accelerated out of a 50kph zone towards a point where the limit changed to 70kph and anticipating this, a *gendarme* leapt out of a bush waving his speed gun, gleefully pointing out an infringement of about 4kph above the limit. He had been waiting, not where there was a potential danger, but where he had the best chance of bagging a victim, and perhaps a bonus. Having been flashed by other drivers, I often saw *gendarmes,* heads poking out of bushes, hoping to snare a commuter. They reminded me of the *Pontipines* and the *Wottingers*, characters from the BBC's surrealist children's series *In the Night Garden,* with their little peaked caps in the foliage.

My most infuriating experience with a member of *la Police* rather than *les Gendarmes* occurred in Bordeaux. I developed a routine of driving to the local station at the crack of dawn, putting my bike on the train (which, admirably, you can do for free in France) and then cycling to the school where I taught music. Bordeaux is a wonderful city for cyclists. It hardly ever rains in a serious way, there is a generous and winding network of bike lanes throughout the centre and plenty of side streets where you can zip along stylishly, grabbing a free newspaper from a smiling distributor as you pass (which I'd use to light the fire in the evening).

In my first weeks as a cyclist therein, I noticed traffic lights seemed not to apply to French pushbikes. There are some junctions where they are officially allowed to pass a red light if the way is clear, but otherwise, they should wait like everybody else. They don't. As time went by, I nervously joined the legions of cyclists indulging in this mischievous moment of law-breaking and it soon became second nature.

One morning I was warned of a strike which, as already noted, was a frequent occurrence. French train staff call a snap-strike for absolutely anything, although the most common reason is due to a *controlleur* being treated aggressively by a passenger. I suspect the majority of 'aggressors' are baffled Brits becoming infuriated by the surrealist *compostage* system and understandably having a bit of a strop.

"I say old fruit, you really are being most obtrusive," an English gentleman *en route* to a conference in Paris might offer in mild annoyance.

In this event, the *controlleur* would think to him/herself *'Excellente!* I am going *chez moi* for an early *aperitif* today' and claim aggressive behaviour. No-one would dare to contest the claim as the weight of the entire nation's unions would be behind the employee, regardless of the evidence or indeed, lack of it. The result would be the meltdown of the entire rail system. Next time your European mini-break is disrupted by yet another air-traffic controller strike in Paris, do a little research. You may find the origin of the dispute was the raised voice of an exasperated commuter.

The consequence of this particular day's strike action was that I had to go to Bordeaux at an absolutely ungodly hour as the first train was the only one running. When I'd arrived in this magnificent metropolis, it was still dark. I decided to make the best of the situation and, as there was at least an hour to kill before anyone would be at the school, I went for a gentle pedal through the picturesque side streets.

It was a pleasant morning and the clear sky promised a day of fair weather. I was freewheeling down a little decline whistling happily to myself, believing all was good with the world when suddenly, my *reverie* was gate-crashed by the sound of a powerful motorcycle overtaking me and blocking my path. It was a gentleman from *la Police.* He dismounted from his vehicle and told me I had just gone through a red light. Without thinking, I told him I had done at least forty since leaving the station before realising this was not the most intelligent course of action. Soon recognising I had met a policeman who had no sense of humour, I decided to change my tack. I am fluent in French but I figured the 'ignorant tourist' approach would be my best bet. I deliberately spoke in my worst English accent.

"Bonjour monsieur… Je m'appelle Daniel Jones… où est le Syndicate d'Initiative?" I mumbled alongside other schoolboy French clichés.

It could have worked but, when he asked me for identification, I was deep in *la merde.* My driving licence, and therefore my address were French.

"But, I say! You live here!" exclaimed *Monsieur Zero-Humour. Mais alors! Vous habitez ici!*

Zut alors! I received a ninety euro fine. I was deeply peed off by both the act of idiotic officialdom and the subsequent penalty.

I was feeling thoroughly sorry for myself when I pulled up at home later in the day and was wearing my best 'I am the victim' sulky face, ready to present to anyone daft enough to take notice of it. As I parked I saw André, our 88-year old neighbour who was, as always, tending to his vegetable garden. Delighted to have someone to whinge at, I called him over and recounted the day's injustices. His eyes opened wide and he asked me if I would show him the penalty notice. I willingly handed it over, hoping for sympathy, the offer of a highly-alcoholic beverage and maybe the means whereby I could instigate a national strike in protest against the wrongs I'd experienced. Instead, his face broke into a broad grin and, as he read, turned into a picture of unrestrained mirth. Eventually, holding his sides and bending over double with laughter, he told me he was going to show the offending document to Eliane, as she too needed a good belly-laugh. I was deeply put-out.

Just as in the UK, there are *gendarmes* and police who are good-natured and pleasant. I've enjoyed a good chat with those who have stopped me when I've been returning home from a gig at 1.30am. They've been interested in my career and to hear why my family and I are in France. I translated for the benefit of an elderly British driver and a charming *gendarme* in a car park following an unlikely sequence of events in which no human being was injured but the financial damage probably ran into tens of thousands of euros (why do I appear to attract such incidents?) On the day in question, we were waiting to exit a car park following a most convivial lunch *en famille* in Perigueux when we found ourselves stuck behind a car. The driver and his passenger were experiencing difficulty in correctly placing their exit ticket into the machine which would, in turn, raise the rigid horizontal barrier which was stubbornly refusing to budge. The fact that the two occupants were of advanced years and limited mobility was exacerbating the situation. Eventually, the driver succeeded in inserting his ticket but, by the time he had reinstalled himself in his seat in order to progress, it was too late. The barrier had closed again. I was aware that there was a help button on the pillar so I jumped out of my own car to direct the gentleman towards it. He had had the same idea and laboriously pulled himself from his vehicle for a second time. Regrettably, he had omitted to apply his handbrake and as he stepped away, his car inched towards the barrier. In a moment of agility not experienced by his body for some thirty years, he spun on his heel and dived feet-first back into the driver seat in order to stamp on the brake. His car was an automatic. Such a machine has two pedals: a brake and an accelerator. The chances of a successful outcome were 50/50 and the events which followed illustrate why I am not a gambling man. He regrettably applied his entire body-weight to the accelerator rather than the intended pedal situated a couple of inches to the left of it. Consequently, in a screech of smoke and spinning of tyres worthy of a *Die Hard* movie, the modest 'sensible car' flew forwards at the barrier. At this point, I was just a couple of metres away and found myself covering my face with my hands as the car crashed through the obstinate barrier with a spectacular crunch of metal-on-metal. It could have ended there but sadly, having destroyed the said barrier, his momentum carried him towards a line of innocently-parked vehicles, owned by unsuspecting white-collar workers shuffling papers in the adjacent *préfecture.* He collided with these spectacularly. The result reminded me of Roy Castle's *Record Breakers* series from the 1980's where men with too much time on their hands would create lines upon lines of dominoes and attempt to knock them all over with a single lazy flick of a finger (a fly always appeared to destroy their work during the night at least once). In our case, the dominoes were cars and our friend was the fly-in-the-ointment. He took out, at best, seven of them. An eerie silence followed, only punctuated by the occasional clank of a wing mirror or hub-cap dropping sorrowfully onto the asphalt. I prised my fingers one-by-one away from my face and surveyed the carnage; Perigueux Central Car Park resembled a demolition derby. The elderly driver struggled out of the smoking mass of twisted metal that was once his car, along with his female companion who staggered from the passenger door. They were both English. The couple were fully-paid-up members of that golden generation of Brits who had endured the toughest trials of the Twentieth Century: The Blitz in the 40's, post-war rationing in the 50's and progressive rock music in the 70's. For them, a mere multiple-vehicle pile-up in a city centre car park was a whimsical breeze. As they dusted bits of automobile debris from their smart overcoats, they uttered things such as 'Bad show old girl', and 'I say, what a bore!' As I offered words of sympathy and concern to the driver, Kirsty checked over the equally-aged passenger and enquired as to her well-being; she startled us with her response.

"Oh, don't worry my dear, only last year I drove my car off a cliff and I was stuck in a tree for at least an hour before they pulled me out," she stated in nostalgic reflection as if describing a pleasant summer afternoon nibbling cucumber sandwiches and scones with old school chums.

Kirsty had actually thought that the gentleman was startled by my well-intentioned approach, and feared he had hastily jumped back into the car believing me to be of malicious intent. I was able to correct her on that issue to her immense, visible relief.

The long and short of this tale is that *les Gendarmes* soon appeared and I was employed to act as a translator as the inevitable paperwork was completed (in triplicate). A queue of vehicles backed up behind the now-destroyed barrier and a calm *gendarme* gave my wife authority to act as an impromptu traffic cop, authorising her to remove posts and chains which marked the boundary of the car park and to wave drivers through one-by-one – tasks she fulfilled with the proficiency of a seasoned veteran. One gentleman in a low-slung sporty number tried to exit before his turn and added to the ever-augmenting to-do list of the local garage by grinding his undercarriage against a horizontally poised bollard. My stepmother, always a great advocate of fair play, suddenly took on the role of Community Police Officer, turning back miscreants attempting to use the carnage as an excuse to zip off without paying their parking fees. *Les Gendarmes* were most professional, calm and appreciative. It was impressive stuff. The following week, *la Famille Jones* received a box of chocolates and a beautiful letter of thanks – written in script that can only be employed by those over a certain age – in which the driver explained that he had decided to hang up his driving gloves once-and-for-all (I hope his cliff-jumping passenger had arrived at the same wise choice). He had a son who was apparently a television personality of some note in Australia. He'd been trying to persuade his dad to live closer to him, way on the other side of the planet and, following this minor inconvenience, he'd decided that it was the right moment to make the move. This is another example of how life's challenges can often bring hidden gifts if we only choose to view them that way.

In contrast to this positive *gendarme* encounter, there are others who should command our sympathy rather than derision. I have often endured little men using the power of their badge to inflate a sagging self-esteem (and more-often-than-not, paunch) and the consequences are, at best, tedious. I'd speculate some are wannabe Special Forces trainees who failed to make the cut.

Once a *gendarme* who was training a group of young *gendarmes-to-be* kept me at the edge of the road for a full fifteen minutes as he criticised my crumpled-up driving licence. The fact two of the trainees were female probably contributed to his somewhat over-zealous and macho attitude. I'm messy. If you doubt the verity of this statement, just contact my wife. The licence was valid and, as far as I can recall, there is no law against creased paper. He checked my insurance which in France is displayed by a sticker on the windscreen. Not content with my perfectly good and in-date sticker, he insisted on seeing the full insurance document. This was in a rucksack which was to be found squashed into a ball under the feet of my children, as well as three months of discarded banana skins, toys and car-park stickers. When I eventually dug it out, he criticised me for being so disorganised. I didn't have the energy to dispute the point with him so I nodded earnestly and promised to iron my papers just as soon as we returned home from the lunch he was making me and my family late for. Next, he highlighted the fact that our *carte grise* - the French equivalent of a vehicle registration document which you are obliged to keep in your car in France - had been turned down at the corners making it inconvenient for the reader to observe the page number. I suffered three weeks of sleepless nights due to the guilt I felt at having to make the poor dear turn over five millimetres of paper at the roadside. I promised to replace it immediately, before lunch even, and then having admired his ridiculous and ever-so-slightly camp pill-box cap, we went on our way.

There is a depressing practice I often see in the Dordogne and that is drink-driving. In the UK it is rightly, an absolute no-go. Yes, I have a lot of problems with too much control in society but drink-driving is another ball-game. Young people fail to realise that not so long ago, drink-driving was regarded as a minor misdemeanour. As a teenager, I loved reading the James Herriot stories which told of his life as a young country vet in the Yorkshire Dales. Fellow fans of the original books will recall many of Herriot's stories revolved around taking the wheel of a vehicle with little in the way of brakes after several pints of strong ale and a couple of whisky chasers. It wasn't until 1966 that an official limit was established in the UK and the following year, the breathalyser introduced. Before this, a police officer would ascertain the degree of a driver's inebriation by judging whether he or she could walk in a suitably straight trajectory. I have played hundreds of gigs for restaurants and bars in the Dordogne and beyond; ex-pats will often make up a considerable percentage of the audience. I think many of them have been out of the UK for thirty or forty years and fail to realise how times and opinions have changed. I've frequently overheard comments such as 'I'd better take the country roads tonight' or 'Anyone seen the *gendarmes* around this evening?' In the UK and most urban centres, such remarks would rightly be met with shock and disgust. In our corner of the world though, these comments prompt mischievous chuckles and murmurs of agreement from some quarters. The French police are cracking down hard on this practice and they will target events such as well-publicised gigs, where those at the wheel may be tempted to have 'one-for-the-road'. As drivers pass through a village *bourg* at night, *les gendarmes* will be waiting, hidden around corners, ready to breathalyse as many people as humanly possible at closing time. I once played a gig in a private house during which a member of the catering staff took to the stage to warn the 150-strong audience that there were *gendarmes* parked at the end of the driveway. They were breathalysing every single driver. Consequently, at least fifty people hovered around self-consciously as we packed up the equipment, occasionally glancing out of the window to see if the coast was clear. This was a decent indication as to how many were over the limit. In my thirty-plus years of driving in the UK, I have never been breathalysed. Conversely, I've lost count as to how many times I've been breathalysed in France, bearing in mind you can be, and often are, stopped for no reason. After one gig in a restaurant, I was breathalysed twice in one thirty-minute drive. On another journey to play at a Cuban evening in Aubeterre-sur-Dronne, I passed through the lovely little town of Saint Aulaye. There was a festival happening in the latter town - the *Foire de la Laitière*. This translates as 'Fair of the Dairy' and such events will feature products such as cheese, beef, pork and one heck of a lot of booze. As you drive in rural France, you will often see shops and supermarkets with signs reading *Foire de Porc* or *Foire de Vin*. This tells you they have special offers (probably due to a surplus) on the product in question. *Gendarmes* had created roadblocks at every exit from the festival and were systematically breathalysing all drivers. It broke my heart to see a bewildered and confused line of elderly French country folk sitting miserably at the edge of the road, having their details taken by a *gendarme* forty years their junior. I suspect they'd been attending the event since the 1950's without such interventions. I'm afraid though, we must all keep up with the times, and the times, they are-a-changin'. As a final note on this topic, British drivers risking a glass of wine with their dinner need to proceed with extreme caution as the alcohol limit in France is about half of that in England and Wales.

The Fire Service *(les Pompiers)* in France is a completely different animal from the noble tradition which is the pride of the UK. When I envisage firefighters, I tend to think of characters who are fit, athletic, well-drilled, square-chested, six-pack yielding, chisel-jawed, equipped to the eyeballs, experts in their field and with years of intensive, expert training behind them. Any self-respecting after-shave advert should prove that. In contrast, much of the French Fire Service is staffed by volunteers.

I have befriended a number of gentlemen in my village who generously give up their spare time for *les Pompiers*, yet when I glance at the list of attributes above, it could be headed 'Everything Which Dan's Volunteer Fire-Fighting Friends Are Not'. I'd question whether a couple of them would be able to climb into the cabin of the fire engine from ground level, never mind ascend a severely-angled ladder adjacent to a burning building. Their primary motivation appears to be the opportunity of a heavily-subsidised and highly-liquid series of dinners which pepper the Fire-Fighters' calendar. I'm certain there must be a crack unit tucked away somewhere to deal with real emergencies but I reckon if my home was ablaze, I could do a better job of extinguishing the flames with a leaky garden hose than the bunch of misfits from our neck-of-the-woods.

One autumn day we had reason to call the *les Pompiers* due to a real fire in our house. We had just invested in a new boiler, powered by a log burner. Wood is plentiful, local and cheap in the countryside so this is an excellent way to heat our home and water. Anyway, just one month after its installation, we had a chimney fire. We were about to go out for a lazy lunch *en famille* when I decided to chuck a few logs in the burner to ensure an agreeable, toasty house upon our return. It was almost a disagreeable toasted house. Within moments, thick smoke poured out of one of the joins in the chimney flue which then started to glow bright red. Panicked, I hastily removed stepmother, wife, children, cat, guinea pigs and the odd stray chicken from the house (not necessarily in that order) and phoned the fire brigade. Happily, the blaze calmed down after ten minutes or so; we were indeed fortunate because the 'emergency' services didn't roll up for at least another forty-five minutes. They claimed to be enduring a hectic period but I think firstly, they'd finished a five-course lunch and secondly, got lost. Once put into action, they prodded around the chimney meaninglessly, clumped around our home in muddy steel toe-capped boots, bantered over their walkie-talkies with the lady from mission control, used our back garden as a toilet copiously and finally decided which one of the forty or so waiting calls seemed to be the most pressing before carrying on their merry way. The scene was observed and recounted to the entire village with some rapture by Madame Godefort opposite.

The most extraordinary aspect of the local *Pompiers* though is the source of its funding. I have no doubt *la Republique* directs some its bulging taxation coffers towards what I would regard as an essential service, but it seems the fire brigade requires its Senior Officers to sell calendars door-to-door in order to ensure its survival. Our first experience of this started with a hearty knock at the front door.

"Bonjour!" cried a manly voice.

Upon answering, we were greeted by a tall, muscular and annoyingly good-looking man in uniform who confidently brushed past us, casually noting he was the *Pompiers* before installing himself in the kitchen and accepting the coffee which I hadn't offered him. Next, he produced a huge bundle of calendars and plonked them on the table.

"Combien?" he demanded.

We had no idea what he was talking about so, talking to us as if he was on a community visit to a kindergarten class, he explained he was selling calendars to raise funds for the Fire Service. One could buy as many as one required and the price paid was up to the purchaser. When I asked him to suggest how much per calendar, he volunteered a figure which suggested a level of demand and subsequent scarcity which I'd wager was fictional.

Once I started leafing through the pages though, I could scarcely believe my eyes. The only question occupying my mind was how many Mrs Jones would *allow* me to buy. In our home, we have calendars which are composed of photos of loveable things such as children, goats, river-swimming scenes and the like; usually snapped during the corresponding month the previous year. Other favourites in the world enjoyed by sane individuals include cats, dogs, pop stars, ballet dancers, *Strictly*

Come Dancing contestants, Peter André and the like. My brother has chickens for crying out loud.

Les Pompiers calendar though had images of unspeakable carnage captured by... well, who? Some sick individual who, instead of helping out upon encountering a scene of life-threatening crisis, grabbed his Nokia phone from the 1990's (judging by the picture-quality) and started snapping away. Consequently, instead of 'Aunt Mabel on Her 90th Birthday Surrounded by Her Fourteen Great Grandchildren' for 'January', you could enjoy 'Grizzly Aftermath of a Multiple Pile-Up on the Motorway to Toulouse'. How about replacing February's 'Freddie the Dog and Puss the Cat Snuggled up Together by the Fire' with 'Our Beloved Family Home Going Up in a Raging Inferno'. Other favourites included 'Climber Being Winched Up a Rocky Cliffside Following Devastating Fall' (April), 'Smouldering Remnants of Cornfield Set Ablaze by Vandals' (August) and 'Family Saloon Being Dragged Out of the River Following Misjudgement During Trip Home From *Foire de Laitière*' (October).

Once I'd discussed this noble publication on social media, the orders came flooding in from disbelieving family and friends. *Les Pompiers* raked in significantly more euros that year courtesy of *Chez Jones*; I'd venture the quality of wine at the July 14th *Pompiers* meal increased markedly as a consequence. It transpired that the gentleman who calls at the doors of the houses in our village every December is the Head of the Fire Service in the area. I respect a man who is in charge and yet is prepared to do some legwork. We have become friends and he enjoys catching up with our story each year.

Another excellent service provided by *les Pompiers* is the 'Children's Open Day'. For an equivalent event in cities, children may be allowed to view a shiny, exciting-looking fire engine from a respectable distance, or perhaps watch a computer simulation of an emergency being re-enacted on a monitor. The modest fire station situated in a small town a stone's throw from *Chez Jones*, allowed kids to clamber into the vehicle's cabin, sound bells, sirens, horns and generally have an unforgettable time. They haven't (yet) been allowed to hose one another down but once, a mischievously-sniggering fireman actually drove a group of about forty-seven elated kids down the High Street (which, to be fair, is not exactly the M25), their wriggling limbs poking out of cabin windows and sirens blaring, causing passing motorists to swerve onto the pavement in panic.

As was discussed elsewhere, health services in France are excellent, although not free. We have had one flirtation with the Ambulance Service from an unlikely source - our dear friends Andy and Esther, who we met during our happy years in Pontypridd. In 2011 they came to our first rented home to pass a week of summer fun *Chez Jones*. Andy is a forester. He is a good-looking guy, loves the outdoor life and has abundant energy. He's the kind of bloke who, when someone suggests a barbecue, will rip off his shirt, run into the woods and return with the said shirt acting like a sack, bursting at the seams (literally) with kindling. Andy is also an excellent swimmer and has the physique to match. Makes you sick, doesn't it? One night during their stay, my dreams were interrupted by a sharp tapping on our bedroom door. It was Esther who announced we urgently required an ambulance. Andy had, during his slumber, stretched out his left arm causing him to completely dislocate his shoulder from its socket – a recurring problem due to a longstanding swimming injury. Gingerly, we entered their *chambre* and there lay Andy in what can only be described as an advanced state of discomfort. We made the telephone call and minutes later the ambulance arrived, occupied by two competent young paramedics. The pair breezed upstairs to the visiting couple's room, to be greeted by a now-whimpering Andy. I am bilingual but Andy's demeanour and the distorted form of the offending limb made a translation of the nature of the grievance unnecessary. They started manipulating and wiggling his arm about - accompanied by a sound which strongly implied Andy was finding the experience more than a tad uncomfortable – before concluding an x-ray was necessary. Just as they were preparing to wheel him away, there was an audible 'pop' and Andy's face became the image of pure, blissful relief. In the bat of an eyelid, the offending arm had zipped back into place and once again, all was well with the world. There followed an awkward silence and then the normal 'Thank you so much… would you like a coffee…' but all offers of hospitality were politely declined. Next, completely unembarrassed, *Mademoiselle Ambulance* produced a bill and requested a *Carte Vitale.* Happily, Andy and Esther had thought to sort out their European Health Cards before coming away on holiday so they were spared the trouble of having to re-mortgage their home. I was struck by the lack of romance of it all. I wonder if Florence Nightingale lovingly tended the war-wounded and then asked if they were appropriately insured.

During our first year in France, we endured an upsetting experience when Sam had an accident in the garden. He was probably about fifteen months old and was pottering about in the pleasant evening sunshine when, in the bat of an eyelid, he had tripped and fallen. Sam seemed to lack the instinct to put his hands out in front of him and had landed on his head. We ran over to him and found he had knocked himself clean out. It was very, very frightening but he regained consciousness fairly quickly and seemed as right as rain. We took him, at the kind of speed which would have had *les Gendarmes* leaping out of the bushes in fury, through the rush-hour traffic to A&E in Perigueux where he was seen promptly and efficiently.

There is a policy in France which dictates, in the event of a head injury, a child must be hospitalised for twenty-four hours. Consequently, Kirsty and Sam were allocated quarters for the night. It was a private room with a drop-down bed for Kirsty, and hosted a TV with all sorts of channels (such exoticism for Sam who lived in a house with no television), a bathroom and a gaggle of remote-controlled toys such as self-unfurling shutters and atmospheric lighting options. The only inconvenience of this luxury overnight stay in Wonderland was that Sam had to be awoken and given a series of checks on the hour, every hour, throughout the night.

The following day, Flo and I drove to Perigueux to collect Sam and Kirsty, arriving there at about 4.00pm. Being required to wait until 6.00pm, the children killed some time with a game of table tennis on the rooftop recreation area; they were then read a book by a story-teller employed for the purpose and finally, explored the library, games room and a range of other exciting and stimulating play options which made Hamley's of London look as bare as a voluntary book-keeping seminar held at the same time as a wine-tasting evening.

At 6.00pm precisely, I clapped my hands together.

"Righty-ho children, time to go home!" I called buoyantly.

I was met with wails of protest.

"We want to stay in the nice play centre!" cried my offspring in unison.

I eventually dragged them out to an accompaniment of disgruntled mutters.

I spent the next week or so singing the praises of the French Health Service to anyone with or without the time and inclination to listen to me. On the eighth day, I received a letter containing a bill which almost caused me to faint (which would have necessitated the whole procedure once again). At the time, we were too broke to afford a *Mutuelle* – a complementary health insurance. Therefore, as the state only paid 80% of the cost of Sam's treatment the remainder *facture* for outstanding balance landed firmly on our doorstep. The alarming part of this tale is that Sam didn't require any actual treatment, give or take a couple of teaspoons of paracetamol. Had a serious intervention been necessary, I may have been obliged to sell a kidney. I won't go into figures, but many of my friends have joked that French hospitals are the most expensive luxury hotel in the world. Let's just say we could have enjoyed a family room for four with dinner and breakfast for a lesser outlay. The service was second-to-none but, as they say, you get what you pay for in this life.

***

Bonjour, What's Your Emergency? – The Essential Tips

(1) If you take the train, either go with a Frenchman or grill the guard to within an inch of his life before you board to ensure you've completed the necessary procedures with your ticket.

(2) Mess around on a French train and you might be taken down by the SAS.

(3) Red traffic lights are essentially for decorative purposes if you're a French cyclist. If you're unlucky though, an over-enthusiastic traffic cop will unjustly single you out.

(4) You are likely to hear people with a 1960's attitude towards drink-driving. You'd have to be a complete moron to do it though.

(5) If you want to join a social club that drives around big lorries at speed, *les Pompiers* are for you.

(6) If a driver flashes his/her lights at you, *les Gendarmes* are hiding in the bushes ahead.

(7) The *Pompiers* calendar should be X-rated, not because it has images of under-clad ladies but because it contains distressing scenes of grisly carnage.

(8) Children's hospitals in France could be renamed 'Disneyland'.

11. My Animals and Other Families

Ai vist lo lop, lo rainard, la lèbre
Ai vist lo lop, lo rainard dançar
Totei tres fasián lo torn de l'aubre
Ai vist lo lop, lo rainard, la lèbre
Totei tres fasián lo torn de l'aubre

I saw the wolf, the fox, the hare,
I saw the wolf, the fox dance,
All three were circling round the tree

Traditional - *Ai vist lo lop, lo rainard, la lèbre*
(I Saw The Wolf, The Fox, The Hare – Occitan)

We are frequently reminded of Great Britain's status as a nation of animal lovers. Recent statistics show in 2017, there were an estimated 8.5 million domestic dogs being housed, fed, vaccinated, loved and poop-scooped in the UK. Running a close second are 8 million cats and one can add to the furry equation rabbits, guinea pigs, iguanas, hamsters, mice and a veritable menagerie of other species sharing our homes for our pleasure.

France, as a whole, trumps Grande Bretagne in the pooch-ownership stakes with approximately 8.8 million hounds (a cursory walk around the streets of Paris and you may well believe it) and a whisker-curling 12.7 million moggies. In the French countryside, pet ownership is also *a la mode* and yet attitudes towards our furry friends are very different from what I experienced in my former life in the UK.

Firstly, there is the phenomenon of 'the garden dog'. This practice varies from the bizarrely inconvenient to the downright cruel, as I was soon to learn.

Once we'd arrived in France, we were short of cash so, I took every work opportunity that came my way in an attempt to make ends meet. I taught guitar in people's homes, bouncing noisily through the Dordogne countryside in *le Tank,* leaving plumes of diesel smoke in my wake. Through some local advertising, I found myself a client near the beautiful *château*-town of Bourdeilles. Madame Dupont was a glamorous lady, about my age, who was a great fan of Johnny Halliday and The Rolling Stones (one out of two isn't bad taste-wise). We made an appointment to commence tuition and I was given extensive directions to her home.

After many kilometres of idyllic rural trundling, I found myself rolling up outside a pair of magnificent wrought-iron gates, electronically-operated from within the house. I was opening my door to press the intercom buzzer (the electric windows in *le Tank* were temperamental) when I heard a spine-tingling, ear-shattering, bottom-tightening growl, followed by a frenzied barking reminiscent of something out of a Hammer House of Horror werewolf movie. Cautiously, I rotated my head and spotted a large Doberman/Grizzly Bear cross-breed tearing across the garden, going utterly ballistic at my presence. As the gate opened, I found myself re-entering *le Tank* with considerable haste. I thanked the Good Lord I'd had the wisdom not to attempt to open the window, just in case it had decided not to close again (as had been the case on many other rainy occasions) thus saving my face from becoming a substitute bowl of Pedigree Chum. I don't know what it is about me and dogs. I once had a job delivering leaflets to houses in Cardiff and a dog actually jumped through five-foot long front-door window pane in an attempt to devour me. He was completely uninjured. More astonishing was the owner's response who bemoaned, in woeful tones that (and I kid you not) 'he was always doing that.'

I manoeuvred slowly up the long driveway with my adversary going ballistic around me - running between wheels, in front, behind, maybe even over the top of *le Tank*. I was sure it was going to take out my tyres at the absolute minimum. I eventually reached the front door and waited as the beast sharpened its knife and fork and salivated profusely in anticipation of devouring my right arm. There was absolutely no way in which I was going to leave the safety of *le Tank* with that crazed monster repeatedly hurling his body against the driver door, leaving a trail of doggy-drool on the driver window. After what seemed like six weeks, the front door opened a millimetre and I saw Madame Dupont's fear-ridden eyeball peek out through the tiny opening she had created. Then, to my absolute amazement, a broom handle poked out of the crack, followed by *Madame* herself, stepping gingerly into the death-zone which had once been her front garden.

"Don't worry, he's not nasty!" she shouted in a voice which failed to display either confidence or conviction. *N'inquitez-pas, il n'est pas mechant!*

When the dog's demeanour had changed to one which suggested the state of affairs was merely 'perilous' rather than 'lethal', she edged her way out and, using the broom as a life-saver between Bear-Dog and our backsides, we edged, employing sideways pigeon-steps, into the house.

Why, oh why anyone, I mean *anyone,* would choose to own such a creature is completely beyond my comprehension. Over the following weeks, in between strained renditions of *Angie,* I questioned her as to her reasoning for owning such a death machine.

"Because he is very beautiful and gives security for the family," was her suspect response. *Parce qu'il est très beau et donne de la sécurité pour la famille.*

I mentally questioned both motives. Firstly, Bear-Dog was anything but my idea of 'beauty' and as for the second, well, the French countryside was hardly a hotbed of urban disorder. During the years we've owned our own home in France, I've never actually possessed a key for my own front door. It remains unlocked at all times, although that may need to change following the publication of this book. The car lock was so infrequently applied, the electronic key fobs malfunctioned due to neglect.

Madame Dupont and her family were otherwise perfectly ordinary and reasonable people. Mr Dupont would generally be working in the garden (in a different zone to Bear-Dog I noted) and they had a charming, sporty, good-looking son of about eighteen years of age who appeared to have reached early adulthood without being visibly maimed.

As the weeks went by, a new routine established itself. I would turn up at Madame Dupont's house ten minutes early and wait for Bear-Dog to go through the necessary period of psychotic behaviour. I would eventually exit the car when the consequences seemed to be, at worst, a minor mauling rather than certain death and being leisurely consumed. I would bring a snack or a book to keep myself amused during this period. I did consider adding the time to the bill.

One day, I had exited *le Tank* and Bear-Dog had calmed himself sufficiently to be emitting a mere sustained, threatening growl three metres away from me. By this time, I found myself actually almost liking the beast. Almost. I opened the boot and leant in to gather my guitar. The temptation was clearly too much for Bear-Dog and, without warning, I felt the unmistakable sensation of teeth on buttock as The Beast of Bourdeilles finally fulfilled his *raison d'etre*. It was a feeling I had last experienced as a 15-year old boy when I had a part-time job collecting milk money door-to-door in Cardiff. I entered Madame Dupont's house feeling affronted and annoyed.

One of my weaknesses in life is that I shy away from confrontation. I rather foolishly decided to let it lie and said nothing to my pupil. From that day on I kept my guitar on the passenger seat, avoiding the necessity to expose my backside to the Hound From Hell. A couple of weeks later, he bit my left hand as I closed the door of *le Tank*. At that moment, I decided enough was enough. As a guitarist, my hands are precious to me and I couldn't risk damaging them for the sake of a few euros which, after diesel and taxes, barely made *la Famille Jones* any revenue anyway. With toe-curling embarrassment, I explained this to Madame Dupont who was understanding and gracious. I think she was more interested in health, beauty, well-being and not being pinned to the ground by her pet than she was in the guitar anyway.

As I drove away from *Chez Dupont* for the last time, Bear-Dog did his usual act of tearing around my vehicle, darting in and out of my vision, behind, in front of and underneath *le Tank*. At one point, I knew he was next to my front wheel; all it would have taken was a little push on the accelerator to claim a terrible accident and an unfortunate canine casualty. As I weighed up the pros-and-cons, I spotted Mr Dupont picking weeds from his potato patch. I'm sure he could read my mind but, to this day, I'm uncertain whether he was thinking 'Go on, please do it' or 'Don't you dare'.

Owners of such brutes go to extreme lengths to control them. Just metres from my home lives a gentleman who seems, to all intents and purposes, a lucid and intelligent human being. At some point in the last decade though, he made the somewhat eccentric decision to purchase two drooling mutts who make accessing his property a near-impossibility. Furthermore, he has been obliged to invest thousands of euros in an effort to prevent them from escaping and eating the local children - including my own. Initially, he installed metal fencing. With some practice, and a rampant desire to maim innocent bystanders, the hounds overcame this obstacle. The next step was to install an electric fence which would have cost him about 50% of my annual salary to put into place. This has had the desired effect but, to this day, I've never seen him enjoy the dogs in any way, or let them enter his home.

It's not just large dogs either. Living directly opposite *Chez Jones* is an adorable lady of a certain age who is, without doubt, a genuine animal-lover. Madame Godefort is often to be seen craning her neck from her kitchen window, trying to spot the antics of our goats in our field (and also those of their human owners one may speculate). I have often popped over and invited her to our home to admire our menagerie. She will always accept this proposition and as we approach each species, be it chicken, cat, goat, rabbit or guinea pig, she will emit coos of wonder and admiration. On more than one occasion, she has actually been moved to tears because a goat has stood on his/her hind legs for a stroke. Thankfully, one has yet to head-butt her. Her conversation is more-often-than-not limited to repeated reiterations of how much she loves animals. As I said, she is, without a doubt, a genuine animal-lover.

Madame Godefort owned two small dogs which lived, about 98% of the time, in her front garden. They were by no means dangerous (except to a hamster perhaps) but I'm sorry to say they could only be described as deeply annoying. Their sole mission in life appeared to be to make as much noise of the high-pitched, repetitive, nerve-shredding and ear-splitting type as possible for no evident reason. Their archenemy was the pushbike. As small children trundled home from the *Boulangerie,* baguette artistically poised between bicycle handlebars, all hell would suddenly break loose. The yaps could be heard in Bordeaux and were known to break wine glasses from 100 yards. Actually, I exaggerate. Any dog causing a Frenchman to lose a glass of wine would be shot on sight. More bizarrely, as the dogs went verbally ballistic, one always mounted the other and attempted to, if you'll excuse my expression, shag it in a most disturbingly frenzied manner. I'm pretty sure they were both boys - this is The Twenty-First Century after all - and the lower dog, if you get my drift, appeared oblivious to his buddy's dogged (in many senses of the word) homo-erotic-canine advances, being more concerned with emitting a racket the equivalent of ten pneumatic drills. On one occasion I'd been chatting to Madame Godefort at her garden gate when a pushbike passed causing the whole pantomime to unfold before our very eyes. I found it excruciatingly awkward and desperately sought any excuse to stare at anything other than at the lusty scene being played out on the lawn at foot level.

"Aren't the birds a joy to behold," I babbled, encouraging Madame Godefort to cast her gaze upwards towards a skyline conspicuously devoid of avian life-forms.

Eventually, I was forced to make my excuses and leave the scene.

The racket became a real problem for us when we opened our small cattery in the garden. One of the key features of our advertising was the promise of blissful, rural silence and 'no dogs'. I was once showing prospective clients around the premises when a cycling club rode innocently past the house. The sight of twenty-five lycra-clad Frenchmen on racing bikes was just too much for the dogs *en face;* the subsequent yelping led to me screaming apologies, inches from our prospective clients' faces, in an attempt to be heard over the cacophony. When one of her beloved pooches passed away, Madame Godefort was in deep mourning for weeks. I chose not to share with her the repetitive dream I'd been experiencing. In this, I'd converted the ex-pooch through the posts of *la Stade de France,* winning the Rugby World Cup for Wales.

I do not wish to judge the country which has stolen my heart but, on many occasions, I have witnessed a certain priority of human fancy over animal well-being. The most extreme example was in the little hamlet where we rented our first house in 2010. We lived next door to perfect neighbours - in their fifties, kind, considerate and helpful. They owned a patch of land on the other side of the lane and within this, had erected a small fenced area about the size of the average bathroom. The space housed a beautiful, large dog – a kind of furry Alsatian cross. He had a kennel and various dog toys, ineffectively placed there for his distraction, but he lived within these confines twenty-four hours a day, seven days a week, come rain or shine. The animal was evidently in some distress yet the owners and seemingly everyone else in the area unblinkingly accepted this as perfectly ordinary practice. The dog was fed, watered and frequently verbally admired, but that was about it. He sat in his pen looking despondent with life and, being an animal lover, I was deeply troubled. One day, I decided to ask if I could take him for a walk. Upon making my request, the owners looked baffled and simply failed to understand why I might want to do such a thing. I couldn't push the issue too far as I needed to maintain good neighbourly relations. It was very tricky to challenge the conditions in which the animal was being kept when one could find many other dogs in similar situations within the immediate vicinity. The last thing I wanted was to appear judgemental of my host country.

Similarly, in 2017 Kirsty and I stayed in a little *chambre d'hotes* in the Perigord Noir to celebrate our wedding anniversary. The proprietors were absolutely charming but I couldn't help but notice a sizable dog chained up in a kennel next to the front door. They had spent considerable time and finance on doing up his abode, having stuck such niceties as fake bones and other doggie paraphernalia to the external walls. The effect though was rather like locking up an innocent man for ten years in solitary confinement but, as a compensatory gesture, hiring Laurence Llewelyn-Bowen to paint the walls in order to make the cell aesthetically pleasing.

I could hardly believe that dog-ownership practices could become any more surrealist but that was before I stumbled across *Toilettage.* I discovered this one Saturday morning when ambling pleasantly through the market town of Coutras. I was on my way to teach for the local *Ecole Municipale de Musique* and I'd come to know a number of the Saturday-morning market traders who knew me as *le Guitariste Gallois.* We would share chit-chat in the early-morning chill as I made my way to the music school, and they set up stalls selling everything from live fish to Bob Marley posters. One day, I was discussing *la Coupe de Monde* with a gentleman selling fruit and veg when my eye was caught by a sight which was as disturbing as it was downright weird. In a small shop window, displayed for all to see, was a large dog, suspended inches above a table-top by a labyrinth of chains. I stopped, aghast, open-mouthed, guitar in hand, staring in disbelief. I prodded my veg-vending-rugby-chat partner.

"Regardez, regardez!"

He looked at me, then at the dog, and then at me again.

"Quoi?" responded *Monsieur Veg.*

I could only assume I had uncovered some sort of small-town dog torture ring and, by his clear denial and indifference, *Monsieur Veg* was implicit in the plot. I made a mental note of his principal facial features, ready for my witness report at the local *gendarmerie*, before turning my attention back to the helpless creature behind the glass.

The levitating hound was accompanied by two ladies. One was wearing a smart lab coat and surgical gloves whereas the other was sitting on a stool, chatting amiably to *Madame Lab-Coat.* Closer inspection revealed the dog-victim had just withstood a thorough shampooing with some sort of expensive, smelly designer product, and was now undergoing a blow-dry treatment. The result was the poor beast took on the appearance of a four-legged candy floss and any resemblance to nature's canine creation was brushed aside, along with its dignity.

This was a *Toilettage* boutique. I found myself disproportionately fascinated by the practice and would watch *Madame Lab-Coat* at work through her shop window every Saturday morning. When she had a lethal dog, it was absurdly comical. The suspending chains rendered the animal defenceless and, within seconds, a well-honed killing machine would be turned into a powerless soft toy, vulnerable to the whims of its owner's artistic imagination. I would fantasise it was Bear-Dog suspended there, and visualise him leaving the shop looking like a pair of purple clouds mounted on lollipop sticks separated by a fat sausage. I took to turning up to work five minutes early so I could enjoy my weekly chuckle outside the boutique. *Madame Lab-Coat* habitually waved at me, giving me the kind of smile one reserves for men who are either one-sandwich-short-of-a-picnic or a little bit dangerous. I suspected this enterprise was a one-off small-town eccentricity, but it seems rural areas can't get enough *Boutiques de Toilettage.* Even the small town of Montpon Ménestérol, situated near to my own village, provides sufficient clientele to sustain no fewer than three of them. A cursory glance through *les Pages Jaunes* (Yellow Pages) reveals most small towns will have four or five *Toilettage* centres.

The well-worn cliché of dog ownership in France is of a lady in a mink coat guiding an ornate poodle on a lead through Parisian streets, allowing it to defecate the pavements freely. I did see some small dogs on leads in tiny villages, but this type of animal is the *chien préféré* of the city dweller. Our daughter Flo had a brilliant, artistic and deeply generous ballet teacher who was the doting owner of such a creature. The first time I met her in Bordeaux, we were enjoying a discussion involving the merits of various European teaching philosophies in music and dance, when I glanced downwards towards the small handbag she was holding underneath her right arm. I was startled to see a large pair of eyes gazing back at me and found myself physically recoiling in shock. The owner of the eyes was Gaia, her pet chihuahua, technically a dog but in reality, an anaemic guinea pig. If you are unfamiliar with the breed, the house-elves in the Harry Potter films will go a long way towards helping you visualise a chihuahua. Florence fell deeply in love with Gaia over the following year and I took pleasure in gently winding her up with tasteless jokes about how I loved chihuahuas too – especially when served with a rich *sauce tomate.*

On a number of occasions in 2017, the teacher was invited to teach in Italy; consequently, we agreed to host Gaia at *Chez Jones* for a couple of weeks. I was concerned because of the threat posed by our cat, Badger. I had seen Badger catch and consume rabbits twice the size of Gaia and the micro-mutt would certainly have provided him with a pleasant *aperitif.* Bizarrely though, Badger was utterly terrified of Gaia and we were forced to keep them apart throughout the mini-pooch's entire stay. On the one occasion they inadvertently came face to face, Badger tore out of the house and scaled an immense pine tree in the field next door. It was pretty impressive form for a cat approaching fifteen years of age and who generally spent twenty-three and a half hours per day sleeping (the remaining half an hour was spent requesting food and eating). As the branches had been cut off up to a height of around seven metres, he was well and truly stuck. Kirsty, my father-in-law Dave and I ended up spending hours, well into the night, constructing a lavish escape route out of two ladders and random planks of timber placed at angles of improbable geometrical certainty. He initially refused to descend our improvised contraption, but our efforts did not go unrewarded as the structure won the year's Turner Prize. Thankfully, Kirsty had the inspired idea of rattling his food bowl; Badger subsequently discovered new reserves of courage and was down like a shot. The next day, Madame Godefort recounted the tale to me, step-by-step, revealing shamelessly she had watched the entire *spectacle* from the comfort of her living room armchair, including the moment when I'd fallen spectacularly into a ditch upon returning from a neighbour's house carrying a fifteen-foot ladder on my right shoulder. I began to wonder if she'd bought a video camera and was filming every debacle.

As already observed, cats are popular and much-treasured domestic pets in rural France. I also have neighbours who own barn cats. These are semi-wild and live primarily off mice and rats. Cats earn their keep, keeping down numbers of such pests in an efficient, balanced and ecological manner. When we bought our first home, the garden was rampant with wild rabbits. I would open the shutters in the morning and a kind of brown carpet would disperse in all directions with little flashes of white creating a furry strobe effect. Within weeks they moved on as our cats took charge of the situation. Olive, our female cat, would indulge in a classic stalk-and-chase procedure. It was like watching David Attenborough in miniature, in our own back garden. Badger though had a more efficient technique. He would sleep at the entrance to a rabbit warren and just wait. Once he spent two entire days and nights asleep, just waiting for the moment when a bunny was absolutely convinced there was no danger. Then he would launch himself on his prey and within minutes, would consume everything: bones, fur and all. It was quite disgusting. Neighbour André was elated at their presence. He had spent years trying to protect his beloved vegetable garden and had invested heavily in fences, traps and repellent products with little effect. Badger and Olive were this gardener's godsend.

I'm amazed Badger needed further sustenance, yet our neighbours rewarded his rabbit-hunting efforts with gifts of fine *cuisine* on a daily basis. Knowing he was on to a good thing, Badger could be seen hanging around on next-door's doorstep at midday, on-the-dot, just as lunch was being served. His reward was a piece of *beefsteak* or some other delicacy vastly superior to the budget-brand cat food he received *Chez Jones.* Worryingly, he then took to scratching at their shutters in the early hours of the morning. On one occasion, Eliane gaily informed me Badger had woken her at 4.30am as he had been hungry.

"I'm *SO* sorry," I burbled. "From now on we'll keep him in overnight."

But appearing to misunderstand me, she continued to explain she had risen from her bed and opened a tin of tuna for him. Unable to believe my ears I wondered if I'd mistranslated and she had in fact *thrown* a tin of tuna *at* him.

"He decided against it," she continued nonchalantly. "I cooked him an omelette instead."

When later relaying this tale to my friend Stéphane, he correctly noted my cat ate better than we did. I half considered dressing up in a moggie suit and scratching on next door's shutters at 4.30am.

Wild rabbits have reached astonishing numbers in France due to diminishing numbers of natural predators yet, like in other developed countries, they are used less and less as a staple meat for human consumption. Many of the gardens in our village still have *lapinières* - concrete, stackable rabbit houses - where villagers would raise rabbits for meat. We found a set on our land covered by a mass of foliage but they served to provide our bunnies with palatial-like accommodation rather than us with food.

When we opened a small cattery in 2013 the vast majority of our clients were British. Upon explaining our enterprise to our French friends they would look at me with vacant expressions.

"You mean a refuge? You keep dogs as well?" they would enquire, obviously puzzled as to our objective.

The implication was if you had a cat and went on holiday, you just left it to its own devices for a fortnight, trusting it to sustain itself on vermin. The opposite extreme existed too. We had one French client who adored her cat so much, she couldn't bear to be separated from it during her fortnight of annual leave. Therefore, she took her *vacances* in our village, boarded her beloved moggie with us, rented a *gite* nearby and arranged appointments during the period when she could pay it a social call. The manner in which the cat in question was wholly indifferent to her efforts typifies why I love them so much. The moggie would totally ignore her cooing visits, completely blanking her unless she offered him a cat treat. They are outrageously rude and disloyal pets. I find that hilarious.

We made the decision to open our small cattery to earn a few more euros and also use the huge garden which we had inherited with our modest abode. There was a small, waist-high outbuilding in the back garden which had probably been a chicken coop. We recognised that if it were to be built up to standing height and have an exercise pen constructed around it, the structure could serve the purposes of a cattery very well. It was also an excellent opportunity for me to play with power tools and pretend to be a real man. During the construction period, I took great joy in slipping in masculine comments to those stupid enough to listen.

"Just popped down to the yard to pick up some shuttering timber as we're doing a concrete mix tomorrow. By the way, do you have any spare hardcore?" I'd ask acquaintances while adjusting my tool belt.

The building process, in fact, took a couple of years and nigh-on killed me. That was a learning curve. On one particularly dark day, I was the hanging the timber doors at the entrance to each little bedroom; I had lovingly made these myself, as I'd frequently boast to my newly-discovered construction-worker social group. Hanging a door on one's own is *really* tricky; the cumbersome, weighty wooden blighters seem to have a mind of their own as they flap about in the breeze. Eventually, I found hanging them from the *inside* of a bedroom was a more effective technique when working single-handedly. This was a masterstroke, until the day I got my angles wrong. I had successfully hung a door but then found it wouldn't open – and I was *inside* the little kitty *chambre*. Frustrated, I went about undoing the hinges I had just installed but, true to form, the battery on my cordless screwdriver chose *just* that moment to run out. It was dark, cold and claustrophobic.

At first, I panicked. What if I never got out? There was no way I was going to kick down the robust timber door I'd so lovingly created, not with the amount much blood, sweat and tears I'd shed. I contemplated spending the night there. What was the weather forecast? Would I die of hypothermia? Maybe in three months' time, Kirsty would be showing prospective clients around the new facility (named in my memory following my unexplained disappearance) and discover a skeleton in Unit Three. Thank the Lord for mobile phones. Kirsty, passing a pleasant afternoon in the house with the children, received an unexpected call.

"Hello Dear, how are you?" I enquired.

"Fine. Are you after a coffee or something? Make me a tea while you're at it."

"Not exactly *Cherie,"* I responded. "I was wondering if you could pop down to Unit Three for a couple of minutes."

"Does it really need to be now? I'm rather busy," my spouse replied, reasonably.

"Um, yes. It *really* needs to be *now,"* I said. "Please bring a screwdriver, a torch and the telephone number of someone competent."

"Okaaaaay," said Kirsty, sensing another farce. "Are you alright Dear?"

"Fine. Oh yes, and promise me you'll never utter a word of what you discover to anyone. Ever."

A greater challenge though was the fact I had to complete a *formation*. A *formation* is a training course. If you intend to do any activity in France, sooner or later you'll be required to do a *formation*. The *préfecture* grimly informed me a *formation* run by LOOF *(Livre Officiel des Origines Félines)* was an absolute necessity.

"Il faut," asserted *Madame Faceless-on-the-Phone* leaving me with no room for manoeuvre.

Therefore, I was booked into a three-day training course in one of those characterless business-persons' hotels next to Bordeaux *Gare*. My wallet was lightened notably for the privilege. For the *formation* itself, I expected something fairly straight-forward, I mean, it's not like I was training to be a vet or a brain surgeon. I was hoping it might be generous on the side of exploring the fruits of the *aperitif* and less so in terms of academic rigour. At the end of the day, I reasoned that if a cat became ill during a stay, I'd phone a vet. In my opinion, as in the world of electrical and plumbing installations, it is unwise to dabble in DIY veterinary skills.

About twenty-five people showed up to participate in the said *formation,* making a tidy profit for LOOF. They were a pleasant bunch and we all got along very well. We actually formed a Facebook group to remember our time together and show pictures of kittens and err… well, kittens to one another. The lady who ran the course (we'll call her *Madame Moggie*) welcomed us and then asked us to introduce ourselves. I was the only English speaker. The first lady stood.

"Hello, my name is Evelyne and I want to breed Maine Coons," she announced.

Then the next spoke.

"Hello, my name is Marine and I intend to breed Abyssinians."

The third lady was Axelle who held a passion for Siamese. And so it went on.

As we advanced through the group, it became clear I was the only person intending to open a small cattery. Everyone else was breeding exotic and expensive cats, in the hope of a large financial recompense. When I announced my name and intended project, my co-*formation* buddies, despite their field of expertise and passion, were taken aback. I heard a general murmur of approval:

"What a lovely idea!... That's so sweet!" and the like. *Quelle jolie idée!... C'est mignon!*

Madame Moggie then distributed two enormous volumes of information weighing a good twenty kilos each. Upon opening the first book, I noted the print was absolutely teeny and the content made *War and Peace* look like *The Adventures of Winnie the Pooh and Eeyore.* It was, of course, in French. It was explained that every session hosted a guest speaker - undoubtedly an expert in her field (all the speakers were female) and each speaker would talk for two hours. Every day hosted four speakers so that totted up to a daunting eight hours per day of lectures with each class punctuated by a cursory toilet break. Therefore, three consecutive days meant a terrifying twenty-four hours of intensive study. *Madame Moggie* casually informed us we would be examined on our knowledge immediately after the last session, and the material to be memorised was the content of the two encyclopaedia-resembling volumes - their combined weight causing several table legs to creak ominously - which had been unceremoniously plonked in front of us. The atmosphere had changed notably in the room from pleasant conviviality to sphincter-tightening anxiety. Everyone was thinking the same thing:

"What the ****?!"

Madame Moggie told us to relax and that 'It wasn't all about the exam' but quite clearly, it was. We all wanted the necessary *diplome* so we could venture into our respective pussy-cat breeding/hostelry worlds with no further administrative obstacles, and earn some hard euros.

Speaker Number One took the floor and gave us a mind-numbingly tedious, but, to be fair, very well-informed lecture on tax issues and record keeping when trading feline species. The problem for me was, well, I had no intention of trading feline species. There was an audible gasp and a notable deflation in enthusiasm levels when she revealed a 40% tax rate imposed on the sale of each posh moggie. It couldn't be done 'on the black' as no tax receipt shown meant no pedigree certificate issued.

The second speaker addressed us on the topic of 'genetic mutation when interbreeding certain species in an incestuous manner'. This was both impossibly complex (I flunked biology in school, with the exception of the vital-organ dissection module) and a bit scary. At the merciful termination of this lecture, I gingerly raised a mentally-exhausted hand and asked *Madame Moggie* if I really needed to be there. I was hoping to learn how to use a poop-scoop in a manner which would minimise the risk of repetitive-strain injury rather than the hazards encountered when 'marrying' a British Shorthair with its Aunt. *Madame Moggie* was having none of it.

"Il faut," she announced sternly, and the room nodded in approval.

"Ob-li-ga-toire," they muttered telepathically.

For three days I studied like a madman. I hadn't worked so hard since cataloguing 17th-Century French Guitar Works for my Masters' Degree. I thought that was nerdy but this took things to a new level. I found much of the content disturbing but opted to keep my opinions to myself as I knew the lecturers would be grading my exam paper. Maybe I'm wrong, but in my humble opinion the practice of driving a cat hundreds of kilometres and trying to make her breed with a prize-winning male - when perhaps neither cat is in the mood - is pretty disgusting. Worse is the incestuous breeding of related animals, knowing there is a real risk of still-birth or death, just to save the road trip to an unrelated kitty. I just like cats because they are independent, arrogant, rude and funny.

When the exam arrived, we were told it was multiple-choice but each question could have more than one correct answer. Therefore, a question could have seven options with three correct answers but, if the examinee checked only two of them, the response was marked as incorrect. We were to be given unlimited time for this daunting task. As my peers drifted out of the room wearing dazed expressions, I soon realised I was the last candidate remaining in the exam room. My longevity achievement was in fact won by some considerable margin. As I sat alone, in silence except for the ominous ticking of the clock, my plastic chair playing hell with my buttocks, *Madame Moggie* paced the room, glancing repeatedly at her watch.

"Fini…. terminé?" she enquired for the seventeenth time, wondering if she'd catch the last train back to Paris.

Anyway, I passed and so was able to open our little enterprise.

I learned several of our group had failed and would have to re-sit the exam. At least they'd have time to revise thoroughly as we'd inexplicably been denied the course materials before the commencement of the *formation*. Upon reflection, I felt irritated by the whole procedure. I had particularly grown to like a young man with whom I shared a desk. He clearly loved his animals and enjoyed telling me about what must have been a small zoo at his home. Perhaps he should have been highlighting a passage in his textbook about hereditary eye problems when breeding a Burmese with a Siberian Lynx as I later learned he'd flunked the exam. The problem was, if I may be indiscreet, he was hardly an intellectual. This is no crime in my book - many of my dearest friends are, in fact, quite stupid - and his heart was in the right place. I think he got his diploma on the seventh attempt, like some people with their driving tests. My certificate, resplendent with its official stamp, takes pride of place alongside my academic and performance qualifications in Music. Kirsty inexplicably forbade me to frame and mount it in our living room. I thought it would make a striking focal point, just above the glow of the wood burner.

The requirement to attend *formations* is a constant source of annoyance to my sole-trading friends. One central-heating expert of twenty years' experience explained to me that he is the frequent ungrateful recipient of correspondence requiring him to close up his business for a week and attend a *formation* given by a spotty graduate who would struggle to wire a plug. The privilege will deny him a week's work and therefore, wages.

I heard a story that as British builders emigrating to France need evidence of an appropriate qualification, some enterprising soul set up a one-hour *'formation'* on the cross-channel ferry, complete with an official-looking diploma at its conclusion. It would be signed and boast an impressive-looking stamp so it was good enough for the powers-that-be. After all, *il faut*.

To return to the French and their feline charges, I observed that many French cat owners indulged in the pointless, and pleasingly farcical, practice of putting their pets in a harness and lead, particularly when taking a holiday with their moggie in tow. They harboured a misguided mental image of their human family parading along the seafront, led by a contented, well-exercised sphinx-like beast on a lead, responding to their every command, like a finely-tuned sheep-dog. Of course, the reality is cats dislike strange places and concentrate their efforts on either hiding, attacking the lead or attempting to escape rather than answering to their owners' whimsical requirements. Any experienced cat-lover understands that it's really the cat which owns the humans.

***

My Animals and Other Families – The Essential Tips

(1) If you want a successful business, open up a *Toilettage.*

(2) Keeping a killing machine in your garden rendering it inaccessible to both family and visitors is normal practice.

(3) Small, yappy dogs are apparently lovable and are, under no circumstances, to be used as rugby balls.

(4) Expect to be obliged to attend an expensive *formation* of limited value if you set up in business doing anything, from cleaning houses to practising nuclear fission.

Figure 7 Open for business! The completed cattery.

12. Four Go Wild in *la Forêt*

Oes gafr eto? Oes heb ei godro?
Ar y creigiau geirwon, Mae'r hen afr yn crwydro.

Is there another goat? One that hasn't been milked?
On the craggy rocks, the old goat is wandering

Traditional - *Cyfri'r Geifr*
(Count the Goats - Wales)

Ex-pats in France often take the moral high ground when discussing animal welfare - at times with some justification - yet often through ignorance of practices which have been in place for many generations. There is one topic which rattles my cage annually, and I have participated in heated exchanges with newcomers who are, in most other ways, reasonable human beings. The topic in question is that of processional caterpillars.

Every springtime, a natural phenomenon occurs which I find both beautiful and extraordinary. If you take a stroll in woodland, you may be fortunate enough to come across a trail of small, furry, red-and-black caterpillars making their way nose-to-tail, in chains of hundreds across the forest floor. As they are red and spiny, common sense dictates that if you were to touch one, mild irritation would follow which is indeed the case. Discontent arises amongst dog walkers who use the same pathways to exercise their pets. There have been incidents where animals have consumed the caterpillars resulting in illness or, in some cases, death. It's usually curtains for the caterpillars as well. The result is as spring approaches, crazed messages appear on ex-pat internet forums (of which there is a bountiful supply) reading such pearls of wisdom as 'Processional Caterpillars Seen Near

Mussidan. Destroy Upon Sight!' Dog owners indulge in an orgy of caterpillar destruction during the months of April and May in order to secure the safety of their beloved mutts. I have even heard of people burning down pine trees – the nesting place of choice for the caterpillar – in an attempt to wipe out the species, thus indulging in an act of mind-boggling eco-terrorism. It's a bit like buying an expensive television and then taking a sledgehammer to it because it's too loud rather than turning down the volume. I once gently suggested to a group of anti-caterpillar-league activists that perhaps, just perhaps, a more intelligent solution would be to walk their dogs on a lead during the months in question, or maybe even to avoid forest routes. Such radical ideas were met with scorn and ridicule. I did point out the caterpillars had been in *situ* for several centuries before their hounds but reasoning was fruitless. It was death to the caterpillars at all costs.

If you thought the rights of processional caterpillars stirred high emotions, then I assure you this is peanuts in comparison to the question of the Hunt - *la Chasse.* If you are squeamish about hunting, then I recommend you avoid living in the French countryside as the practice is alive and well. Firstly, I should clarify that hunting is a working man's sport. The targets are deer and wild boar and all kills are distributed amongst the participants for consumption. The origin of the practice would be necessity; a cursory glance at the lot of the French *paysan* will reveal that at frequent intervals throughout history, it's been a case of 'hunt or go hungry'. It is anything but the weird upper-class fantasy indulged in by Britain's aristocracy where people with too much time and money wear fancy dress, play the trumpet badly and pursue foxes with dogs as an outlet for their pent-up frustration at not being allowed to beat up peasants any more. As an animal lover, I could never use a firearm against any creature. Having said this, I am an occasional meat-eater so it is hypocritical to criticise *la Chasse* when the animals taken down are always consumed. I also feel it is inappropriate for me, an immigrant, to enter another country and tell the locals how to behave. I could never be so discourteous. I have friends who are vehemently anti-*chasse*. One markedly carnivorous French friend told me, with some considerable passion, how disgusting he found the practice of shooting a deer.

"After they've shot it, they rip it into bloody pieces for all to share!" he ranted, spitting a little at the edges of his mouth.

I'm unsure as to what he thinks goes on in the average abattoir, but unless he buys his pigs and cows live and intact, I suspect the activities are not dissimilar.

La Chasse is also blamed for missing pet cats.

"They shoot them for the hell of it!" my anti-*chasse* pal will declare to anyone willing to regard a complete absence of evidence as immaterial. I'd speculate the motor car, which according to government statistics is responsible for the demise 230,000 moggies annually in the UK alone, is a more likely culprit.

The reality though, as far as I can make out, is that *la Chasse* is actually a not-so-secret eating and drinking club. Hunt leaders are desperately trying to convey an image of a wholesome family eco-activity, but this is nonsense. I once attended a *commune* meeting in a neighbouring town as I was due to perform a concert for them the following year. The local *Chasse* gave a presentation outlining their proposed activities for the forthcoming season, and a kindly gentleman gave out a leaflet with dates and statistics for the past year. On the cover was a photo of a young glamour model, dressed immaculately in a spotless wax jacket and wellingtons, with conditioned hair blowing gently in the wind. She had one arm draped casually around a handsome, similarly-attired young boy. In the other, she held a cocked firearm which, judging by its condition, had just been taken out of a box for the first time. The two of them were staring at a fictional horizon as if searching for a small fluffy creature to lovingly blast to smithereens. So utterly fantastical and far from reality was this image, I failed to hold back a large derisive snort when I cast my eyes upon it. I was forced to mutter an apology to the speaker who was in the process of explaining how many elderly stags had been taken out that year or something similar. The picture was the most nonsensical kind of marketing deception imaginable. I know this because, during the winter months, I see *la Chasse* out-and-about every weekend. Practically everyone is a white male of post-retirement age with a ruddy, red complexation which suggests a lively and active relationship with the local wine merchants. There is a distinct absence of glamour models and children.

A day with *la Chasse* usually starts with an alcohol-fuelled breakfast. Coffee is drunk with the liberal addition of a local hooch known as *eau de vie* (water of life). I was once given a bottle of *eau de vie* by neighbour André, as a gift. The fact his name was stamped on the bottle suggests he and a group of friends had an industrially-scaled enterprise, of dubious legality, underway in a barn hidden amongst the sunflowers. As advised, I knocked back a generous nip with a swift reverse action of my right forearm. For a moment, I knew how a fire-eater feels when his act goes wrong. A robust bout of retching and spluttering was followed by five minutes of partial blindness. After I'd sufficiently recovered, I complimented him on his creation but declined a second glass. The bottle gathered dust in the corner of our kitchen, only to be brought out for unsuspecting visitors.

"Is it really *that* strong?" they'd ask as I got the video camera ready.

I think it was eventually used to good effect when we had a mains drainage blockage. In later years, I was interested to learn the Scots use the Gaelic term *uisge beatha* for whisky which also translates as 'water of life'.

Anyway, to return to *la Chasse,* the hunters will make their way to open countryside where one group will act as 'beaters' in the forest and others will stand in fields awaiting the exit of a suitably-startled animal. The net result is a day out with *la Chasse* will often mean standing in the drizzle, alone, holding a cocked firearm and an antique flugelhorn for hours at a time. The monotony is only broken by intervals of eating, inevitably accompanied by unrestrained quantities of ropey *vin rouge.* It did not escape the notice of hunt organisers that the participants had become more successful in shooting one another than they were the furry inhabitants of *la forêt,* such is the predictable outcome of mixing alcohol and firearms. This became such a problem it recently became law for hunters to wear fluorescent clothing, to try to avert the frequent tragedies which occurred on hunting weekends. What I find inexplicable is hunters still wear camouflage clothing underneath lurid orange vests and hats, as if they would remain invisible to their prey by wearing military-style jungle outfits concealed under their hi-vis garments. I suppose they could dangle upside-down from orange trees. The problem is still unresolved and much-disputed. During the meeting mentioned above, an incident where a child's bedroom window was smashed by a bullet (thankfully, with no injuries sustained) only added fuel to what is already a highly-emotive fire.

If you do purchase a property in the rolling French countryside, you may well simultaneously yet unwittingly become a substantial landowner. It is absolutely the norm to have a couple of acres chucked in as an afterthought, even with the most modest of abodes. Such was the case with our little bungalow. We found we had acquired a long, thin parcel of land, the size of a couple of football pitches, along with our home. Before we took possession of the land, a retired farmer had been given permission to keep some horses there in order to keep the grass down. Employing his spectacular digger, he generously helped us to fence it off when we were ready. Soon after, we realised land management was a full-time job so we decided to obtain some livestock to keep the land in trim. Within a year we had built up a small petting zoo due to our susceptibility to say 'Oh, go on then' when offered ownership of a small fluffy beast.

We soon earned ourselves a reputation. Having played in a *ferme auberge* one Sunday lunchtime, *la Famille Jones* drove home with full bellies, our pay cheque, a small abandoned bunny in a cage, a guitarist/driver gripping the steering wheel a little too tightly while muttering words along the lines of 'I can't believe we've taken another one' (that was me) and two elated children. The bunny in question was called Peter by the original owner and renamed Peta following a visit to the vet which revealed an error in the original gender designation. Peta had been hand-reared by the owner of the *ferme auberge.* She had been neglected by her mum (the bunny, not the owner) so *Madame Auberge* had raised her in the kitchen, next to the warmth of the oven, with every intention of popping her into the very same device once she was plump enough. Peta though escaped this unhappy fate through her charm and enormously-friendly nature. She lived in our garden, running to us like a loyal dog as we approached and putting herself to bed in her hutch at night.

The previous owner of our property had built a number of outbuildings on our land, so we decided to acquire chickens to inhabit them. André drove me to a supplier to purchase some *pondeuse* (layers) and together, we returned with six squawking fowls in cardboard boxes and a large case of wine André picked up from his *cave* on the way home. Chickens are immense fun, hugely ecological, keep the grass in trim and lay the most fantastic eggs you'll ever eat. Once we'd installed ours in their little coop, they remained there in a huddle for about five days before gingerly venturing out into the garden. That fifth evening I recognised, with some wariness, I'd need to put them away for the night. My unease was justified. I spent a stressful half an hour (for me and the chickens) chasing them around the garden like a madman, arms and wings respectively flapping in the evening sun. Once I'd grabbed a couple, I'd open the chicken-house door with my foot, only to be engulfed by my earlier captives who would cascade out in a tidal wave of feathers and squawks. Eventually, I succeeded. Traumatised and feather-beaten, I staggered back into the house. As I wiped chicken poop from my face, Kirsty and I mused on the fact André next door never appeared to have such difficulties.

The following day, I explained my dilemma to my guru-neighbour who, in a characteristic wave of guffaws, explained to me they would put themselves to bed at sunset.

"I can't believe that André," I said as we poured a second glass of *porto*.

"Mark my words," he said. "They follow the rhythms of the sun and the moon. They know when to retire for the night."

That evening *la Famille Jones* watched, for the first of many times, as our hens calmly and peacefully put themselves to bed in their chicken house under a reddening sky. They retired slowly, unhurriedly, their leader, Chirpy, being the last to enter. They made a very special, soulful cry which seemed to lament the parting day. It was fantastically beautiful. I should mention that our chickens were named by the children of our extended family. This explains why I was often to be heard calling out 'Racing Car' in our garden, that unfortunate bird having been named by a four-year-old boy.

Of course, collecting eggs is an activity no child ever seems to tire of. Every successful search for a newly-laid prize is like a little miracle to them. Flo, Sam and I were once rather mischievous towards a cousin who came to stay at Easter. We told the young lad we'd fed the hens cocoa powder over the previous weeks so they would lay chocolate eggs on Easter Sunday. When the big day arrived, we sneaked down to the chicken house and popped a handful of chocolate eggs amongst the straw bedding. Later on, I casually asked the cousin in question to collect some eggs for tea and we watched, sniggering somewhat cruelly, as he exited the chicken house, eyes like saucers, holding the chocolate eggs in one hand, complete with shiny foil wrap. Whilst we're on the subject of seasonal child-deception, I should point out that the Easter Bunny fails to include France when delivering chocolate eggs. At the end of the day, there's only so much confectionary a rabbit can be expected to distribute in twenty-four hours – he's not *Amazon Prime* for heaven's sake. The upshot is if you ask a French child whether the Easter Bunny visited their house in the night, they'll probably run away and report to Mum that the new *Anglais(e)* next-door is a fruitcake. I have heard there is an old French custom which says when the church bells ring, chocolate eggs will appear in the garden for children to seek out, but I have yet to see it acted out.

But to return to the smallholding which we were unwittingly assembling. The jewel in the crown of our menagerie was the pair of goats we took ownership of in order to keep our field in trim. When one discusses goats with those who keep them, or have done so in the past, the reaction tends to be one of two extremes: either undying lifelong affection for these wonderful creatures or a dropping of the jaw, rapidly followed by dire warnings against such an acquisition. There appears to be little middle ground.

I acquired an adult pupil who kept a broad range of livestock, but his experiences with goats led him to believe they existed purely to drive human beings insane. James had never played an instrument in his life, but for reasons which were clear only to himself, he was desperate to learn the tenor banjo. I, like most guitarists, enjoy being very rude about the instrument. Its main attribute is that it is extraordinarily loud which explains its popularity in early Dixieland jazz bands. Aside from that, it is difficult to credit it with many other musical attributes. Here's a joke, should you wish to irritate any banjoist friends.

Q: What's the difference between a banjo and an onion?

A: No-one cries when you chop up a banjo.

James' approach to learning the banjo was one of pure endeavour. He believed if he endured sufficient agonising repetition of a piece (usually a little Irish jig or something) he would eventually master it. Any input offered by me would be a mild and irritating disturbance to his incessant assault on the tune in the hope, by sheer trial and error, it would all suddenly click into place. At the end of each session, he'd pass me the instrument and ask me to run through his repertoire. I would do this reluctantly as I am frankly a fraud, neither owning nor playing a banjo. James was perfectly aware of this deficiency on my CV but we mutually enjoyed the sessions and ultimately, a banjo is a big, noisy guitar with odd tuning.

When I announced to James our imminent goat-acquisition, he nearly fell off his seat. He practically dropped to his knees and begged me not to go there. James had added a handful of goats to his menagerie of beasts and soon discovered they are expert escapologists. One stormy November evening he'd been snuggled up in front of the wood burner with Jane, his wife, about to take in a light movie as they polished off the evening meal's bottle of red, when he caught sight of four or five goats galloping past his living room window *en route* to the village centre and undoubtedly, the neighbours' vegetable patches. Having shrieked in horror, he set off in pursuit and spent an altogether unforgettable night (for all the wrong reasons) pursuing his livestock. At 4.00am, drenched to the bone and covered in bruises, horn marks and mud, he returned the last one to its pen. The next evening, exactly the same thing happened. If you are sensitive in nature, you'd do well to skip the remainder of this paragraph as James rounded them up once again but this time, directly into the back of his lorry. The following morning they made a one-way trip to the abattoir and came home in freezer bags.

Another of my adult pupils, Christophe, had at least twenty goats which he kept and bred for pleasure. He promised me first choice of the crop once a litter was born. A friend, Tracie, was also a goat owner; she had hand-reared hers and we decided to take one of those as well.

As the big goat-acquisition weekend approached, I prepared their area with a suitably sturdy wire fence (or so I believed) and arranged a network of planks and beams, mounted between wooden stakes for their amusement and recreation. On the big day, I drove, with my hefty muscle-bound assistant by my side (Florence, my then nine-year-old daughter) to Tracie's house to collect our first specimen. When we arrived, a herd of goats was quietly munching away at the grass in the distance. I rolled up my sleeves, donned leather gloves, and faced Tracie's husband, Alex.

"OK, how are we going to do this?" I asked while chewing a blade of grass, trying my utmost to convince him I was an experienced farm-hand.

He gave me a quizzical look, ambled casually up to a young female (whistling a merry air all-the-while), picked her up, placed her neatly in the back of the car and closed the door. It was that simple. Florence and I then gently drove the few kilometres back to *Chez Jones* accompanied by loud bleating, but aside from that, we experienced no real difficulty. It says everything about our village when I tell you the presence of a goat in the back of our car turned very few heads. I recall we even pulled up outside the bar for a casual exchange of pleasantries with acquaintances; the beast in the boot barely drawing comment. Once goat number one was safely delivered we stood to admire our handiwork in a self-satisfied fashion. Suddenly, the inimitable voice of Madame Godefort was heard crying from across the street.

"You need another one!" she yelled shamelessly. *Il faut une autre!*

Suitably impressed yet unsurprised it had taken her just ten seconds to notice our new acquisition, I assured her that the arrival of goat number two was imminent. I dutifully phoned Christophe to see if I could collect the animal from his herd but his response alarmed me considerably. He said he'd been attempting to catch the goat in question for days and had severe lacerations to his knees as a consequence. He suggested ropes, a team of burly aides or even a tranquiliser for the task at hand. I reflected on his words for a moment and then called Tracie to see if she had another one of her mellow goats to give away which indeed, she did. I thanked Christophe profusely for his time and effort and, in a cowardly and more-than-little shameful fashion, placed the phone onto its receiver and drove off to collect another super-easy goat from Tracie and Alex. The second journey was equally uneventful - aside from the fact that goat number two was a lively, substantial and quite magnificent male who bounced around in the back of our Vectra Estate for the entire trip. Once home, I reversed the car across the garden to the goat pen. It had all been going swimmingly until the last metre when, in an effort to avoid being horned in the side of the head, I lost my bearings and reversed with a sickening plastic 'crunch!' into a concrete washing-line post. This stirred elevated levels of excitement in goat and human passenger alike. As I gingerly moved the car forwards, there was the inimitable sound a bumper makes when it is being lazily ripped from its holdings and dragged across the grass.

If you are considering becoming goat owners (and we can't recommend this enough) Madame Godefort is quite correct. They must live in a herd to be content, even if it is a herd of two. They are beautiful, sociable animals who give hours of pleasure. I was unsurprised to learn they were one of the first species to be domesticated by early humans. Neighbour André though gave dire warnings against goat acquisition.

"If you want to be irritated, get goats," he declared, shaking his head woefully. *Si vouz voulez etre embetté, prenez des chevres.*

Our two were very easy to handle as they had been hand-reared and consequently, they actively sought the company of human beings. They were rather impulsive and unpredictable though which is much of the fun. Whereas horses are 'equine' and cows 'bovine', goats are 'caprine'. The word 'capricious' derives from this, illustrating precisely the personality of our mini-herd. I soon learned goat owners have to show their animals who is boss. They will often challenge you, rearing up as you approach, or trying to overtake when you amble through the fields with them. The misunderstanding is that people believe their goats *want* to be in charge. I'm certain all they want is to understand their place. If they are second-in-line, that's fine, as long as they know it. We soon grew quite obsessed with our acquisition, talking about them endlessly to bored yet obliging friends and family. I loved the fact our neighbours did not judge us negatively upon our bizarre choice of pets but regarded their procurement as an obvious step.

Our goats needed names so we named our female Darcey, and our male, Bussell - in homage to Florence's dancing idol. This choice led to one of the most surreal conversations of my entire life. Ms Bussell, as is common knowledge, owns a beautiful

château in the Dordogne. She doesn't live there, but her brother
(whom I'll call Tim) and sister-in-law (Ann) maintain and run it
as a stunning wedding venue. A significant part of my work as a
guitarist is playing for wedding ceremonies so, over the years, I
was fortunate enough to visit this particular *château* many times.
I became good friends with Tim and Ann, and we would enjoy a
chat after my day's plucking was complete. Out of politeness, I
never mentioned the venue's celebrity owner, thinking it in bad
taste to do so. Following one wedding, I noticed Tim had
acquired sheep so I shared with him the fact that we'd taken
ownership of two goats. His eyes lit up and he questioned me in
detail about issues of goat ownership for a good half hour. Only
when we were deep in conversation did it dawn upon me I had
named our goats after his sister and indeed, our male goat shared
his own surname. I kept on nearly naming them during our
discourse, verbally slamming on the breaks as the syllable 'Buss'
left my lips. I don't think he ever knew the truth.

Darcey and Bussell initially lived in a fenced area alongside
our freely-roaming chickens and rabbits. Soon after their arrival,
it became clear Darcey was the mischievous one. She was
constantly seeking out weak places in our fence and, after a day
working at a vulnerable spot, she would escape from the
compound. We learned of her *sorties* not because she galloped
away and caused havoc but because she ambled her way up to
the house, seeking us out. There were regular instances when
we'd hear a bleating at the back door.

"Darcey's out!" the children would cry in lethargic tones as if
they were announcing the arrival of the postman or something
else somewhat run-of-the-mill.

Another day she escaped when we were at work. Upon failing
to find human interaction *Chez Jones,* she trotted across the field
and visited our distant neighbour, Jean-Claude. He had just
finished his coffee when he heard a tap at the door. Upon opening
it, he was more than a little taken aback at the sight of Darcey,
who amiably wandered into his kitchen seeking treats and
affection. Once he had shooed her away, she made her way to

Madame Godeford's house - much to her eternal delight. Bussell had exactly the same opportunities to escape as Darcey, but usually couldn't be bothered. On the afternoon when both goats ran off due to a gate failure, they went to visit André and Eliane next door who were enjoying their late-afternoon *aperitif.* The goats, spying nibbles, hovered around them for ten minutes or so until Eliane lured them into her garage with a bucketful of corn.

Animals are truly extraordinary and I find it difficult to accept the cold and impersonal explanations for much of their fascinating yet logically-impossible behaviour. For example, one of our rabbits, Ella, and Darcey the goat indulged in sophisticated teamwork. Having several hundred square metres of grass was obviously insufficient for Ella and she clearly believed it was greener on the other side of the fence. I watched, transfixed, as the two species made a highly-successful cooperation pact which reaped rewards for both parties. Ella would gnaw away at one strand of the fence as Darcey stood behind her, waiting patiently. Once there was the slightest bit of damage, Ella would step back and Darcey would 'work' the same hole with a horn. Then the procedure would recommence with another adjacent strand of fencing. By the end of the day, the hole would be big enough for both to escape. They would pass the evening eating exactly the same things as they would have done had they stayed within their area. Then at nightfall, they'd re-enter their compound through the same hole when they were good and ready.

We're also at a loss to explain how our cats knew they could eat wild bunnies *a volonté,* yet understood Ella and Peta, as well as our guinea pigs, were out-of-bounds. A further mystery is that they would hiss and spit at a cat visiting the garden but seemed utterly blasé about those in the cattery. Once, I tried to take Badger into the empty cattery to pose in a heated cat bed for a publicity photo. The instant I crossed the threshold of the building, he panicked and attached himself to the wire mesh, spread-eagled like a fly on a windscreen.

One cold, drizzly January evening, I was sitting on my backside in the wet mud, mending a fence which had been damaged by the

Ella/Darcey pact. I was trying to find my dropped pliers in a puddle, while simultaneously musing over at what point pneumonia or even frostbite might set in when I became aware of a presence over my left shoulder. Darcey had trotted out to see what was going on and, as I had positioned myself lower than her, felt it appropriate to challenge me for dominance. She delivered a head-butt to my forehead which would have made a Glaswegian pub-crawler on a Saturday night proud. Dazed and angry, I dragged her, bleating madly (her, not me) into the little wood cabin that was their shelter, and closed the door. I then staggered back to finish the job in peace. Eventually, shivering, damp and with hands as red as beetroots, I headed back eagerly for the sanctuary of the house and the warmth of the wood burner. Unfortunately for me, as Mrs Jones will freely attest, I am an inherently untidy person. Earlier in the day I had been raking some leaves and had, predictably, left the rake lying prongs-up on the floor. Inevitably, I trod on it in the darkness. I remember a huge whack to my already bruised face and then lying on my back in the sodden grass, staring at the clouds above. I was seeing double for three days afterwards and probably should have gone to A&E, but I just couldn't face the moment of explanation to the doctor.

"Well, injury number one came about because I was sitting in a pool of muck doing some nocturnal fence reparation at 10.30pm on a winter's night when my goat butted me. The second is where I trod on a rake hiding in the thicket ten minutes later."

Any self-respecting *medécin* would never have believed me and may well have had me sectioned.

André had warned us.

"Si vouz voulez etre embetté, prenez des chevres."

One should always listen to the advice of elders.

But Darcey and Bussell saved their most startling surprise for a cold January evening in 2016. The Sunday before that fateful day, we were invited *en famille* to go ice-skating in Angoulême. We were passing an agreeable afternoon when Kirsty slipped, landing smartly on her backside. I snorted loudly and reached for my phone to photograph her in this undignified position, but immediately chastened myself when I spotted a glare in her eyes which suggested there was a serious problem. Twenty-four hours later, we were in A&E in Sainte-Foy-la-Grande where a fractured ankle was confirmed. Kirsty was ordered to remain immobile for several weeks, leaving me with the duties of running the household, maintaining a smallholding, tending to the guests in the cattery and coping with two highly-active children; all-the-while holding down full-time employment as a guitarist and teacher. The Friday evening following these events, I rolled up outside the house, drained and exhausted. I sat back in the driver's seat, closed my eyes and took a deep breath to meditate upon the tasks which needed to be completed over the weekend. Suddenly, I became aware of Flo, Sam and a friend tearing up the garden in a state of extreme excitement.

"Darcey's had *babies!"* they cried, bouncing on the spot and clawing at the windows of my car.

I couldn't quite believe my ears. It appeared I now had to add 'learn goat midwifery' to my to-do list, just after 'clear week's backlog of washing up'.

Moments before, Flo and a friend from school had ambled down to the goat paddock and stumbled upon a new-born kid, barely minutes old. Having heard a commotion, Kirsty broke doctor's orders and limped down the garden to investigate. There she discovered a second kid, concealed in the goat house. In a dazed state, I staggered to the paddock to meet the new arrivals who were already venturing into the outside world. There, Eliane and Kirsty stood with hands clasped, cooing over the utterly adorable bundles of fluff who'd just gatecrashed our lives. It seemed that I was the only person in the company who felt any reason to be anxious, or even mildly concerned. From over the garden fence, André simply shook his head and chuckled to himself in an 'I told you so' manner. Desperate to do something at least a little bit responsible, I telephoned Christophe the goat man (he of the psychotic caprine new-borns) for advice. He asked if the new arrivals were feeding and, once I'd confirmed this was the case, advised we just left them alone and allow nature to take its course. To put a halt to my fretting, we decided to go out for a meal at a local bar where I displayed photos of the new-borns to bemused strangers enjoying their *entrecôte et frites*.

I should say at this point we had wished to avoid such a circumstance, having deliberately chosen a female and a castrated male – I do possess some foresight. It seems Darcey must have mated within the herd almost on the day we had picked her up nearly five months before. Now I come to think of it, I do recall seeing a billy stretched out on a *chaise longue* smoking a cigarette. The next day, I phoned a retired vet who had been taking guitar lessons with me. This wonderful gentleman came straight over to *Chez Jones* and confirmed we were the proud owners of boy and girl kids.

The children named them Billy and Sugar respectively. As a family, we agreed to give them away to worthy homes once they were weaned. Fat chance. Inevitably, *la Famille Jones* fell deeply in love with our little goats and soon after there was no question of living without them. Baby animals of all species possess a special kind of magic, and the next three months were some of the happiest and most memorable times, not just of our stay in France, but my entire life. I can't begin to tell you the fun we had with these playful creatures. I have films of them standing on our heads, jumping between our laps and trying to rear up at us in a ridiculous clumsy manner, all captured to a soundtrack of children's laughter. I recently saw a film of a yoga club in the US which has introduced sessions where kids (of the goat kind) are brought into class to climb over, jump onto and utterly charm the participants. They are said to inspire and improve the well-being of all present. How I can believe that.

More goats meant a larger area was required to house them. With further assistance from our neighbour and his splendid machinery, we fenced off the remainder of our land. Having constructed a new cabin from waste timber we set about creating a playground for our goat family. A local garage owner was only too pleased to give us a large supply of old tractor tyres as they are expensive to dispose of commercially. One thank-you gift of a bottle of red later, Flo and I were to be seen driving our Vectra through the country roads with a large rubber pyramid strapped to the roof. We then designed and created a labyrinth of muddy hillocks, tyre-mountains and rickety beams for caprine amusement. Upon our return to France, we intend to become owners of Ouessant sheep to relieve me of the necessity to drag the lawn mower out of the shed in the summer months, but that project will have to take a back seat for a while.

A side effect of keeping rustic animals (to use the French expression) is children are able to grasp the natural cycles of life. How unwise we are to shield youngsters from the joy of new life and the inevitability of death. We have lost animals and, inescapably, such moments cause immense sadness. These experiences though have initiated open and honest conversations about our finite time in this world and the importance of living each day to the full. I am proud of the fact that my children understand where babies come from. I would prefer them to learn about reproduction from witnessing horses in season in an adjoining field rather than one of the many desperately-grubby programmes on TV where so-called 'beautiful' people indulge in intimate contact for the public to gawp at and gossip over.

Despite the fact that many of our neighbours owned livestock purely for pleasure, a utilitarian view of animals, coupled with old-school cultures, can yield the unsavoury practices of yesteryear. Nowhere was this more evident than in a family business which became legendary, or notorious - depending on your point of view - in the Dordogne and beyond: *Madame Mystico's* Circus. It was a travelling circus with performing animals; a tradition still present in the area, but which is slowly dying away.

The first time I was treated to the *Mystico* experience, they were putting on a free show in the glamorous setting of a supermarket car park. Being a renowned skinflint, the word *'Gratuit!'* (Free!) emblazoned across the garish neon posters which had been pasted liberally throughout the *commune* immediately appealed to my nature, so I took the family along for a 'treat'. I loved it because it was so gloriously crap. To be fair, the acrobats were impressive. Kirsty sat in absolute terror, unable to watch a single airborne feat as, in true French countryside Health-and-Safety style, it was shockingly, yet compellingly dangerous. A young girl performed a range of airborne stunts – free from the tedious restrictions of a safety net - as her younger brother held on to a 'security' rope which had obviously doubled as a washing line for the previous decade-or-two. I think he was only holding the rope with one hand and eating a hot dog with the other. In the interval, *Madame Mystico* dropped her magical persona and wandered around the modest crowd, attempting to sell sugary snacks and luminescent sticks made in China, which I suspect had steered a wide berth of interested Trading Standards Officers. As the *finale* approached, I sat bouncing on my bleacher with child-like excitement as *Madame Mystico* presented the *pièce de résistance*. She whipped back the curtain, almost causing it to crash down upon her head, and in ran a magnificent horse, artfully dodging the odd abandoned shopping trolley as it entered. The crowd applauded enthusiastically. As it trotted a few circuits of the ring, I wondered what it would do: tightrope walk, sing a song, jump through a flaming hoop... After thirty seconds of circumnavigation though, it exited. It was simply making an appearance. I felt ripped off. Mind you, I hadn't paid a *centime*. The full *Mystico* show was an evening do and to attend, we'd have been required to cross *Madame's* palm with silver in the form of a not-negligible sum of euros. I couldn't fork out that much for an ironic laugh, undisputedly tempting though the proposition was, so it remains an unknown entity to *la Famille Jones*.

A few days later, I was driving past Mussidan's fire station (there were no firefighters to be seen - they were probably in the local bar) when I noticed a couple of lorries parked up on the forecourt attracting a disproportionate degree of attention. Closer inspection revealed one of the vehicles held a couple of *real-life* lions in the open-sided cargo hold. I did a huge double-take and nearly crashed into the forecourt of *Intermarché.* The poor creatures were held behind bars and made a sorry sight. What was equally incredible though was the 'security' in place to protect the considerable body of onlookers who were gathering to gawp at the unfortunate creatures. There were a couple of bollards put up at either end of the truck, and a piece of tape hanging loosely between them, flapping in the breeze, and that was pretty much it. I recall a couple of infants were using it as a skipping rope. A handful of circus guys were ambling about carrying out routine tasks but nothing, absolutely nothing was in place to prevent a small child from approaching the cage and offering hungry little kitty a stroke. Obviously, *Madame Mystico* and her crew were displaying the big cats as a publicity stunt for their *spectacle.* They also appeared to own a wealth of livestock which, as far as I am aware, played no role in their performances. Some of these were standard fare such as goats, chickens or modestly-sized alpacas. Others were altogether more ambitious in scale. Upon a Friday visit to market one early spring morning, Kirsty and I ambled around a corner to be confronted by a full-sized camel tethered to a patch of grass next to the bloke selling kitchenware. The creature seemed oblivious to its circumstances, grazing away quite contentedly. More extraordinary was the indifference of the locals who continued purchasing their goods, as if the beast was a Jack Russell on a lead. Happily, a number of animal-rights groups have directed their collective attention to these practices; *Madame Mystico* and other travelling circuses are gradually adapting their *spectacles* to suit modern expectations.

Having touched upon the topic of the *marché,* markets make a wonderful morning out, especially in the summer. Once again though, the squeamish may want to prepare themselves for an unsentimental approach to the origins of our food. Most markets will have a fish stall where clients are invited to select supper from a water tank. At this point, their evening meal will be still-

Dan Jones

living, although indisputably approaching the end of their journey in this realm. The proprietor will grab the victim with a net and give it a neat clonk over the head as he/she wraps it up for the customer. Once, in Coutras market, I watched, revolted, as a young assistant reached into a huge sack of slime containing hundreds of wriggling eels before plonking a bare armful onto a scales for her hungry client. The fishmonger stalls are extraordinary and I have a disproportionate compulsion to stare at them, second only to the *toilettage* boutique. One market day, I was holding Flo, who would have been about six years old, showing her the amazing range of species available for *la table*. On impulse, I picked up a red snapper with my right hand and turned it to face her. Using finger-pressure on the gills, I was able to make its mouth move slightly. I coupled this with the deft application of left-to-right wriggling actions, thus completing my spontaneous fish-animation. Putting on a squeaky voice, I said something along the lines of 'Hello Flo-Jo, my name is Mr Snappy. Please don't gobble me up!' Since that day, she has refused to touch a single morsel of fish. This tale is not unlike my venture into balloon-animal modelling which has left her with a mild phobia of all things inflatable. I'm sure Social Services have a file on me somewhere.

Visiting a French country vet is a similar experience to that in the UK. Badger's annual 'check-up' would consist of a torch in the eyes, a thermometer where the sun doesn't shine, and a token poke in the ribs. For this 'service' I found myself driving home with a disgruntled moggie and a much-depleted bank account. I adore the fact one can turn up at the vet with a goat, and no-one bats an eyelid, just as if you'd arrived with a guinea pig. When Billy went for his castration, he unceremoniously shat all over their shiny white floor, almost as if he was giving his opinion on the procedure which he was about to undergo. Interestingly, if you keep 'rustic' animals for pleasure in the French countryside, rather than for commercial reasons, vets are very flexible when it comes to vaccinations. Rather than taking the view that if the pet isn't vaccinated, it will surely die in agonising fashion, our vet will ask about the animals' lifestyle and recommend accordingly. Badger's only treatment was de-worming due to his rabbit habit. Friends in the village who kept horses, sheep and goats actually believed vaccinations *weakened* their animals. Once again, the modern world may sneer at such a view but I did note their livestock, who lived free-range and ate at nature's table, never seemed to become unwell.

***

Four Go Wild in *la Forêt* – The Essential Tips

(1) Caterpillars are lethal in the eyes of some ex-pats.

(2) If you dislike hunting, you may wish to live elsewhere.

(3) Please do not offer me any more abandoned baby mammals. I will probably accept the gift when placed under pressure by my children.

(4) Goats and rabbits have telepathic properties.

(5) Life is incomplete without hens.

(6) The travelling circus in France is reminiscent of those of Victorian Britain.

(7) Fish are, under no circumstances, substitutes for puppets.

(8) Goats will lead you to extremes of emotion, at either end of the spectrum.

Figure 8 Can anything be more magical for a child than a new-born goat?

Figure 9 Kirsty and Bussell

Figure 10 Kirsty 'The Chicken Whisperer' luring escapee hens back into their area.

Figure 11 Sam and the new goat house, mid-build.

13. Etiquette and Questions of Love

My mother tell'd me to gie him a kiss
Ha, ha bit I would nae hae him
If you like him so well, you can kiss him yoursel'
Wi' his grey beard newly shaven

Old Grey Beard – Traditional (Scotland)

Pedalling my bike through Bordeaux at the end of a school day, I encountered a dialogue shared between a girl of about eight years of age and her mother.

"You sure as hell better have brought me a *goûter* because I'm starving!" barked the little girl by means of welcome to her parent.

In response, Mum scrambled around in her designer handbag, seeking out a sugary snack before being further berated for being too tardy in her reaction time. *Maman* appeared to have an acute case of the modern urban illness which leads victims to believe that being a good, compassionate parent means you should cater to your child's every crudely-delivered whim. In stark contrast to this woeful state of affairs, rudeness to parents is something I have hardly ever witnessed in our village. Of course, there are mums, dads and carers who face the everyday challenges of parenthood, but for the most part my experiences of young people have been very positive. This is because the vast majority of parents display daily courtesy which their children imitate. They remember the word 'discipline' has the same origin as the word 'disciple' meaning 'follower'.

I have found common courtesy is of great importance in rural areas and this is something which I value very much. Having said that, questions of daily interaction, love, eye-contact, kissing, small talk and going to the toilet all contribute towards a social minefield which those moving to the French countryside must traverse. Upon meeting someone, be it for the first time ever, or the first encounter on any given day, outsiders will encounter complex and potentially error-strewn behaviours which must be practised in order not to seem like *Monsieur* or *Madame Rude.*

In French village life, the practice of *les bises* (kissing on the cheeks) is absolutely alive and well. For us reserved Brits, this can be the root of sleepless nights and several years of trauma counselling. To make things even more perplexing, certain *departements* and *régions* will have different practices to those of their close neighbours. By means of example, in the Dordogne where we live, one kisses once on each cheek, yet In the Charente (half an hour north) it's three kisses (right, left, right or left, right, left).

Below, I have created a handy guide to *les bises* which I hope will enable you to avoid the squirming moments of embarrassment and social *faux-pas* which littered my early years in the region.

(1) If you are male or female, it is always appropriate to kiss a child of any gender. In the Dordogne, a child will approach you upon introduction (and subsequent encounters) and expect to receive two kisses, one on each cheek. Which cheek to kiss first is irrelevant in my experience. If you fail to deliver the expected kisses, you will confuse the said child and they may believe they've done something wrong.

(2) When males or females meet adult females, kisses are usually appropriate. The first time I met an adult pupil of either gender, a handshake was regarded as correct, but I had to use my perception to understand when it would be appropriate to offer a kiss. Watch out for nuances of body movement. If a lady gestures her head towards you, she's probably going in for *les bises.* After three or four meetings/lessons, just go for *les bises*

if they are yet to happen. It's OK and, unlike in the UK, you will be safe from prosecution.

(3) When adult males meet adult males, a handshake is appropriate. I've never experienced a physically-painful handshake in France, whereas attempting to injure your new-found buddy through crushing small bones is the norm in the UK. The latter practice appears to be some weird alpha-male hangover from Neanderthal times which is most galling for me as a guitarist. What's fascinating in France is the handshake is only part of the necessary social interaction. As you shake hands it is *imperative* to *make good eye contact* and say *'Bonjour'* as you shake. After a while, it will become appropriate to kiss your male friends as well. This is scary for us reserved Northern-Europeans. In my experience, the boundary between hand-shake-land and male-on-male-*bises*-land appears to be traversed once I experience some kind of social interaction with the person outside a professional setting. This could be an *aperitif* or possibly something as simple as crossing paths at a village event. The fact you acknowledge one another's existence as men capable of activities other than working at diminished seventh chords makes one worthy of a kiss. If you are a musician working in the arts, expect to kiss male counterparts immediately. When rehearsing with our village big band, I usually come home to my wife having kissed around twenty males. Now *that's* a sentence I hadn't anticipated writing in 2010.

(4) There are some tricky moments to navigate in terms of the kiss-recipients' age. I can't help but notice that after retirement age, some ladies appear to expect a gentle handshake rather than a kiss. I find this agonising and opt to kiss regardless of the years under the recipient's belt. It's almost as if not to do so suggests they are no longer pretty. I can imagine a lady would

feel awful the day she receives her first handshake. I am against ageism. Granny-Kissers of the world unite!

(5) There is another awkward corner to be encountered as young boys reach adolescence. When does one kiss and when does one shake hands? A killer. Like many music teachers, I have witnessed young boys in June carrying superhero-type plastic figures skip gaily out of their lesson, singing a little regional *chanson* in choirboy falsetto tones only to return in September carrying a mobile phone, sounding more like Barry White than Aled Jones (when they do actually speak) and preferring Metallica over Mozart. In such cases, boys will find it a compliment if you shake their hands rather than kiss them, as it acknowledges their newly-discovered manliness. A few will habitually go in for *les bises* though and embarrass themselves immensely in the process. Mind you, even the act of breathing in their presence appears to be a source of extreme embarrassment for most adolescents.

(6) Parents usually insist their offspring go through the ritual of thanking their teacher and saying, '*à la semaine prochaine*' which is a stock parting pleasantry at the close of a lesson meaning 'until next week.' One time, a newly-transformed teenager shook my hand and muttered '*à la semaine prochaine*' at the close of his session with his father watching some twenty metres away. Moments after I'd closed the door, he was frog-marched back into the room and repeated the parting words for the second time. I hastily assured his father that he had made the required polite statement the first time around, but Dad was dissatisfied as 'he'd said it but didn't mean it'.

(7) It's easy for ladies. Kiss everyone.

(8) If entering a committee meeting or some other gathering of multiple persons, it is appropriate to go round the table and

either kiss or shake the hands of everyone present. Brits tend to walk in, obviously having stood paralysed outside the door for at least twenty minutes, mortified about the whole *bises* thing, and do a sort of on-the-spot jocular dance, throwing mimed kisses in all directions so as to avoid the necessary process which goes against every instinct in their Anglo-Saxon body. That's inadequate and simply weird in anyone's culture.

(9) Please avoid doing a loud *'mwaah'* sound and making a big physical gesture – both of which are an attempt to conceal embarrassment. It only makes the situation worse for all present.

(10) At the end of the day, *les bises* are an issue for Brits and not for the French. As a male, you may well mistakenly kiss your sixteen-stone rugby-playing plumber in ignorance. Consequently, you'll curl up into a ball of agonised embarrassment for the next decade every time someone mentions a U-bend, but I guarantee the plumber will have forgotten about it moments later. It's our issue rather than theirs.

(11) Finally, remember this: Inaction is impolite. Getting it wrong shows good intent.

I enjoyed gently mocking Kirsty when we first arrived in Scotland as I witnessed her, through habit, 'going in for the kiss' on multiple occasions; the potential recipient being completely ignorant to her intentions. Once, upon being introduced to a 'Playground Mum', she approached with her head leading towards the victim's face before realising she was no longer in France and subsequently employing a swift rear-guard action, pretending she had lost her balance. I think the new acquaintance thought she was a jealous wife going in for a 'Glasgow Kiss' (Scottish slang for a 'head butt'). Interestingly, as we've joked about these incidents, our new friends have said they'd have loved to have received a kiss. Maybe we should start a cultural trend north of the border.

A behavioural code which, strangely, I have found far more complex than whether to kiss a man or not, is the question of whether to use the '*tu*' or '*vous*' form of the second personal pronoun 'you'. You will probably remember from your schooldays the French have two ways of saying 'you'. There is '*vous*' which is polite and formal, and is also used for when you speak to a group; '*tu*' is employed when you speak informally and with familiarity to people, and is always used when addressing a child.

The French in rural areas maintain the formality of a certain detachment within a professional situation. I think I must be old-fashioned (or maybe I have French genes which would explain a lot) as I dislike over-familiarity without my permission. Upon occasional visits to restaurants or bars with family and friends in South Wales, I've found serving staff referring to our group as 'guys'. I feel this is inappropriate when some of the group are senior citizens, articulate, very well educated and deserve a little respect. Even worse is the present fashion for 'babe'. In a British corner shop, a young lady recently addressed me saying 'Hi babe, how can I help?' I understand she was being warm and friendly, but I find the assumption I will be OK with it rather discourteous - or perhaps she mistook me for the little pig in the 1995 comedy film of the same title. I assure you this would *never* happen in French village commerce.

When working with French adults, I always use the '*vous*' form of a verb. All of the *How to Live Life in France* books always tell you *only* to use '*vous*' in professional situations. A cue to switch to the '*tu*' form will be if your pupil uses '*tu*' when addressing you. Some of my younger, more radical adult pupils have used '*tu*' from the word go. Often, a French acquaintance will simply ask '*tu/toi?*' which is a proposal to use the familiar form and is actually a compliment to you. Accept it. One of my adult pupils has been to my home out of professional time, come to see me in concerts, shared a drink with me and been nothing less than a friend as well as a guitar student, yet he retains the *'vous'* form when we converse. I have taken the bold step of addressing him as *'tu'* before having been given the green light to do so, but with no reciprocation, so I suspect I've messed that one up. A good escape route if you meet this oft-encountered dilemma is to employ *'on'*. In English, this is the rather posh indefinite pronoun 'one'. In French, it is common in everyday language so you won't end up sounding like the Queen of England. Therefore, if you are a guitar teacher, you can niftily sidestep the *'tu/vous'* decision. 'One places the second finger on the note A' *On place le deuxième doigt sur la note la,* can be said Instead of, 'You place…' *Vous placez…*

France has, unfairly I believe, a reputation for liberal attitudes towards all things relating to sexuality. As a British teenager on vacation, I recall a certain astonishment (and admittedly, delight) at the habit of topless sunbathing on the beach. I genuinely didn't know where to look. I also remember a group of three or four English boys around twenty years of age persuading a couple of generously-buxom and topless French girls to play piggy-in-the-middle with them in the shallows. The scoundrels clearly had the intention of making them leap around in the water, creating the dual effect of excessive bounce and splashing-of-water-on-upper-body. Their scheme triggered immense amusement on their part and the apparent indifference of the girls. Now I am older, and perhaps a little wiser, I suspect *les filles* knew exactly what they were doing and were enjoying both the attention and tantalising the fellows in question.

One will also observe the public flaunting of flesh in the most unlikely of environments. I have mentioned my post as a guitar teacher in the marvellous market town of Coutras in earlier chapters where, in late spring, the approaching months of extended holidays are celebrated by the arrival of a travelling funfair. In small-town France, these are very much like their British counterparts (but with live animals thrown in for good measure). You can expect the regular fare of the fair: the smell of diesel, teenage ride-operators with attitude problems, older ride operators with a story to tell, and shooting stalls where success is nigh-on impossible - although these tend to be altogether more pleasingly dangerous, featuring proper air-rifles with little or no restriction on the direction of fire.

A notable difference though can be seen in the artwork displayed on the more daring of white-knuckle rides. I recently attended a travelling funfair in South Wales, and the more-extreme rides featured sub-GCSE standard paintings of movie stars alongside supposedly-erotic images of female icons – the likes of Wonder Woman or Pamela Anderson. These good ladies were, predictably, modelling bikinis several sizes too small for them in their artistic depictions. In France, they don't mess around with false modesty. The Wall-of-Death ride in Coutras (in my book known as the Rapid-Vomit-Generator) was tastefully decorated with an image of a lady, not instantly recognisable to my eyes, sporting a pair of breasts of improbable proportions free from the restraints of swimwear, skimpy or otherwise. The effect was tastefully topped off with LED lights at the peaks of her nipples - flashing colourfully and brilliantly in time with the accompanying *Europop*. Her pouting lips and half-closed, generously-lashed eyes suggested she was finding some erotic excitement in publically sporting her unique and magnificent *techno-boobs.*

I'd wager such high-brow artistic adornments embellishing a roller-coaster in the UK would draw crowds, open-mouthed in amazement. Furious protests from *Daily Mail* readers would follow, with the finger of blame being pointed firmly at immigrants. When one takes a moment to reflect though, I truly believe the French are simply more honest when it comes to flaunting the delights of human sexuality. What is the point of putting a modestly-dressed Ms Anderson on a funfair ride in South Wales? I suspect the given reason would be to add 'glamour', but this is a code word for 'sex'. The small-town French just cut to the chase, pulling off the wrapping and making the whole package available to those wishing to admire it.

As Lucy Wadham notes in her book, *The Secret Life of France,* It is an extraordinary fact that the majority of recent French presidents have had extra-marital affairs, and even more astonishingly, no-one seemed to mind very much. There is a magnificent *château* in the Dordogne where I perform regularly, which boasts a sumptuous suite named after a former French president. He apparently loved this particular getaway and was a regular secret visitor there. I have no evidence to support this but, as it is in a remote, leafy and deeply romantic setting, maybe *Monsieur le Présidente* used it to entertain guests other than the First Lady. It is now public-knowledge that *Monsieur le Présidente* had a pretty serious fling – one that lasted thirty-two years in fact - and that the relationship yielded a child, but the press decided that the whole affair was none of their business. Can you imagine if David Cameron had popped off to a Premier Inn in the Lake District with a young PA while Samantha held the fort at home? Even more unthinkable is the concept of our gutter press not bothering to report it… for thirty-two years. Wadham goes on to describe attending dinner parties which, unbeknownst to her were actually evenings for those indulging in the practice of 'swinging' (unrelated to gymnastics or jazz). In the improbable event of your considering moving to France in the hope of some lusty and diverse extra-marital entertainment, I can only advise you, dear reader, the scene is very different in the countryside (thank goodness). I can only presume such behaviour remains the domain of the city dweller.

In the rural area where we've set up home, it has struck me that attitudes towards relationships are far more conservative than those I've witnessed in today's speed-dating culture. Loyalty and fidelity are valued enormously. Many French friends of my age appear to have met their life-partners at a younger age than I'd regard as the norm for their British counterparts. Also, far fewer of them are divorcees. I make no moral judgement here, but the modern-day phenomenon of 'seeing how it goes if we shack up together for a few years' is conspicuously absent from my immediate social group.

As a fourteen-year-old boy, my school chums and I participated in a fortnight-long French exchange in the *commune* of Yerres, to the south of Paris. With regards to the fairer sex, the boys in my class still regarded them primarily as objects to be mercilessly tormented yet in contrast, upon shyly descending the bus at *l'école* which would host us, I was astonished (and I confess, a little intrigued) to note that French teenagers spent the majority of their spare time locked to one another's faces by the mouth. I can confirm with some authority that this remains the case. My British side continues to cringe at such behaviour; I sometimes wonder how they find time to converse or breathe even. Actually, the former question is answerable as they appear to disengage only to check their smartphones upon which I presume they send one another indecipherable, acronym-laden text messages via snap-face-twit or something (lol). Despite this, young people are allowed to be 'young' for much longer in the French countryside than their counterparts in urban areas. It is very refreshing to see early-teenagers interested in sport, nature, crafts and running like crazy people across fields rather than stressing over whether their latest posts on social media have received sufficient 'likes' so they can feel loved. I do enjoy social media and have 'befriended' some of my former child-pupils of bygone years and of varying nationalities. I really want to know how they are getting along in life but instead, as they are now teenagers, I am obliged to follow emoji-laden declarations of eternal love for their new-found sweethearts. Excruciating.

The final, peculiar social topic upon which I'd like to enlighten you is that of using the toilet. My experience with the *fosse septique* has already been discussed at length elsewhere so I apologise if I appear obsessed with the subject. When I was a teenager travelling through France, I was amazed at the oft-witnessed sight of people taking a pee at the side of the road, without bothering to locate heavy foliage to conceal themselves. It seemed so brazen. So impolite. The bottom line is that it's often *polite* to pee outdoors, rather than in someone's loo. Why? Because in the warmer, southern areas of France, water is expensive. Therefore, a flush costs your host a lot of money. I am amazed at twenty-first-century attitudes towards relieving one's bladder. Like many readers, I was captivated and moved by R J Palacio's beautiful book *Wonder*. In one chapter, a group of kids get into trouble for urinating in the woods. What on earth do the parent-characters think the bears and squirrels do? Maybe they believe there are gender-separated animal sanitation blocks amongst the trees - bears to the left, racoons to the right - installed safely out-of-sight behind an ancient oak? When playing sports, kids of both genders are frequently sent to the trees to pee *en plein air*. They do the necessary and then dive back into the game. You know what? No-one dies. When we arrived in Scotland, I found myself constantly having to remind Sam that in the UK, the 'correct' thing to do was to run 200 metres to an outbuilding and relieve himself there. It was tough for him to learn, and even tougher to justify.

***

Etiquette and Questions of Love – The Essential Tips

(1) Children are polite because their parents set the precedent.

(2) If in doubt, kiss. If you mess it up, it's less of a big deal to the French than it is to the Anglo-Saxon.

(3) If you intend moving to the French countryside in the hope of vigorous and athletic extra-marital activities, buy yourself a flat in Ibiza, or even 'Shagaluf' instead.

(4) French teenagers can apparently breathe through their ears.

(5) To *'tu'* or to *'vous'*? That is a tricky question. If in doubt, use *'on'*.

(6) Electronically-animated boobs are a frequent sight.

(7) Taking a pee in the garden is both ecological and polite.

14. Love Thy Neighbour, Love Thy Life

Nid wy'n gofyn bywyd moethus
Aur y byd na'i berlau mân
Gofyn wyf am galon hapus
Calon onest, calon lân

Calon lân yn llawn daioni
Tecach yw na'r lili dlos
Dim ond calon lân all ganu
Canu'r dydd a chanu'r nos.

I do not ask for a life of luxury
The world's gold or fine pearls
I ask for a pure heart
A happy heart, a warm heart

A pure heart full of goodness
It's fairer than the pretty lily
Only a pure heart can sing
Sing day and night.

John Hughes and Daniel James - Calon Lân
(A Pure Heart – Wales)

Within the routine of living in a French village, we soon learned it was necessary to re-evaluate the role played by neighbours and friends in everyday life. Maybe it was due to the sense of isolation, but there was a natural interdependency which provided security and a feeling of mutual well-being. Could it be in this world we are so focused on ambition, financial success and status, we forget things which are central to making us happy? For newcomers, indeed outsiders, like ourselves, we found a sense of belonging and community were very precious indeed. I benefited from innumerable acts of kindness in our village. There was never a sense of 'you owe me one' - it was just understood that helping out a pal was more fulfilling than staring at a screen. I often made too much of a big deal over an act of generosity; I now see this led to embarrassment. One lives and learns.

When we were installed in our home, I became friendly with a neighbour who lived about 100 metres away. He and his family had an air of being outcasts. They lived in a bungalow which was a ramshackle affair (even more so than our own) and it reminded me of JK Rowling's depiction of the Weasley family home, with its abundance of livestock and improvised add-ons. I wouldn't have been surprised to have caught the inhabitants de-gnoming the garden in springtime. It was quite the everyday occurrence to encounter a chicken in their living room or to park oneself on an egg which had been discreetly laid beneath a cushion. The gentleman of the house was Alain - a scruffy-looking man who was disproportionately preoccupied with telling me at least fifteen times a day how much he loved the British. He had been a long-distance lorry driver and had travelled the world before setting up home in our village. Nothing pleased him more than to call in *Chez Jones* to pass the time of day and, if I were indulging in some DIY, he would instantly join me, sharing his expertise and time with passion. He had a philosophy of 'give, give, give' which was both genuine and warming. Alain's problem though was he partook in the French country tradition of the appreciation of all things fermented with somewhat unfettered abandon. One afternoon I was attempting to rectify a leaking chimney pot when Alain passed the house on his way back from the bar. Delighted to see a project was underway, he was up the ladder and at my side quicker than you could say 'bloody dangerous'. As you will have no doubt observed, my attitude towards all things 'Health and Safety' veers towards an approach with a certain elasticity in the rules, but even I would never consider mounting a roof after a pleasant few hours consuming *Pelforth* in the late-morning sunshine. I have two friends in France who are wheelchair-bound, paralysed from the chest down, due to falls from roofs. Thankfully, we both got down safely (and did a pretty good job on the chimney too).

I felt uneasy about my relationship with Alain and his family. He was often ridiculed by friends in the village as he recounted wildly-adventurous stories about his past life as a trucker. To me, they were perfectly feasible as I have learned long ago that real life is always more extraordinary than fiction. He claimed to have a pilot's licence and would expand lavishly upon his experiences at the controls of small aircraft. It was this claim which attracted most derision behind Alain's back. I found that upsetting. One morning, Kirsty and I attended a *vide grenier* (a car-boot or jumble sale) where I spotted a little golden model aeroplane, about the size of my thumb, so I acquired it for Alain. He was visibly moved when I gave it to him and it took pride-of-place in his ancient Renault Five, suspended from the rear-view mirror. I would see it glinting in the sunshine as the rickety vehicle, which made *le Tank* look like a Bentley, trundled down the lane past *Chez Jones*.

Alain's lifestyle habits though were often painfully humiliating. One day Eliane, our kindly and elegant neighbour, was sharing a chat with us in our garden. I think we were discussing chicken health or something similar.

"Salut!" came a boisterous call from the front of the house, announcing that Alain had dropped in for an exchange of pleasantries.

As I beckoned to him to join us around the back, both Eliane and I noted his route towards us could only have been described as 'scenic' as he meandered crazily into washing lines, vegetable patches, children's toys and pretty much any other obstacle unlucky enough to be within fifty metres of the direct route. He was clearly plastered. I had to physically catch him a number of times as we attempted to string together some kind of conversation. Sadly, the dialogue - no doubt inspired by the morning's over-indulgence - consisted primarily of declarations of eternal brotherhood and manly love. Touching though this might have been, there's a time and a place for such things. Tuesday morning in the presence of a sophisticated, kindly and gentle lady neighbour certainly wasn't it.

"You are my best friend Dan… I *love* the British… and *you*… are my *brother!*" he decreed as Eliane became disproportionately interested in a patch of nettles on the other side of the garden.

"That's very kind Alain, can I get you a strong coffee?" I said, doing my utmost to change the subject.

"No, but *listen!* In my heart… and my soul," at this point, he thumped his chest, "You are my *brother!*"

And so it progressed, for far more time than was desirable.

I became nervous when Alain occasionally asked me for money. In the first instance, I had not a *centime* on me. The second, I had the small amount requested and I handed it over, not expecting to see it again. In fact, it was returned to me just a few days later, accompanied by a thank-you gift of ten jars of home-made jam. Alain and his family confused me. I say 'and his family' as his wife was also prone to calling around asking for similar favours such as lifts, child-care and short-term loans. Some acquaintances maintained that we were being used and mocked our naivety, but we were *always* paid back and rewarded handsomely with unsolicited gifts of the food type as interest. Alain helped me with one-hundred-and-one DIY projects and loaned me Lord only knows how many tools. As time has gone by, I've realised the family will never adhere to the image of 'good living' imposed on us by the contemporary world. They are very open-hearted and they live in the moment; I sense the spirit of the vagabond within them. They are in fact deeply generous and genuine people, trying to find their place in a world which is full of codes and pre-determined formulae for behaviour which, even if they wanted to, they couldn't fulfil.

In rural France, significant annual events are celebrated in a more-restrained and tasteful manner than I've witnessed in urban centres. Christmas decorations go up in December rather than the day after Hallowe'en. *Le Père Noël* (Father Christmas) is wholly active in France – I point this out as I am aware that some European countries have gifts delivered by the Three Kings, and in Catalonia, presents are pooped by a log. During our frivolous days as music students, Catalonian friends (the same friends we visited in Barcelona in the 1990's - see Chapter One) subjected the aforementioned log to a month of force-feeding in order to generate a games console or some other consumer desirable – a kind of festive *gavage.* Good to see Santa is spreading the load, particularly as he reportedly has a terminal sherry and mince pie habit.

Our village knows how to put on a show at Christmas and, considering France is officially a secular country, the commune makes an extraordinary annual effort to celebrate the birth of Christ. The nativity scene in Saint Cecilia des Dames now enjoys near-legendary status of international standing. This fame is due to, in no small part, my films of it in action which I posted online and which subsequently went somewhat viral. Throughout the week preceding its unveiling, retired men with cordless drills, timber and bottles of wine are to be seen hammering and sawing away next to the cavernous doors of the church. The result is, at first glance, a fairly run-of-the-mill nativity scene with the standard Jesus, Mary, Joseph, shepherds and array of furry (and notably European-looking) farm animals. How looks can deceive. As the unsuspecting member of the public approaches the scene, all suddenly bursts into life (courtesy of gnome magic, although some killjoys claim there is a movement sensor tucked away somewhere). Firstly, the farm animals - in all their two-dimensional animatronic glory - nod up and down, as if consuming the hay which has been artfully super-glued to their snouts. As if that isn't enough, angels actually descend from above, their fishing-wire suspensions barely visible behind rickety plywood clouds. The *tour de force* though is saved for the end of the cycle. The baby Jesus - looking suspiciously like a discarded *Tiny Tears* doll from the 1980's wrapped in a knitted sleeping bag contributed by the local ladies' activity group - *rises up* before... well, lying back down again. I interpreted this as a theological anticipation of the risen Christ but my friends, in apparent disagreement, told me to 'shut up and get a life you weirdo'. Now small coachloads of sightseers turn up to witness our *spectacle*, rivalling Lascaux Caves and Saint Emilion as tourist attractions, especially after nightfall when the effect is enhanced by some nifty lighting. It lacks music at present but, at the next *commune* meeting, I intend to propose the addition of Christmas-themed *Europop*.

It troubles me deeply that the local church appears to be disengaged from these endeavours and other community activities in the village. I have yet to see a priest in a frock and hi-vis jacket, hammer-in-hand, contributing to the above-mentioned construction. When I look back at the dozens of concerts we've organised in the church building, never have I seen a member of the clergy present. We are obliged to write to the boss-priest in begging tones to ask permission to hold concerts in the building and to submit a programme to ensure all music performed is morally appropriate. We have yet to be dignified with a response so we just go ahead anyway.

One Spring, I was asked to perform a concert in a huge church in Mussidan. I was delighted to have been invited but, a fortnight before the event, I received a call from a lady who was part of the church committee. I had been summoned to outline my programme to the priest-in-charge, to ensure it was suitable for delivery in the hallowed surroundings of 'his' building. I was being scrutinised and potentially, censored. Not since the 1990's had I been asked to do anything like this. On that occasion, I was touring in Brunei with a group of Welsh artists on behalf of the British Council who were promoting UK education. There was to be a concert in a large hall to celebrate our visit and, the day before the performance, we were obliged to go to the venue and perform our programme, donning our full concert dress, to a panel of three censors. I am a confident performer but playing for three humourless blokes in a hall capable of holding five hundred people was supremely weird. The strangeness was heightened by the fact that they were in Arab dress and I was wearing black-tie;

communication was impossible due to the lack of a shared language. I played like a donkey. Anyway, I must have done something right as we were allowed to proceed with the gig.

So I went to *Monsieur le Priest's* home with a feeling of *déjà vu.* As I walked in, he barely acknowledged me, seemingly more concerned with eating cheese and bread than welcoming a guest. The lady from the committee explained the event to him and I listened, like an invisible spectator, as my programme was unveiled. A murmur appeared to suggest my performance would be acceptable, not that *Monsieur le Priest* was going to attend the event at any rate. Upon leaving his cavernous home, I failed to shut the door properly and his two large and frisky dogs escaped. They took off in the direction of the *route nationale* towards Bergerac. I felt I had other things to do rather than help to catch them.

On a Sunday, a mass in our village will pull twelve or so elderly folk, rattling around in a space capable of housing over two hundred worshippers. It strikes me a smiling priest at a concert, bursting at the seams with a non-church-going public, would have a great opportunity to meet people, build relationships and develop a congregation. We'd happily let him say a few words of welcome beforehand and even advertise a mass or two. The Catholic Church is dying in France. Recent research estimates only one in twenty French attend masses regularly, and the vast majority of attendees are elderly. Baptisms have fallen by 25% since 2000 and Catholic marriages by 40%. I believe the reason for this lies wholly at the church's own doorstep. It seems to have forgotten the original word 'church' translates as 'a gathering of people' and has nothing to do with bricks and mortar. I have no wish to be unfavourable in my observations of the French Catholic Church, but I am genuinely bemused as to the thinking behind the closed-door policy I have witnessed.

In a long conversation with a saxophonist from our village Big Band, I was quite aggressively challenged regarding my own faith. We were at a post-rehearsal *casse croute* – an expression which translates as 'break crust' - and surrounded by laughter and warmth as we spoke. She told me the gathering which we were attending at that moment was her 'church'. I couldn't have agreed any more with that definition. How could I defend an organisation which had made no visible effort to bring the community together?

There is a church in Aquitaine which was set up in 1825 to serve the long-standing English-speaking population in the area. The Chaplaincy of Aquitaine does extraordinary work and we have met many spiritual and genuinely-caring people who serve there. It couldn't be more different from the sorry picture I've painted above. The Chaplaincy uses old Catholic Church buildings in small villages which were falling into ruin. It organises meals, quiz nights, walks, talks, book exchanges, children's activities, cultural events and more. Many Anglophones, and increasingly French, find community, comfort brotherhood and sisterhood within this fine organisation. We were deeply touched when, at the height of our financial crisis, we received help in the most powerful way from the congregation and friends of The Chaplaincy of Aquitaine. I was working every available hour to complete our cattery building while holding down a day job and trying to be a good Dad and husband. One January, I was exhausted and depressed. Out-of-the-blue, we received an email from a friend at church who had arranged a chain-gang to come to our home for a day (with our blessing of course) bringing tools, expertise, energy, good humour and food. For eight hours, ten men and ladies hammered, screwed, nailed, lifted, joined, glued, pinned, laughed and ate at *Chez Jones*. Some of them were even worse at DIY than I am, but it didn't matter. This is church and the experience reaffirmed in my mind what the essence of the Christian faith should be.

Hallowe'en has crept into French culture just as it has in the UK. Sadly, even during our time in France, we've noticed the supermarkets becoming increasingly packed with plastic Hallowe'en junk during October. In our village though, the evening is beautifully managed. We tend to make it a group event and tag on an excuse for a glass of something reviving at its conclusion. In some urban environments, Hallowe'en has become a menace – a kind of authorised form of extortion. Before we left for France, I grew sick to the back teeth of my door being rapped on October 31st by bored-looking teenagers in no apparent costume of any kind demanding 'trick-or-treat'. This translated as 'give us a quid or we'll egg your car'. I must say though that Scotland, where I am living and working at this moment, wins the Hallowe'en prize hands-down. Here, children are required to earn a treat. This may be via a song, a dance or a joke. It's genuinely charming. In rural French areas, many of the older folk had no concept of Hallowe'en. Rather than allowing kids to knock on anyone's and everyone's doors, we tended to do a reconnaissance trip beforehand and forewarn certain households whom we knew would welcome the youngsters. We also limited the activity to about an hour so we could go back to someone's home and kick off the serious activities of eating and drinking.

For our last Saint Cecilia des Dames Hallowe'en, the responsibility of the post-trick-or-treating refreshments fell to us. A group of children in a range of gruesome outfits gathered in the living room to examine the diabetes-inducing sugar feast which they had amassed, and we adults popped open some Breton *cidre doux* in the kitchen. It was all most convivial.

'Kaboom!!!'

Without warning, the house was rocked to its foundations by one of the almighty explosions which appear to be a fairly run-of-the-mill occurrence in Saint Cecilia des Dames. This one was so impressive though, people from several households dashed into the street. Across the way from *Chez Jones,* standing in an empty cornfield, an enormous bonfire raged with the remnants of a nuclear-mushroom-like cloud dissipating into the night sky. In the distance, staggering away in a zig-zag fashion could be seen a local farm-hand. After a few minutes, it was clear the show was over, and there was no apparent opportunity for a free drink, so we all returned inside.

It transpired the young farm-hand in question had decided to light a bonfire on Hallowe'en to burn some garden waste. It seems he selected the wrong accelerant and had also mistaken 'millilitres' with 'litres' when distributing what must have been surprising quantities of fuel on to his pile. He'd then casually chucked a match at it. Joking aside, the incident necessitated a hospital visit, but he was OK, give or take a few flash burns. His eyebrows had been completely obliterated in the flames, as had his fringe. Upon his return home later that evening, his hairdresser wife decided the only way in which he could look remotely respectable was to shave off his entire thatch. On the school run the next day, he looked like an ostrich egg which had fallen asleep on the beach in Benidorm. Rather than offer concern and sympathy, the menfolk of the village (myself included) took the p**s mercilessly. As I've said elsewhere: boys will be boys.

Maybe it relates to the French love of a *spectacle,* but some people really go the extra mile when putting on a Hallowe'en show. In 2015 a family who owned an acre of woodland proposed a Hallowe'en knees-up. As a 'treat', the gentleman of the house spent a few days preparing a spooky walk through the forest to delight and entertain the village children. He became rather carried away with the project and ended up with a sound system hooked up in the trees emitting a range of howls and screams. Ambient lighting concealed in gnarled tree stumps and obliging friends hiding in the bushes added a certain authenticity the eerie installation. His masterpiece though was a zip wire suspended twelve feet above the ground which guided a white dress mounted on a coat hanger between two trees a good forty metres apart. The fruits of his creative imagination were funny and rather charming in a 1950's-retro-house-of-horror kind of way in the light of day, but when they were released upon ten tired, sugar-fuelled and already-spooked primary-school children in the blackness of night, the effect was altogether different. The first twenty minutes of that particular party was spent pacifying trembling and sobbing infants. Thankfully, at least half of them had been too terrified to enter the woods in the first place – their caution justified by the reaction of their peers.

Other traditions from the Anglo-American worlds have also taken hold in France. The tooth-fairy for example, is wholly Anglophile but she (fairies are always girls, right?) delegates infant-dental-collection duties to a mouse in rural French areas. The *souris* is expected to leave a handful of euros for each milk tooth gathered.

Aside from such tomfoolery though, we found our beliefs, habits and interests changed with our new rhythms of life. Kirsty grew some amazing vegetables in the patch André had helped us to prepare some years before; he also shared his advice with passion and boundless generosity. In one conversation over the garden fence, Kirsty asked him when she should plant her carrot seeds. He paused and thought for a moment, appearing to be doing some mental calculations of a mathematical nature.

"On April 4th, but in the afternoon, not the morning," came his reply.

We laughed, thinking he was making a kind of surrealist joke but he was, in fact, absolutely serious. André gardened by the rhythms of the moon and followed these to the hour. It sounds like medieval nonsense but every time someone challenged his unscientific approach, my wordless response would be to lead them to the edge of our garden and invite them to look at his vegetable 'patch'. It was the size of half a football pitch and permanently groaning with produce, whatever the season. Before long, we were the proud owners of gardening volumes giving year-by-year planting instructions aligned to the position of the moon. These were available from the local supermarket rather than a hippy website.

What a joy it is to grow one's own food! Kirsty successfully grew melons, carrots, radishes, leeks, onions, courgettes and potatoes to name just a few. We planted our spuds *en famille* in the springtime and I can still recall the magical day when we harvested them; the children enraptured by the bounty of goodness which nature had generated, out of sight, beneath the soil. They learned how the earth can act as a natural larder for potatoes and would often join me to dig up a few for that evening's dinner.

André had dug a well in his garden in the 1950's. He had been assisted by a local gentleman employing divining rods to locate the source of water running some seven metres underground. For more than half-a-century, through the most severe of droughts, he has never been connected to mains water and has enjoyed an unlimited supply. I use André's well water for my homebrewing activities as the taste is far superior to the chlorinated alternative. When admiring this facility during one garden *aperitif,* André gave me the telephone number of a diviner who enjoyed sufficient trade to own a small shop in nearby Mussidan.

We learned to observe and acknowledge the wonders of nature. In particular, the bird-life is truly astonishing in South West France. Each summer, a pair of storks comes to nest on L'Isle and we would watch in awe as they soared overhead, seeking food for their young. For three consecutive years, we also hosted a pair of redstarts who had constructed their nest on a shoulder-high shelf in our garage. What a joy to show our children the little heads and frenzied beaks of the new-born chicks as they squawked for a meal of maggots and moths. Their mum would dive-bomb us if we came too close so we soon learned to maintain a respectful distance. After a couple of weeks, the fledglings would nervously fly around the rafters of the garage, apprehensive of confronting the world until eventually, making their break to freedom.

We were deeply fortunate to witness bird-life of incredible beauty and scarcity, but I am embarrassed to say that much of it had completely bypassed our notice until we welcomed friends from Pontypridd who are keen twitchers. Lesley and George were on holiday in France and had called by to share a barbecue when, without warning, Lesley leapt from her chair sending potato salad and ketchup flying into my lap.

"Golden Oriole!!!" she exclaimed in a peculiar whisper-scream.

"Actually Lesley, it's Golden Pride, but I'm glad you like it," I replied, a little confused.

"Not the beer you dimwit!" she said uncharitably, "It's a Golden Oriole!"

In the field adjacent to our garden hovered a beautiful bird with the most incredible golden chest and head set off against deep-black wings and eyes that appeared to sport heavy eye-shadow worthy of a 1960's Soul Diva. This bird is so rare in the UK that the RSPB actually count the number of individuals which pass annually. At the time was writing, the last count was eighty-five. No wonder she was excited. We later realised, a little ashamedly, that this little bird was one of a breeding pair. Spotting such a combination was, in the life of the average twitcher, the equivalent of winning the lottery twice. They had been our near-neighbours for many weeks, annual visitors for years, and we'd heard their shrill, flutey whistles as part of our everyday soundscape. Due to our preoccupations with the necessities of life, we had neglected to stop and actually take notice of them. From that day on though, we appreciated them fully - as we did the hoopoe bird, with its uncanny resemblance to Woodstock from *Peanuts,* which arrived from Africa every springtime, and the collared doves who successfully reared a clutch of chicks on our outside floodlight. I refrained from switching on the light for a few months, lest we ended up with dry-baked eggs as a consequence.

Every spring and autumn we were blessed with a phenomenon which could bring either joy or gloom in equal measure. Our area of South West France is part of the slender migration corridor taken by cranes as they fly between their breeding grounds in the Scandinavian countries and Spain. They are an utterly majestic and awe-inspiring sight. One afternoon, I counted literally thousands as they passed overhead in flocks of around fifty or sixty. More extraordinary though is the eerie song they make as they pass - possibly for navigation purposes. The locals cheerily refer to this as 'the cry of the souls of the dead'. During the day it is beautiful and mystical; at night though, the sound is rather spooky. One evening, I was carrying out my oral-syphoning-of-heating-oil-into-the-fuel-tank duty when they passed low in the night sky. It was drizzling slightly, the misty air creating an atmosphere akin to that of a campfire ghost story. The haunting cries distracted me enough to swallow sufficient fuel so the next day's bathroom visits were undertaken well-clear of naked flames. The contrasting emotions allied with the cranes were because their journey south, undertaken in late autumn, announced the coming of winter, whereas the opposite journey in spring heralded the arrival of the warmer seasons. Their passage acted as an uncannily-accurate barometer.

The real living in the French countryside takes place well after the cranes have headed north, that is to say during the glorious summer holidays. Oh, how we adored the months of July and August, where every day seemed to be hot, lazy and full of laughs. Family and friends came to visit and together we built precious memories - epic games of crickoot (a football/cricket hybrid game Sam and I invented) in the garden, improbable stunts involving trampolines and rubber rings in our above-ground swimming pool, and grappling our way up trees, grabbing at the deep-red bunches of cherries which were *just* out reach of the ladder. In the evening, little green frogs would attach themselves to our French doors (or are they just 'doors' in France?) and the patio would attract meaty, warty toads when rain fell. The French word for toad: *'crapaud'* – pronounced 'crappo' - remains one of my favourites.

The hot season awoke a wealth of wildlife. We commonly encountered sizeable snakes in the chickens' area which would give us quite a start as they slithered away - some deep-rooted instinct warning our brains that the snake equalled danger. The vast majority of French snakes are harmless and in fact, they are the preferred snack of chickens, so it was the serpent who had everything to be afraid of. It is apparently the small snakes or *vipers* which have the potential to deliver a nasty bite. Kirsty once uncovered one when lifting a tarpaulin from a rabbit hutch and my father-in-law, who is converting our garage into an apartment, came eye-to-eye with another when standing on a ladder holding a trowel full of cement (my father-in-law, not the *viper*). In the evenings, the air would be thick with the sound of chirping crickets and croaking frogs. The noise was so loud, some nights we'd be unable to sleep. It didn't matter though. The cacophony was more bewitching than any man-made musical masterpiece.

On Tuesday evenings in July and August, as already mentioned elsewhere, we attended a food and drink festival hosted by little village of Le Pizou. Diners brought along their own plates, cutlery and glasses, and then ambled around a gallery of stalls where local vendors offered an amazing array of local produce: snails, *anduoille,* chilled sweet white wine, deep red *Merlots*, *frites,* steaks, *confit de canard* and *pain de campagne.* Once we'd purchased sufficient foodstuffs to supply the New Zealand First XV, we joined literally thousands of other diners to feast, installing ourselves on long lines of shared tables and benches. As the evening progressed and the wine flowed, the focus turned to the grand stage set up at the centre of the village square. Here, acts of outstanding entertainment and novelty value took to the *scene,* usually offering songs of the traditional or *Europop* variety with a few phonetically-reproduced English-language classics thrown in for good measure. In the latter case, the entertainers clearly had no idea of what they were singing which made it all the more entertaining for us Anglophones.

One year, Kirsty's uncle and his family were visiting us for their *vacances* and had joined us for the inimitable Le Pizou experience. I was in a particularly good mood having enjoyed the spectacle of seeing him attempting to consume a snail and nearly spitting it in the face of the chortling lady who had offered him the sample. Tony is a fine chef, a writer and he knows his music, but I bet he'd never seen anything like this. A girl/boy vocal duo took the stage to entertain us. They were the type of singers who perform to backing tracks and they dished out every cliché known to mankind. Resplendent in a *diamanté* double-belt, deep-blue eyeshadow, rose-red lipstick and a pink, body-hugging T-

Shirt, singer number one certainly turned heads. The young girl who followed him was pretty good too. My own favourite performer though was a handsome and youthful virtuoso accordionist whose fingers flew around his highly sequin-adorned instrument, like Joe Satriani and Eddie Van Halen on speed. For a profoundly memorable part of his act, he ran the length of a dining table, sending snails and baguettes flying, to the wild applause of the youths and simultaneous curses from ladies of a certain age, all the while shredding the riff to AC/DC's *Thunderstruck* on his squeeze-box.

The months of fine weather also sees the culmination of the *vide grenier* or *brocante* season. *'Vide grenier'* translates as 'empty attic' and such events are enormous car-boot and jumble sales. A *brocante* usually suggests a specialist shop or gathering of traders, like a bric-a-brac or antique fair. We took Matthew and Sophie to a huge *vide grenier* in Montpon Ménestérol where I introduced them to one of my favourite pastimes – seeing who could locate and, finances permitting, purchase the most useless item of the day. The more unfathomable the purpose of the item, the higher the points tally. After ten minutes of sniffing around, I leapt in delight as I spotted a forlorn-looking gentleman at a stall selling a huge sack of surprisingly life-like plastic pigeons, each one mounted on a stake which had been artfully shoved vertically between its host's legs.

"Combien?" I asked the seller, hopping from left to right like an infant needing the toilet.

"Vingt euros," replied the vendor speculatively. He was clearly the most surprised person in town.

"Twenty euros! What a bargain!" I exclaimed to my wife whose face wore an expression which suggested that the proposed transaction was unlikely to come to fruition, but I was undeterred.

In my mind's eye, I envisaged planting a series of dummy pigeons around the garden and then concealing myself in a specially-constructed dugout to learn what would happen when the cats charged at them. As already discussed, both our moggies enjoyed a good bunny-hunt and they would also launch themselves at the flocks of birds which settled on our field. I was desperate to see what would unfold if a cat tore towards a flock which remained immobile as it approached. Would the cat attack anyway or would it turn on its paws and sprint off, befuddled by this change in the pecking order, so to speak? As my mind raced, I imagined advancing my inert pigeon army inch-by-inch towards the house in the small hours, even organising them in Roman-Legion-inspired military formations such as a triple line, wedge or classic pincer arrangement to really mess with the cats' heads.

"It will be *scientific research!*" I argued unconvincingly. "Think of what the children will *learn* by witnessing this unique reversal of roles in the natural world! They will have a *huge* advantage in biology class!"

"Oui! C'est vrai!" chipped in the vendor encouragingly, barely able to believe his luck.

"Pleeease!" I ventured, going for the 'whinging child approach' in my effort to prise open the *Famille Jones* wallet (I think the vendor may have joined me in a spontaneous chorus).

For reasons which I am unable to fathom, the deal failed to materialise and I can only assume that it will be someone else's children collecting a Nobel Prize in thirty years' time, the seeds of their scientific passion having been sowed by a sack of fake birds and the mistreatment of domesticated animals.

Select your *vide grenier* with care. *La Famille Jones* attended a few which were little more than a couple of families trying to flog off three-limbed Barbie dolls for a fiver apiece. The disappointment of such an eventuality is usually tempered by the inevitable presence of a bar and *grillade* where one can gather, eat, drink and stare at the perhaps ill-judged purchases which had seemed like such a good idea only minutes before. The truth is one man's *vide grenier* can all-too-easily become another man's *remplir grenier* (fill attic).

Rural areas are attracting a new type of inhabitant. In recent years, we have witnessed an influx of actors, artists and those interested in the organic movement. These are people who recognise there is a genuine alternative lifestyle to be lived out there, and this might mean something other than communal living in a tepee with a heavily bearded guru wearing sackcloth called Dorian Rainbow.

In our final year before leaving France, we befriended a couple of actors who had moved from Bordeaux. This extraordinary pair had, within a year, turned a rickety old barn into a fully-functioning theatre, and had started putting on *spectacles*. The villagers have attended their shows in droves and wholeheartedly back the enterprise.

People are seeing the value in living life at a different pace, countering a society which has become obsessed with convenience, where shopping must be completed at lightning speed and every whim catered for. The weekly shopping trip remains a social routine for many in the Perigord. Like in 1980's Britain, one can expect to wait in a queue at a till, but most people enjoy the opportunity to exchange pleasantries and *bises* with other shoppers. In our area, supermarkets supply goods which are in season and the prices of these fluctuate accordingly. Consequently, you may find it difficult to locate an Asian root vegetable in mid-winter in a French supermarket, never mind how much you may want it for a special dish. Food is expensive and, as my organic farming friends would argue, so it should be. We must ask ourselves what kind of world we have created when we saturate the land with pesticides so we can have cheap, seedless grapes all-year round, regardless of the consequences. Even more bonkers is that if we discovered pesticides limited internet connectivity, we'd be howling to have them banned. As all they do is slowly poison us and our eco-system, we're prepared to let them go. It still tickles me to find baked beans in the 'foreign foods' section, next to the Marmite.

In contrast to this sedate existence, I've observed a type of behaviour which I've named *Wannabe Urbanism*. This is where families who have lived rurally for generations work like mad to obtain modern-day trappings, conveniences and so-called luxuries for their kids, mistakenly believing this to be 'progress'. I taught a charming young pupil called Luc for many years and watched him grow from a cheery young boy to a strapping teenager. He's undoubtedly a fine lad with likeable parents who truly want the best for him, yet week-upon-week I cringed as Luc breezed into my teaching room – empty-handed except for a state-of-the-art phone - closely followed by a staggering mum carrying his guitar, a wriggling toddler and shopping, like a Peruvian llama treading a mountain trail. At the end of the lesson, he would stand, walk briskly past mum, and leave her to pack up the instrument, toddler, baguette and who knows what else. Our little music school is situated on the first floor of the village primary-school building. To access it, one must climb a rickety staircase with a lethal narrow-stepped bend, as well as the odd squashy step. In the UK it would be closed down immediately and the children sent home to learn music staring at an app on a screen. As Mum apparently believed any minute physical exertion was inappropriate for her twenty-first-century city-slicker son, she allowed his burden-free exit to pass without question, despite being obliged to load herself up to the hilt and negotiate the staircase-of-death unaided. One week, I could stand it no longer and called Luc back. He looked genuinely surprised when I suggested that perhaps he could carry his own instrument rather than leaving Mum to balance a toddler on her head as she attempted to avert extreme injury or worse. Mum argued vehemently against my radical proposition, perhaps believing that to ask him to exert the tiniest iota of effort would be akin to setting him to task in the fields gathering the grape harvest in 40-degree heat for eight hours. Maybe she was devising a way in which she could carry Luc as well.

In our village, more mature members of society participate in enriching social activities with vigour. As already discussed, *associations* will set up schools, clubs and societies in more remote areas and they are usually well-subscribed. It is a joy to see ladies well beyond retirement age (although that may be in their mid-fifties in France) participating with energy and vigour in Zumba evenings, philosophy clubs, choirs and yes, taking up the classical guitar. There is no hint of self-consciousness amongst the grey generation. Maybe it takes until this point in life to release oneself from the shackles of the *je n'arrive pas* mentality.

It is important to understand the sense of humour of a country if one is going to integrate seamlessly. I've read a number of rather insulting accounts of French humour, accusing it of being childish and banal. I'm inclined to disagree. The humour I've encountered has felt very much like that which I experienced in my British social circles. There is one recurring joke, of which I am the butt that I first experienced when I was teaching in Coutras. My teaching room was the old *Syndicate d'Initiative* and therefore had a large glass frontage in a very public place. One evening, I was finishing up a lesson and the next pupil was waiting outside with his family. Out of the corner of my eye, I could see they were glancing at me and enjoying a good snigger. When the scallywag eventually came in, I pressed him to share the joke. Reluctantly, he explained.

"Eet is just, that you ees lookeeng like zee… Top Gear man… Reechard Hammond."

My apparent resemblance to Richard Hammond is a joke which I hear over and over again in France. When the pupil brought a couple of mates along the following week to glance at Mr Hammond's *doppelganger,* I took it on the chin. Turning up with his granny and her neighbours pushed it too far though. Some of my so-called friends have suggested my face resembles Mr Hammond's in the immediate aftermath of one of his spirited accidents which appear to be the cornerstone of his *raison d'etre.* Incidentally, pals in the UK have suggested I'm a dead ringer for Neil Oliver, presenter of the BBC's *Coast,* especially before I had my hair cut. Whereas the original *Top Gear* is as hugely popular in France as it is in the UK, *Coast* remains an enigma here, so the French have yet to spot that one.

France's less-populated areas are enjoying a rise in cooperative economics. We have had the pleasure of witnessing the fruits which can be harvested when an *entrepreneur* acts selflessly. About five kilometres from our home is a family-run dairy farm. The owner, a warm and always-smiling gentleman, had the idea of allowing children to come and watch his cows being milked at 6.00pm each day. This was free of charge. Many attended, as did schools and interested adults. Then he made his fresh, unpasteurised milk available at any hour via a large tank and a tap. You can go along with a receptacle, fill it up and then pop a euro into an honesty box. Children can literally trace the journey from the udder to the pipe, to the tank, to their bottle. How refreshing. Next, *Monsieur le Fermier* laid on a few activities for the kids in his field. This started off with a couple of football goals and a badminton net. Then, the enterprising soul constructed a go-kart track out of tyres and bought some pedal karts. As if this wasn't enough, he designed a maze within his cornfield and planted accordingly. In 2016, he created a foot-golf course in the local woodland. All these activities are free of charge. He just loves sharing good times with people, and believes the rewards will sort themselves out. Sort themselves out they have indeed. As an aside, the farm started making ice-cream. It is stunning and quite simply the best ice-cream on Planet Earth (and perhaps beyond). He set up a wooden shed next to the activities field to allow visitors to seek refreshment at a fair price. Soon after, he had the idea of inviting local food producers to sell their wares on a Thursday evening. Within a month or two, his Thursday events had reached a scale to rival Tuesdays at Le Pizou, although this had never been the intention. All that it is lacks is an accordion-hero. *La Famille Jones* started frequenting the farm when it was a modest ice-cream shack with pleasant activities for the kids. Last year, I sat with friends under an orange sky, drinking my home-brew *(Monsieur le Fermier* is happy for people to bring along a picnic) and wondering where the kids had disappeared to when I spotted our host. He was strolling across the grass, smiling as always, but looking a little dazed. He had just completed a ball-park head-count and, upon reaching eight hundred folks, decided to go and lie down for a bit. This year he has turned a defunct combine-harvester into a climbing frame and slide. I'm just waiting for the tractor roller-coaster.

***

Love Thy Neighbour, Love Thy Life – The Essential Tips

(1) Being polite is good but being passive and disproportionately grateful is simply annoying.

(2) Rural folk are often different. If they are sincere, go with it. Avoid judging.

(3) An animatronic all-singing, all-dancing nativity scene is an excellent proposition as a destination for your local taxes - far more important than weekly bin collections in my book.

(4) The English-language church in the Dordogne is a great organisation, full of good, non-judgemental people who speak their faith through their actions.

(5) Shut the door properly when visiting a priest, especially if he owns large dogs.

(6) Help organise a good, wholesome Hallowe'en event and host the party afterwards. Look out for rogue explosions.

(7) Take time to observe nature and its unexplained phenomena. You will feel awestruck and inspired.

(8) The summer is at the heart of Rural French life. Live it to the full.

(9) Seek out *Europop*-inspired accordionists. Your musical tastes will be changed forever.

(10) Support cooperative economics. You'll be amazed and privileged to witness what happens.

Figure 12 Flo and Sam planting potatoes.

15. War and Peace

Fain wad I, fain wad I hae the bloody wars to cease,
An' the nations restored again to unity an' peace;
Then mony a bonnie laddie, that's now far owre the sea,
Wad return to his lassie, an' his ain countrie.

Andrew Scott - *The Young Maid's Wish for Peace* (Scotland)

We had lived in our little village for a couple of years before I became aware of the area's dark history during the years of World War II. Saint Cecilia des Dames is situated only a few kilometres away from the boundary between German Occupied France and the so-called Free Zone or Vichy France and many harrowing events had passed just a few kilometres from our doorstep. It seemed every town, village or hamlet held its own secrets from the era.

Through one of my frequent discourses with neighbour André, I began to understand the war's direct impact on the inhabitants of our village. On one particularly revealing day, we had taken weekly delivery of a vegetable box from a local organic farmer. Part of the pleasure of receiving the box was that we never knew quite what it would contain; the content and quantity of vegetables received would vary according to the season. Often, we'd discover plants which were completely alien to us, but this obliged us to be more creative with our cooking and to develop our tastes. One such box contained something which resembled a purple cricket ball. We had no idea what to do with it so, as a lame excuse for a pre-lunch *aperitif,* I popped over to consult André who was the indisputable veg-expert of the Dordogne. We comfortably installed ourselves on his patio, sipping a glass of my latest homebrew.

"Now, what can I do for you today Dan?" he asked me.

I pulled the mysterious vegetable from my pocket and handed it to him.

"I was wondering if you could help me identify this please André."

André took the item from my hand and fingered it gently. Some moments passed as he sniffed it and slowly rolled it between his gnarled hands, establishing its texture. He then looked at me, slightly glassy-eyed.

"Did you pay for this?" he asked.

"Bien sur!" I replied, wondering if he thought I'd pinched it from his garden in a nocturnal veggie-raid.

Slowly but surely a broad smile worked its way across his features; then he started to laugh. As was the tradition when I did something daft he called Eliane to share in the mirth.

André told me a revealing anecdote. He had lived in the area during the Second World War when he was just a boy. At the conclusion of this dire conflict, the infrastructure of Europe was destroyed and in rural areas, there was no food. André described how he and his friends learned to grow food and also to forage, not as a hobby but out of necessity. The vegetable which I was holding was easily grown and therefore eaten most days, yet was detested by the youngsters of the time. It was a rutabaga - a turnip to all intents and purposes. How fickle and shallow are we in this modern age? The beggar's food, due to its novelty, has become *haut cuisine*. Not for the first time, I felt awestruck conversing with a man who had watched SS vehicles rumbling past our homes, looked into the eyes of their drivers, and heard gunshots emitting from their weapons before he was out of his teens.

The town of Mussidan, just a few kilometres from our village, has a museum dedicated to its history. The majority of its contents show the ancient tools which worked the land in bygone years. In 2015, I had performed a very pleasant yet taxing concert there with a flautist and a harpist. After we'd packed up, one of the volunteers at the museum offered us a personal tour. Having just given a two-hour recital, preceded by three days of intensive rehearsal, I was *absolutely* in the mood for looking at a vast collection of rusty scythes at 10.00pm. Anyway, my co-players seemed genuinely riveted at the prospect so off we went. Some distance into the tour we approached a collection of military memorabilia; I saw one small exhibit which humanised an appalling yet compelling series of events.

In 1944, a Nazi armoured train was attacked by the *Résistance* in Mussidan. A raging battle ensued with heavy casualties taken on both sides. The train and its cargo of weapons were destroyed. As an act of retaliation, the SS took fifty-two men and shot them in broad daylight, in front of their friends and families, on the steps of Mussidan's town hall. The museum's exhibit was a little book which attempted to identify and honour the victims. The age-range caused a shudder pass through my body. Some were of post-retirement age, others were mere teenage boys. What really moved me though was, in assembling the book, the writers had attempted to find photographs of each of the deceased. Many had black silhouettes where their images should have been. If you were a working man in 1940's Mussidan, taking pleasure snaps would have been well down the list of priorities. In my mind, these silhouetted men had been erased from existence in every way possible. I was deeply touched and found myself silenced by a lump in my throat at this representation of young lives, never given the chance to live, love or be recorded in image.

If anything to raise a smile can be gleaned from such a dark tale, it is a rumour which is rife in our little corner of France. The train is alleged to have contained money and gold, as well as military equipment. Legend has it the bounty was stolen and buried in the woods nearby. Consequently, metal detector enthusiasts have explored la Forêt de la Double with more than the usual zeal and tenacity but with little success. It is said though, some families living humble lives in *la Forêt* became inexplicably affluent in the years after the war - turning up to local markets in sports cars and dressed in the latest designer-*chic* fashions of the day.

The Jewish community endured petty prejudices at the time which were grotesquely magnified with the arrival of a diabolically anti-Semitic aggressor. There is a pretty village about twenty kilometres from our home called St Privat des Pres. One Sunday, we visited friends who live there and after lunch went for a walk, particularly to see the beautiful church which is its centrepiece. I inspected the interior and enjoyed its incredible acoustic yet upon departing, I noticed a modest memorial stone to the side of the building. Closer inspection revealed it to be a monument to fifty victims of the war. There is an inscription on the stone which I have translated below.

In July and October 1942, in this village, 50 people, including 18 children were arrested by the Vichy Police, because they were born Jewish, deported and assassinated at Auschwitz by the Nazis.

Then the names and ages of the victims are listed which include the following:

Henri 2 ans, Eliane 2 ans, Isidore 3 ans…

And so it continues.

As if this woeful tale could worsen, a little research revealed these people were betrayed by their community. Feeling threatened, the Jews sought escape and refuge. They were apparently told to meet 'friends' in the centre of the village on a set day at nightfall, where they were in fact met by the military who took them away, never to return. There had been a history of petty jealousy and financial feuds between cultures, yet I find it impossible to believe the non-Jewish villagers would have been prepared to send them to their deaths. Maybe I'm being charitable but I want to believe that the villagers anticipated restrictions on the Jew's business activities and perhaps a hike in the level of taxes imposed on them. It is worth noting fifty people would have been a very substantial percentage of the entire village's population. One can walk its length in less than fifteen minutes. I wanted to know more about this particular event and had the idea to compose an elegy for the victims. I wrote to the village council to ask for more details. I received no reply.

I sense these prejudices mirror those experienced by the Muslim community today, fuelled by the incomprehensible agenda of the Le Pen family. Mr Le Pen appears to have issues against any ethnic group differing from his own: Muslims, Turks and Jews - you name them, he's insulted them. Le Pen has famously and publically described the Holocaust as a 'minor detail in history' on a number of occasions. Maybe if it were his kids who were gassed in a filthy, freezing concentration camp, he'd feel differently. The *Front National* claims to stand up for the ordinary working French family and implies the country's woes are due to immigration. Perhaps a portion of the culpability should lie at the doorstep of those who enjoy millions of euros worth of property assets, as do the Le Pens. Strangely, the ranting speeches to the ordinary folk of *la France* given by the present leader, Marine Le Pen, fail to highlight this fact. It seems that there is serious money to be made in the hatred game. Marine Le Pen has made strident efforts towards making a right-wing nationalist party fuzzier and more cuddly, as if she is the kind of nationalist who hand-rears abandoned chinchillas for the benefit of orphaned children. Her last general election campaign used the slogan 'Restoring Order to France', in an attempt to appeal to the *'il faut'* mentality. Laughably, every time she eased her party towards something resembling credibility, her retired father would pop up like a stubborn rash, and re-indulge his preferred hobby of making insulting and racist remarks. The delighted reaction of the party's followers indicated that the leopard may have been wearing a glamorous new overcoat, but the spots underneath were well-and-truly unchanged. Ultimately, as Marine watched the fruits of her PR department's efforts unravel agonisingly before her very eyes, she was forced to do the unthinkable and expel her dad from the very party he founded. That must make for an awkward Christmas dinner at his multimillion euro mansion in the leafy Parisian suburb of Saint-Cloud (did he fail to mention that one as well?). The problem for Marine is, although *Papa* is no longer a member, he continues to seek attention, like a resentful, needy bully in the school playground who picks on the weak and vulnerable. Gullible and disillusioned listeners continue to gather whenever and wherever he and his unrestrained mouth choose to make an appearance. I bet Marine wishes he would back crawl under the stone from whence he came - out of sight and mind - at least that's one point of view she shares with minority groups.

I speak occasionally with one of my former lecturers who is very knowledgeable in history, as well as music. He was able to locate a book for me, in French, which is a tribute to those who had been the victims of Nazi barbarism in the Dordogne: *Mémorial de la Résistance en Dordogne… Sous la terreur Nazie.* (A.N.A.C.R. Dordogne, 1985). This little book is both profoundly moving and deeply shocking, revealing the horror and brutality experienced by even the tiniest of hamlets.

As I make my way through the country lanes of la Forêt de la Double, I pass villages such as Saint-André-de-Double, St-Etienne de Puycorbier, St-Barthélémy-de-Bellegarde, Saint-Martial-d'Artenset and hundreds of others. These places are very much 'blink-and-you-miss-them' but every one holds secrets of unspeakable cruelty. The main Nazi tactic appeared to be that of hostage-taking. For every soldier lost on the field of battle, the occupiers would take a man and publically execute him. This would often be preceded by horrific torture, and after death, the body displayed publically as a grisly warning to others.

Maybe villages in our area are trying to move on from what happened, or perhaps they are still trying to understand their own role in the events which unfolded, but I was struck by how many *communes* appeared to have chosen *not* to contribute to this publication. I feel that a community has to find the correct balance between acknowledging the past – be it in memory of those lost in combat or accepting catastrophic misjudgements – and looking to the future with a spirit of acceptance and cooperation. The fact that the ever-deceitful extreme right enjoys worrying popularity in many of this magnificent, cultured and diverse country's rural expanses suggests that there are adjustments to be made.

***

War and Peace – The Essential Tips

Hindsight is easy. Avoid judgement. Respect others.

Figure 13 Monument to Jewish victims of the Nazi occupation.

16. I Am the Music Man, I Come From Far Away

Je cherche des musiciens,
De quel instrument jouez-vous ?
Nous sommes des musiciens
Et nous jouons de la guitare
Guit guit guitare

I am looking for musicians
What instrument do you play?
We are musicians
And we play the guitar
Guit guit guitar

Traditional -*Je Cherche des Musiciens*
(I am Looking For Musicians – France)

The guitar has been central to my very being ever since I can remember. The fire was lit in my musical heart by *Here Comes the Sun* by The Beatles - my late mum being a great fan of the Fab Four. The flames were further fanned by John Williams' rendition of the beautiful *Cavatina* by Stanley Myers, with which I fell in love as a child watching *The Gallery* during the legendary art TV series *Take Hart.* After my ninth birthday, I commenced classical guitar lessons but, during my teenage years, the lure of the electric instrument and its potential to command the attention of the opposite sex (or so I prayed) had me hooked.

Upon leaving school, I thought I should probably get a proper job. The 1980's, as anyone old enough to remember will recall, were a time of crippling unemployment in the UK. During my education, the importance of finding a stable career was drilled into us day after day. Earnest-looking teachers in jackets, which frankly needed a visit to the dry cleaners (the jackets rather than the teachers) gave doom-laden assemblies warning of dire consequences should we find ourselves a One-in-Ten.

In 1987, I started working for a high street bank. It was fine, but deep down I was struggling to understand why I was there. I was assured I would have a long and fruitful career, rich in financial reimbursement, and I'd also have a mortgage tied around my neck at a preferable rate. Personal happiness was skated over as a minor detail. In 1992, following great changes in my private life, I succeeded in gaining a place at a music conservatoire as a classical guitarist. I remained there for a total of eighteen years, firstly as an undergraduate student, then for postgraduate studies before finally becoming a tutor upon graduation. Upon reflection, I'm grateful for my experience as a youthful electric guitarist and my years in the nine-to-five working world. When I entered into full-time music training, what I lacked in proficiency was partly compensated for by a significant amount of real-life experience and a burning desire to prove myself.

During my formative years as a classical guitarist, I soon came to understand that a formal concert in a British, urban environment is a structured and rather predictable affair. There is a code of conduct which attendees follow religiously: it is inappropriate to applaud between movements of a piece, a concert will start at 7.35pm if it is billed as 7.30pm and the performer will receive an encore - regardless of whether the audience enjoyed their evening or otherwise. How different my experiences were in our little corner of France.

Upon arrival in the Dordogne, I was a musical unknown. I needed to expand my pupil base pretty sharpish and to present myself as a guitarist for concert work as there were mounting bills looming on the near horizon. The music schools for which I worked were kindly and energetic in organising events where I could showcase my playing. One of my first concerts was in the beautiful *Eglise Notre-Dame-de-la-Paix* in Ribérac. Here I was to share the programme with an organist, a pianist and also accompany a violinist. Upon arrival a couple of hours before the event I was thrown into a world of loosely-organised chaos, more akin to a rock gig than a classical concert. The pianist was using an electric instrument and brought along a degree of sound equipment better suited for Megadeath at Glastonbury rather than Chopin at Ribérac. There was also the preparation of the microphone for the Master of Ceremonies or, as he/she is known, the *animateur* or *animatrice*. This was my first of, sadly, many experiences of the phenomenon I refer to as *Monsieur/Madame Micro*. Attendees of concerts in small French towns appear to believe an evening is incomplete without a local 'character' bellowing benign information down a microphone at a volume akin to strapping one's head against the landing gear of a Boeing 747 in take-off mode. More on this in a moment.

As the starting time of 8.30pm approached - notably later than in the UK - I was prepared. I had changed into a snappy suit and red shirt, completed my warm-up routine, and was poised purposefully on a pew to the left of the stage. At 8.35pm, the pianist was still unloading more equipment - reversing up a truck to the ancient oak door and gathering a team of roadies to stagger in with a second batch of bucket woofers. There was no audience. By 9.00pm, I was anxious and my normal zen-like pre-concert state had evaporated. I felt uneasy at such a casual disregard for the starting time. At least though, the church had gradually filled up nicely. It seemed the French audience knew the protocols just as a British audience knows theirs - they were just singing from a different hymn sheet. In small-town France, there is *no way* that a concert starts at the billed time. It is mutually understood that at 8.30pm, an audience is tucking into *dessert* which will be followed by an *espresso* and the obligatory *digestif.*

Eventually, at 9.15pm, *Monsieur Micro* took to the stage to rapturous applause. I sensed his performance was of equal, or perhaps greater importance to that of the musicians. He proceeded to introduce the performers at a volume which would have made Pete Townshend wince, giving lengthy biographical details of each of us. This was completely unnecessary as he was simply reading the same programme notes which had been handed to every audience member in print, but it was all a necessary step in the procession of events. Whereas I was bored and mildly vexed at this further meaningless delay to the music-making, the audience appeared enraptured, nodding encouragingly at every already-communicated fragment of information. I soon found myself staring vacantly at the ancient stone domed roof above us, concerned the massive vibrations emitting from the PA may cause structural collapse and kill us all before a note was played. Suddenly, I became aware of a sustained round of applause. I looked at the audience and saw all eyes were on me. I had been introduced and, due to the mixture of 10,000 watts of power and my rudimentary knowledge of the language, I'd rather missed my cue. I hastily stood, grinned gormlessly like a kid with his hand caught stuck in the cookie jar, and took a bow.

The first performer was the organist. He was around ninety-seven years of age and barely able to lift his upper body, never mind place the necessary limbs on the organ's keyboards and pedals. Once he had installed himself at his instrument, with generous help from a couple of gentlemen in the audience, I looked at the programme to see the works he was proposing. With considerable surprise, and admittedly some apprehension, I read that he would be offering pieces by Charles Gounod. These virtuosic and massively musically-complex works seemed an extraordinary choice of repertoire for an audience who looked more as if they were up for a touch of easy listening, and a performer who would perhaps have been more at ease in charge of a Zimmer frame.

He commenced, with the volume predictably turned up to eleven. As he crashed his way through the rich, dissonant harmonies – some Gounod's, others of his own inadvertent invention – I found my face wincing into a range of contorted expressions of which I had no idea I was capable. I lost three years' worth of tooth enamel due to a subconscious grinding induced by each wrong note. At every page-turn, he would stop, raise an arm, and agonisingly turn the sheet before continuing his war with the keyboard. The time taken to do this necessitated a substantial pause which suggested a somewhat elastic interpretation of Gounod's rhythms. Some pauses occurred for no immediately apparent reason. At one point, I wondered if *Monsieur l'Orgue* had met his demise at the instrument which would, I suppose, be quite a rock 'n' roll way to go, but no, happily (or otherwise, depending on your musical tastes) he jerked back into life and launched into a new phase of his attack. At least these pauses allowed us respite to grab a tissue and dab at the blood discharging from our eardrums. *Monsieur l'Orgue's* performance was met with rapturous applause – a standing ovation even. I have no idea who was more surprised, me or him.

From this, I learned an audience in the Dordogne *love* to hear works by a French composer. It is perhaps a reassertion of the might of their culture. Bearing in mind many in the audience were elderly, it's possible they remember the war and therefore value their 'Frenchness'. Secondly, I learned the French like to see a bit of effort - they recognised the gladiatorial element of the performance. Yes, all the notes were there (but not necessarily in the right order) but the audience wanted blood, sweat and tears - as if they were watching a monstrous bearded-bloke from Latvia pulling an articulated lorry in *The World's Strongest Man* rather than marvelling at the subtleties of phrasing in Gounod's melodic counterpoint. I think it also relates to the passion they have for a good *spectacle,* the artistic consequences being immaterial. Interestingly, the French also *adore* music of a Celtic origin. I arranged many traditional Celtic songs and melodies for solo guitar and placed these within a classical programme. They went down a storm. Some of them, such as the beautiful song *The Water is Wide,* have been rewritten with French lyrics. *The Water is Wide* has been reproduced as the massively-popular *La Ballade Nord-Irlandaise* by the French singer/songwriter *Renaud.* Whereas the original is a tale of lost love (aren't they all?) *Renaud's* offering is a pacifist song referring to the troubles in Northern Ireland. The other items, including my own offerings, passed off very well – the audience loving my attempts to tell them about the pieces (Bach, Weiss and Villa-Lobos I believe) in French. *Monsieur Micro* looked rather affronted as I was stepping into his territory.

I was interested to see and hear the courteous and reverential silence which one habitually experiences during the actual pieces was absent during this concert, and the dozens of similar events I performed at afterwards. It was regarded as perfectly acceptable practice for a group of ladies to noisily drag a table across the back of the church during the slow movement of a *sonata,* in preparation for the inevitable post-concert *aperitif, digestif* or rather charmingly named *pot d'amitié* (pot of friendship) which is a diplomatic way of saying 'any excuse for a glass of hooch'. To omit this element would be akin to omitting the presence of musicians or even worse, *Monsieur/Madame Micro.*

Concerts were habitually of agonisingly-long length. I would frequently share programmes with choirs in the area and, during pre-concert planning meetings, I would drop to my knees and beg them to discard some of the proposed items. The response would be that the audience would enjoy such-and-such a piece or this would be a nice contrast to that piece, but when buttock has been installed on hard pew for an hour, *Monsieur/Madame Micro* is in full flow and you had that second glass of wine during the pre-concert *aperitif,* believe me, an unbroken hour of music is too long. I played at a choir festival in Perigueux and the well-meaning organiser allowed a young folk singer with a guitar to do 'a small spot' at the beginning of the already-groaning-at-the-seams programme. The result was the young fellow, charming as he was, did that maddening thing all folk guitarist/singers do where he mumbled indistinct introductions, telling stories which went nowhere, all the while strumming airy chords and making meaningless adjustments to his instrument's tuning. We heard about half-an-hour of chit-chat and seven minutes of songs, all before the actual scheduled programme had begun.

One completely surreal event occurred when I shared a programme with a choir in a glorious rural church near

Perigueux. The choir was accompanied, and directed, by my friend Jean-Marie – he who had received the regular dousing in *le Tank*. It was on April 1st and I had turned up to the concert in our Vauxhall Vectra. The French too celebrate this day with practical jokes. Rather than 'April Fool' the French refer to *poisson d'avril* (April Fish). This originates from the practice of attaching a small paper fish to a victim's back with a piece of sticky tape.

I was ten minutes into a challenging section of my programme when I heard the church door bang open in an unceremonious fashion. I recall thinking it was rather early to be preparing the interval drinks, but soon the initial disturbance was followed by raised voices. As I battled on, trying my hardest to retain concentration for the second half of Bach's Gavotte in A minor, the *melée* intensified. Even the regulars - who were accustomed to unscheduled interruptions - became interested and heads began to turn. Eventually, I felt obliged to stop as a full argument was breaking out.

It seemed a gentleman had a grievance as a parked car had blocked about one inch of the driveway to his house. He was the kind of fellow who would put up a 'No Turning' notice at the entrance to his property – even if it was 100 yards from his abode and at the end of a narrow country lane. Audience members berated him in sympathy for the guitarist whose performance had been so rudely interrupted. As I sat there, looking superior, waiting for the owner of the car to be identified and the problem rectified, I overheard part of a sentence, in French, which made my heart sink.

"A grey car with English number plates." *Une voiture grise avec des plaques anglaises.*

And the sickening realisation dawned that it was, in fact, my car.

In a raised whisper, I called Jean-Marie who was about to wade in and eject the fellow forcibly, and explained the rather awkward predicament in which I found myself. He paused, stunned, and I thought for a moment he was going to forcibly eject me instead. Thankfully though, he restrained himself.

"Where are your keys?" he growled, through gritted teeth. *Où sont tes clés?*

Having directed him to the pocket of my discarded jeans, he nobly went to move my car the hair's breadth necessary to pacify the gentleman. The audience settled and I poised myself to restart. But it was impossible. The moment had been destroyed. Instead, I stood and made an announcement in my Welsh-accent-laden French.

"Ladies and Gentlemen, I suggest we share the pot of friendship early," to tumultuous applause and the eternal wrath of *Monsieur Micro* whose toes I had well-and-truly danced a jig upon.

Now, at this point, you may be anticipating these events were an elaborate *poisson d'avril* prank. If only. The whole thing was a reality and demonstrated once again that real-life is much weirder than any stunt humans can devise. To make matters worse (if that were possible) Jean-Marie had devised a prank for the last piece which, in comparison to earlier events, was lame. To close the programme, the choir had sung an arrangement of a comic song by the great Georges Brassens. During the piece, a co-conspirator in the basses had imitated having 'had enough' of the conductor (Jean-Marie) and had stormed up to the rostrum. There, he shoved Jean-Marie out of the way and conducted the remainder of the song himself. Once the piece had concluded, the entire choir pulled paper fish from their pockets and waved them in order to demonstrate all was well and reveal the prank. The problem was that following earlier events, had a UFO landed in the church and abducted two elderly altos for examination by internal probes, the public wouldn't have batted an eyelid. Therefore, the joke fell rather flat.

In 2016, I organised and participated in a tour with my former teacher, John Mills, and his wife Cobie. John is simply one of the finest guitarists of his generation. He is a living, direct link to the greatest players who've ever lived, including Andrés Segovia and John Williams, and has taught at all of the UK's major conservatoires and overseas. His influence on my own musicianship has been immeasurable – I sound like a second-rate John Mills when I play. Cobie is a guitarist of elegance, precision and sheer class.

Travelling by plane with high-value concert instruments is a complex affair. Increasingly, concert guitarists are borrowing instruments from luthiers once they arrive at their destinations. We were very lucky when a highly-gifted guitar maker from Perigueux, Jean Verly, allowed John and Cobie to use two of his exquisite, hand-crafted instruments for the tour. The spirit of kindness and generosity was also apparent when no fewer than three acquaintances offered their homes to host the visiting couple for the entirety of their visit.

We gave five concerts in churches across the Dordogne and the Lot-et-Garonne. Perhaps the most extraordinary evening was when we performed in the *Église Monolithe* in Aubeterre-sur-Dronne. This incredible underground church was hewn out of the rock by monks in the 12th Century, although work may have originated some 500 years earlier. It was concealed by rock-falls until the 1950's when its 20-metre high caverns were, once again, revealed. To give a concert in such a spiritual, timeless place, playing alongside such brilliant musicians was indeed, humbling.

For musicians playing with rock or pop bands, the working life in the French countryside is markedly different from that in urban centres. My extensive experience in the UK demonstrated that bands who played the usual repertoire of done-to-death cover versions found a regular stream of work, but were relegated to living life as human jukeboxes. Anything creative or original was relegated to rough venues oozing with character but little in terms of financial reimbursement. It was a pretty thankless pursuit.

When I was about twenty years old, I was desperate to 'make it big' playing original songs with a band I'd formed with friends. We would travel to London mid-week to play in the coolest of venues. The proprietors, knowing no-one would turn up on a regular Tuesday evening, would invite bands from all over the

UK to perform. We'd actually have to pay for the privilege. I had been away from the electric guitar scene for some time as I'd been focussing on my classical playing and had no real intention of going back there, but fate had other ideas.

In a search for pupils and concerts, I played at a number of open-mic nights in the area which I normally avoid like the plague. I find the endless blues riffs and attempts to out-do other musicians tiresome at best. One particular night was legendary in the Dordogne: that held on the first Tuesday of the month in *la Gavotte* bar and restaurant in Ribérac. The feature which made it so wonderful was the fact that the venue was run with outstanding incompetence by a French couple of advanced years. This lovable, ever-smiling pair usually catered for passing lunchtime trade and those enjoying a coffee on market days, but their open-mic session would attract crowds of literally hundreds. On beautiful summer nights, listeners would spill out into the square to take in the musical offerings under the stars. It had clearly escaped the notice of the elderly *propriétaires* this was a chance to make a financial killing as, in response to the one hundred-fold increase in their client numbers, they did absolutely nothing. *Rien de tout!*

The majority of the *clientèle* were Brits who were used to having some level of service. It was a lost cause asking for food. Having heard your order, without having made any apparent record of it in paper form, the owner would nod his head and then amble along to the next table. He either had an incredible memory or, judging by the lack of materialisation of foodstuffs, he just forgot not only your order but your very existence. I used to wonder if he asked people what they would *like* to eat as a conversation gambit rather than an invitation to select a meal from the menu.

Eventually, a queue of agitated Brits would form inside the little restaurant, clinging to a vague aspiration of being able to order a *petite carafe de rosé* at a minimum. They were faced with a psychological dilemma. They wanted to enjoy the slower, relaxed pace of life offered by the Dordogne, yet at the same time, they rather fancied the drink which they'd ordered some thirty minutes earlier. As they queued, I'd observe strangers making light quips of disapproval about the service, each party taking care to avoid crossing the invisible boundary into very uncool jingoistic remarks.

As I awaited my turn to perform, I watched one gentleman queue for a good forty minutes, hoping to make a modest purchase of one small beer. Upon eventually reaching the counter (there was no bar as such) he thirstily placed his order. The owner unhurriedly started pouring the client's hard-earned prize but, mid-dispensation, spotted a friend in the street. He gently put the glass down, waved and went outside to chat with him. I sat, spellbound at the sheer cruelty of it all, as the two elderly buddies exchanged *bises* and discussed the weather. The client's half of lager remained a tantalising quarter, froth dissipating in agonising fashion like the parched gentleman's spirits. When the pals started exchanging photos of their grandchildren, I thought the would-be-drinker was going to break down and weep. Those who did by some miracle of fate have drinks brought to their table would often not receive a bill.

On the evening I played at *la Gavotte*, it was about 10.30pm when I took to the stage. The light was fading into a magical palette of reds and oranges, and the air had become pleasantly damp and cool. For those who are *au fait* with the repertoire, I offered some Barrios and Piazzolla. I gave out a few business cards and made many new friends.

A year later, *la Gavotte* closed down and became a pharmacy. This humble establishment, which provided folk with such happiness and well-being, became yet another outlet to sell prescribed drugs - intended to provide happiness and well-being.

Some days after my modest performance, I received a call and invitation to lunch from a gentleman with a broad Lancashire accent. Richard was a tall, tough man who had enjoyed a career in the military before setting up a successful travel company for sports teams with his lovely wife Pat. Richard had a plan to create a small acoustic/pop trio to play in the ex-pat laden bars and restaurants in the area. I was attracted to Richard's honesty and old-school sense of humour so, along with another local musician, Stuart, we created *Redwood*. Richard is a natural-born businessman and consequently, he was able to employ his formidable skills to earn us a gig schedule akin to a fifteen-month world tour undertaken by Madonna.

The group's success instigated jealous attacks from other bands in the area. They struggled to comprehend why bars were reticent to employ hairy ex-rockers playing Led Zeppelin covers at testicle-grinding volume for the entertainment of retired couples indulging in a tipple before dinner, or families with young children enjoying their annual fortnight in the sun. Our mix of country pop, warm humour, and sensitivity to the fact the audience may like to have a chin-wag as they masticated the evening's culinary offerings earned us a solid reputation in the area. Consequently, we were able to gloss over the unlikely combo's innate musical deficiencies. I understand we earned nicknames amongst the 'musician' fraternity in the region: *Jedwood* being a humorous tip-of-the-hat to the large-haired, contemporary duo *Jedward*, and my personal favourite: *Deadwood*.

The group created a formula hitherto unwitnessed in the region, or indeed, elsewhere in the known musical universe. I would sit with my guitar in classical posture offering occasional backing vocals. Where appropriate, I'd play some popular classical works pre-gig to showcase my solo CDs. Stuart is a technology buff. His guitar would be wired up to a MIDI synth, as would his microphone headset. This meant he was able to add orchestral effects and automatic backing vocals to his offerings. He looked like he was flying a *Euro Fighter* rather than playing the guitar. Richard sang and played the ukulele. He was also responsible for a seemingly endless barrage of bad jokes and expressions which he delivered impeccably.

We decided to sing all our repertoire in English. I felt uncomfortable about this but, when we attempted to sing in French, the Lancashire/French combination sounded so ridiculous we felt it was better to let sleeping dogs lie. We researched repertoire meticulously and selected material which would be familiar to all cultures. Happily, the French, Dutch and British (these being our main client groups) adore songs by artists such as *Simon and Garfunkel, Bob Dylan, Neil Young* and the like.

This formula proved highly effective, but there was one element which I felt needed improvement. Richard is a natural wit and our lack of musical sophistication was more-than-compensated-for by his warm banter with the audience. The snag was, although the majority of our audience was Anglophone, a small number were solely French-speaking and they were obviously being isolated. Richard's French was unfortunately on a par with my Swahili, so I asked him to pause after he'd delivered each gag to allow me to translate (my French by this time was pretty fluent). Of course, what I lacked was Richard's comic timing - the gags only really ever working due to their quick-fire delivery with his warm Lancashire accent. What's more, when translated into French, the result was surreal rather than amusing. When, during one anecdote, I translated the expression 'he was as much use as a one-legged man at an arse-kicking contest', the French speakers looked at me as if I'd completely lost the plot. All that was lacking was a ball of tumbleweed bouncing across the stage. I soon put that idea to bed.

One summer, we came tantalisingly close to landing the kind of gig working musicians dream of. We'd successfully performed in a restaurant and, the following day, Richard received a call from *le maire* of a large *commune* on the west coast. He had loved the band (he was somewhat musically illiterate I suspect) and offered us a residency in a chain of restaurants and beach-front bars for the following season. The pay was generous and we would also be provided with accommodation for both ourselves and our families for the duration of the contract. We celebrated wildly and it confirmed my long-term belief that miracles do actually happen. Soon after though, *Monsieur le Maire* asked a killer question.

"You are all, of course, *Intermittents de Spectacle?*"

Our collective failure to fulfil this requirement resulted in the cancellation of the contract. I suspect that by employing only *intermittents, mairies* could never be accused of passing back-handers in cash to employees. Swings and roundabouts as they say.

Playing on campsites was enormous fun. The *clientèle,* being on holiday, were always in the mood for banter and a frivolous evening of wine-induced silliness. I was relaxed when I played and enjoyed really going for it at the instrument. One particular night I felt on great form and was zipping up-and-down the neck like greased lightning. A young boy, about five years of age, installed himself at my side and spent the most part of the evening taking photos of me with his dad's phone. After the gig, I approached the dad, my ego swollen to dangerous levels, and suggested his little boy had taken me for a rock star.

"It's not that," his dad revealed, "he actually thinks you're Richard Hammond."

My fondest memories of gigging with *Redwood* must be reserved for the many nights we played at a restaurant called *la Terrasse de la Rivière*. The owner was a glorious, energetic and ever-eccentric gentleman named Pierre. You couldn't help but love Pierre. He was endlessly full of dreadful jokes, as well as anecdotes about the golden age of Welsh rugby, and he loved our little band. As the restaurant's name suggests it was situated on the banks of the stunning river Dronne. As I sat there strumming away, watching the birds dive and fish leap, enjoying the final warmth of the evening sunshine, I felt any worries life may have held melt away. It was bliss.

A practice which I know will astonish any musician working in the urban rat race is that the band, as well as receiving their fee, was properly fed. We would be offered a full meal (including starter and dessert) as well as drinks. There was no negotiation or pre-arrangement of this. It was just understood to be correct and polite practice. We would usually eat our *entrée* and *plat* before the first set and polish off a *dessert* during the interval. An *espresso* was normally offered before taking down the equipment. Non-drivers could enjoy a cheeky *digestif.*

Pierre possessed a characteristic which I've to be found unique amongst *restaurateurs* before and since: he would argue with you over your choice from the menu. Upon choosing something such as a chicken dish, Pierre would look affronted.

"Why not the beef?" he would say, stabbing a finger at the menu.

"Well, I just fancied chicken," I would answer.

"But *what* is *wrong* with the *beef?*" Pierre would question accusingly.

"I'm sure it's very good Pierre," I'd reply, backing down somewhat.

"Then you'll have *beef!*" he'd exclaim, with finality.

"Okay Pierre, if it makes you happy."

I actually saw him do this to paying customers on more than one occasion. If you were a regular, part of the charm of going to *la Terrasse* was arguing over your meal selection. For the one-off visitor though, it was baffling, or even intimidating for those of a coy disposition. I witnessed British holiday-makers looking perplexed as they tried their utmost to make their own food choices only to be pummelled into submission by Pierre's incessant suggestions to the contrary. I loved taking my family to *la Terrasse* to listen to the music. Pierre would invariably feed my children on-the-house, as well as the band. I have no idea how he made any money, but I do know he enjoyed filling children to bursting point with hearty grub more than he loved filling his bank account. Flo adored his *frites* above anything else and, when we tried making them at home, she would declare they were good but not as good as Pierre's. When I recounted this to Pierre, he was elated. On our next visit, she was whisked into the kitchen as an honorary guest for a whistle-stop course in *frite* preparation – the secret being to cook them, rest them and then cook them again so I'm reliably informed.

Being a member of the mighty *Redwood* also gave me unparalleled insight into some of the lesser-known cultural celebrations of South West France. At the end of one teaching day, I was approached by a local doctor who asked if we would provide the entertainment for the annual dinner of the Guitres Chicken Appreciation Society. On the day of the performance, we pulled up outside a modest *Salle des Fêtes* where a life-sized, beaming fibre-glass chicken was poised at the entrance by means of welcome and confirmation that we had arrived at the correct venue. It always amazes me how these statuettes feature creatures seemingly elated at their imminent slaughter.

Having been served an *aperitif* from specially-commissioned wine bottles bearing a content, plump-looking hen on the label, we played our first set and then settled down to eat at long, communal tables. I enquired of the pleasant gentleman poised to my left as to the reason for the existence of a Chicken Appreciation Society.

"We just really like chicken." He responded factually. *Nous aimons vraiment le poulet.*

Unsurprisingly, the cook served a variety of poultry-inspired recipes which, as one would expect, were deeply appreciated by the gathering. The *entrée* was a chicken noodle soup which transported me with a wave of culinary nostalgia to my childhood; the main course was a little less daring - a traditional chicken breast with vegetables.

"I'd like to see what she'll conjure up for dessert that employs chicken!" I quipped to my bandmates.

Moments later, the cook and her assistants emerged smugly from the steaming kitchen bearing fifty-or-so portions of egg custard tart to the rapturous applause of the attendees, each and every one smilingly shaking their heads at the genius of her invention.

Festivals celebrating the imminent demise of edible birds are all part of the social fabric of France. A small village no more than an hour north of *Chez Jones* holds an annual turkey festival which attracts crowds of literally thousands of keen punters. The initiation ceremony is a parade where a few hundred birds are processed into *le bourg,* closely followed by a musical ensemble who perform on a range of mysterious traditional instruments such as metallic clarinets, drums and hurdy-gurdies. Naturally, as an outsider, I was concerned about the issues of cruelty. Forcing one's children to endure such a racket was subhuman in my book. Contrarily, the turkeys seemed quite unperturbed by the experience as the sound emitted by the band closely resembled that of a hormonally-rampant gobbler in full season.

Once installed, a series of highbrow activities commenced for our entertainment. My particular favourite was led by the inevitably present *Monsieur Micro* who invited members of the public to imitate a turkey call (no instruments were permitted) through his microphone. The participant who received the greatest vocal response from the birds held in nearby pens was crowned Turkey Imitator of the Year. I lost.

I also played with an excellent jazz quartet called *The Dottie Bart Jazz Quartet.* Dottie is an incredible lady. She has a beautiful, expressive voice and is a consummate story-teller; her background in theatre and television shining through when she performs. As if that weren't enough, Dottie is also a very fine painter. I love her bold-coloured oils which capture the very essence of the Dordogne landscape - in particular, her representations of the seas of sunflowers and poppies with which nature blesses us every June and July.

The Dottie Bart Jazz Quartet aimed their set at a different client group from *Redwood.* Audiences would be a clean split of French and Brits. Many of them were of retirement age and loved to hear standards by Gershwin, Cole Porter, Rogers and Hammerstein and the like. We played in the classiest of restaurants – Dottie's loyal following ensuring the establishment would have as good a night as we did. We were also booked annually for one my less-glamorous engagements: a gig in the car park of a major supermarket. This being the French countryside, every supermarket would have a decent eatery attached.

A fond memory of playing with Dottie is performing on the terrace of the restaurant at the *Grand Etang de la Jemaye*. Friends of ours were fishing on the other side of the lake and, upon hearing music, recognised the ensemble. Rather than going to the inconvenience of walking around the lake to come and say hello, they disrobed and swam across it. Half-way through *Fly Me to the Moon,* I glanced up to see the arresting spectacle of a posse of speedo-clad men stepping out of the night, like jazz-loving mermen. They exchanged *bises* with us, grabbed a few startled female diners and danced away for a few tunes. The ladies were either shocked or delighted (or maybe a little of both) to be asked to dance by dripping-wet young fellows sporting their inevitable skimpy swimwear.

The Quartet became well-established enough to record an album. We did this with Stuart, the high-tech guitarist from *Redwood.* His idyllic country retirement home had slowly but surely morphed into a studio which would have made George Martin look twice. Recording can be a stressful process, but these sessions were relaxed and full of good feeling.

My ever-increasing employment as a guitarist for my concert career, weddings, jazz groups and *Redwood* created some tensions in my working life. In July and August, when gigs were abundant, I would be pulled in a number of directions by the different ensembles or agents for whom I played. At the end of the day, it was a good problem to have. On a couple of occasions, I played three gigs in a single day, playing for a wedding ceremony at 2.30pm, the first half of a classical concert at 8.30pm and then zipping off in *le Tank* to catch a jazz gig. Opportunities exist for musicians but they have to be open-minded as to what they offer and to whom. I had accumulated a programme with a charming French jazz fusion guitarist called Samuel and he once found us a gig playing at a Hell's Angels festival. That day marked two 'firsts' in my career: it was the first and only time I have performed to the accompaniment of enormous immobile motorcycles having petrol thrown down their improbably-bulbous exhausts to a cacophony of explosions and flame fountains and secondly, it has proved to be my sole engagement as a support act for a *sexy défilé* which was essentially a parade of girls wearing next-to-no clothing tottering clumsily across the stage in stilettos. Every mention of this part of the *spectacle* was greeted howls and wolf-whistles from three hundred hair-rich, tubby men in leather waistcoats. The mere thought of it was rather sad actually; I successfully made my excuses, gathered my pay cheque and escaped before it kicked off.

The most insane time of year for the working musician in France is around the 21st of June. I state that particular date because this is *la Fête de la Musique*. Coupled with end-of-year concerts and the start of the summer gig season, I found myself living in permanent crisis-management mode, staggering from gig to gig like a music-making autobot.

The all-inclusive ethos and generosity of spirit behind *la Fête de la Musique* are heart-warming. Professional musicians are expected to offer their abilities for free, and most are delighted to do so. Keen amateurs are also given permission to strut the boards; consequently, terror-struck individuals can be seen strumming away awkwardly on stages across France, fighting against temporary amnesia and wayward vocal cords, reluctant to respond to the wishes of their owners. I was truly struck by the generosity with which audiences received such acts. One June, I had the masterstroke of coupling *la Fête de la Musique* with an end-of-year performance for a group of about thirty guitarists whom I taught in Coutras. We chose to air our offering in a little bar which I'd selected due to its immediate proximity to the *toilettage* boutique where I was hoping to catch a glimpse of a mutt-victim being shaved before going onstage. It also meant parents could quaff a sneaky beer as we strummed. It was a win/win situation as the sight of thirty guitarists playing together guaranteed the required *spectacle* and consequently, a standing ovation.

Before we played, a gentleman took to the stage with a Casio keyboard, microphone and the inevitable 10,000 watt PA system. He was interpreting original compositions which was most admirable, and prior to unleashing each oeuvre onto his unsuspecting public, he gave a rambling, quasi-philosophical introduction to assist us in grasping the meaning behind each and every opus.

I should point out that I understand and appreciate atonal and polyrhythmic music. I agree it wouldn't be my first choice at a wedding party, but I respect it for its technical brilliance and inevitability in the advancement of music history. What followed though was a rendition of Casio's entire 'auto-accompaniment' catalogue, coupled with a disco beat, alongside melodies undoubtedly devised on-the-spot. The fact the said tunes bore little or no relation to the harmonic or indeed rhythmic fields of the afore-mentioned accompaniment held little consequence in the mind of this *artiste*. The gentleman wore an expression of earnest concentration throughout each painfully-elongated number, which was seemingly sufficient for the punters as they all applauded enthusiastically (perhaps out of relief) at the close of his programme. In discussion afterwards, listeners noted how 'unusual' and 'clever' the offerings had been. The former, yes. As for the latter, the jury remains well and truly out in my book.

This generosity of spirit offered towards those proposing repertoire of a challenging nature fascinates me. I ask myself how a similar programme might be received in a pub in downtown Stockport. In fact, I shudder to think of the consequences for performer and Casio keyboard alike. Perhaps it's due to the fact that French-village primary schools see it as part of their educational mission to expose their charges to abstract theatre, the type usually reserved for single PhD students and Guardian reporters. In her first year at French primary school, Florence arrived home one evening excitedly telling us her class were going on a trip to see a *spectacle* the next day. In my experience as a parent in the UK, this would normally entail a show written, directed and performed by newly-graduated drama students, the content generously employing custard pies, hand puppets and the words 'look behind you'. Upon her return, she looked somewhat perplexed. We pressed her as to the subject matter of the afternoon's entertainment and eventually, after some interrogation, learned the show was a monologue given by lady dressed in a saggy beige gown, outlining a perspective of the world from the point of view of an egg. On a later occasion, Sam was the victim. Kirsty had nobly offered to accompany the class as a parent-helper and was treated to an hour-long *spectacle* of shadow puppetry. The performance resembled a hyperactive octopus conducting Beethoven's 9th Symphony behind a sheet; frenzied arm movement appearing to be of greater artistic value than the formation of any recognisable shape, or indeed something discernible as a plot.

If a musician is really struggling for work, he/she can form a group to serve the still-buoyant – for now at least - *Thé Dansant* circuit. These enjoyed their heyday in the 1920's and 30's when local bands played classic tunes of the era in the local *Salle des Fêtes* on Sunday afternoons. Young farmers and the girls of the quarter would dance together, under the watchful eyes of their parents, sipping light refreshments and nibbling *pâtisseries*. It was essentially a means of finding a wife. In countryside areas, they remain popular, but audiences are inevitably dwindling with the passage of time. The repertoire could be described as 'cheesy' in English. French musicians use the term *'la soupe'* rather than *'fromage'*.

Along with friends and teachers at our village music school, we also formed an instrumental jazz group. On top of this, Kirsty and I created a quartet with our friend Stéphane and his daughter Charlotte - *L'Ensemble Arisan* - to perform Celtic and French music. The *Ecole de Musique* used these groups as a basis for an annual gig organised each July adjacent to *L'Ecluse de la Filolie,* just down the road from *Chez Jones.* The canal lock would be emptied and we set up tables, chairs, a bar and nibbles for the community to come and enjoy.

Monsieur and *Madame Micro* also blessed the popular-music world with their unique gifts. Their job, in their eyes, was to bully people into having a good time, this being the case regardless of the wishes of the clients. On one holiday in Saint Georges de

Didonne, the little campsite where we were staying put on a karaoke evening. The restaurant was pleasantly situated adjacent to the pool and a children's play area, and that evening around eleven or twelve groups of people sat in the sunshine enjoying a pizza or *moules frites*. At around 8.30pm a heavily-tattooed and somewhat muscular lady dragged a karaoke machine from a cupboard and booted it up. I actually rather like karaoke. I'm all in favour of people humiliating themselves in public, as long as it is done in the correct spirit. I regard myself as an expert in this field.

Slips of paper were handed out for campers to jot down their names and song requests. Subsequently, the first victim was called up and the track commenced. I think it was some *Europop* ditty from the splendid back catalogue of *Jean-Jacques Goldmann.* All too predictably, as the drums kicked in, the sound system was cranked up to the kind of volume which caused a small tsunami to kick off in the pool. *Madame Micro* was keen to encourage the spectators to be involved with performance.

"Come on!!! I can't hear you!" she bellowed, causing small birds to fall out of nearby trees. *Allez!!! Je n'entends rien!*

The fact that the vast majority of the audience were attempting to eat a meal, or even indulge in light conversation, appeared to have bypassed her notice. I'm often amazed at how obliging the French are to the whims of *Monsieur* and *Madame Micro* as, in an instant, everyone dropped their cutlery, whooped and clapped along. What made the whole experience more galling was as soon as the crowd 'got going', she collapsed into a chair and lit up a cigarette. The second anyone dared to be silent, or even take a mouthful of their dinner, she was upon them in a flash.

"What are you doing? I can't hear anything!!!" she screamed in a tone approaching hysteria. *Qu'est-ce que vous faîtes?! Je n'entends rien!!!*

At which point paying customers were obliged to drop their forks, cheer, and spray Margherita pizza into the faces of their beloveds. After a few hours of this, she took a break and sat down to tuck into a burger and chips. I felt like going up to her as she raised her heavily-laden fork to her mouth and yelling in her face.

"Qu'est-ce que vous faîtes?! Je n'entends rien!!!"

At midnight, as I was lying in my sleeping bag a good 500 metres away from the bar, she kicked off once again. I was able to hear every last grotesquely-amplified syllable. I had to admire her stamina.

Of course, I'm just playing at Mr Grumpy. I love the fact the French are so willing to participate in an event and to try their hardest to have a good time. In fact, although they have a reputation for a certain detached *je ne sais pas* in everyday life, when it comes to holidays, the French are extraordinarily well-behaved and rather conformist. At times, I was reminded of grainy black-and-white films of communal activities in 1950's British seaside holiday camps. Children's clubs, sporting activities, quiz evenings, bingo, dance routines and the like remain popular. Cynicism is dead in small-town France. Participation is absolutely *a la mode.*

That holiday was completed with a near-miss which reminded me of how vulnerable senior citizens are to the predatory claws of certain sections of society. The campsite was run, pretty much single-handedly, by a lady who should have retired long before. I was at the reception one evening, making use of her wifi, when she approached me with a question.

"What are the laws like in England?" she asked.

I considered her question carefully and answered as truthfully as possible.

"I think they are fairly similar to those here in France, albeit a little less strict in the swimwear department. Why? Is there a problem?"

She explained a friend of hers was on holiday in the UK and had run into a spot of bother with the law. She was wondering what the consequences might be. Quite what misdemeanour the friend had indulged in was none of my business, so I assured her the penalty he would face was likely to be similar to what he should expect in France, unless he'd over-cooked a steak which, in France, is punishable by ten years' imprisonment. That seemed to satisfy her so we both went on our way. At the end of the week, she approached me once again.

"Do you know a British town called Mali?" she asked.

I racked my brains, which were, admittedly, somewhat befuddled as I'd lost several hours sleep courtesy of *Madame Micro*. The cheap *vin rouge* was an error as well.

"Madame, as far as I can recall, Mali is a Central African country, unless there is a small village which shares its name," I replied, although anything may have been possible for a country with a village called 'Upton Snodsbury'.

"OK, thank you," our hostess responded, apparently satisfied.

I was returning to our tent, carrying a toilet roll concealed in a towel, as one always does on camping holidays, when I put two and two together and an awful sense of realisation dawned over me. I tore back to the reception at improbable speed, given my delicate constitution.

"Madame," I asked, panting slightly. "May I ask where you heard that Mali is a British town?"

As you may have perceived more promptly than I had, *Madame* had received a text at the beginning of the week from an old friend. The phone belonging to the 'friend' in question had obviously been hacked or stolen. She was on the verge of sending several thousand euros to a bank account in Mali, supposedly to bail out her pal who had been arrested in the UK. It took me a good ten minutes to explain the scam and persuade her to cancel the transaction, so convinced had she been of its authenticity. It shows how scammers and hackers can succeed in their activities - their often elderly victims usually being the most generous-of-heart.

***

I Am the Music Man, I Come From Far Away – The Essential Tips

(1) It's a miracle if your concert starts less than an hour late.

(2) Go for quantity over quality. The French love a hero-performer.

(3) *Monsieur* or *Madame Micro* have absolute power and are of equal importance to the performers. In fact, they are also performers.

(4) Expect to play through a PA system set to ball-breaking volume.

(5) Take care when parking your car upon arrival at a gig.

(6) Rock musicians are treated as human beings.

(7) You may well encounter abstract theatre and polytonal music at your primary school's end of year show.

(8) I can think of no job I'd rather be doing more than having a career as a performing musician in the French countryside. Actually, quality-control management in a Saint Emilion *château* may come a close second.

Figure 14 Performing a solo slot as part of a choir festival in the Dordogne.

Figure 15 Kirsty and me performing an outdoor concert in the summer.

Figure 16 Visitng luthier, Jean Verly before a trio tour in 2016. From left to right, seated, Cobie Mills, standing, Jean Verly, me and seated right, John Mills, one of the finest classical guitarists of his generation.

Figure 17 Finishing a jazz gig. I am on the left and standing next to me is my great friend, Stéphane.

Dan Jones

17. Man and Machine

John Henry was a railroad man
He worked from six 'till five
Raise 'em up bullies and let 'em drop down
I'll beat you to the bottom or die

John Henry said to his captain
You are nothing but a common man
Before that steam drill shall beat me down
I'll die with my hammer in my hand

John Henry was hammering on the right side
The big steam drill on the left
Before that steam drill could beat him down
He hammered his fool self to death

Traditional – *John Henry, Steel Driving Man* (America)

As the months and years passed, I couldn't help but notice I was changing. Owning a property with so many minor flaws obliged me to learn how to sort these things out myself, albeit with the help of neighbours. I soon found myself adopting male stereotypes – becoming more interested in power tools and gathering items such as timber, pallets, old doors and anything which could be reused for potential upcycling projects.

I observed how in my previous urban life, I'd subconsciously felt discouraged from being well, masculine. I noticed an ever-increasing number of television adverts showing incompetent males attempting DIY tasks and failing spectacularly. In one such offering, a gentleman installed a shelving system which duly fell apart the moment an object was placed upon it. As he stood over the collapsed structure wearing an aghast expression, his wife and children tutted, knowingly shook their heads, picked up a phone, and called in an expert. The family were then shown sitting on a sofa, in front of a large television set, with the shelving successfully attached to the wall in the background. The modern world encourages us to outsource such odd jobs, leaving us at liberty to while away the hours with activities I'd propose are less life-affirming and enriching. Today, I would like to see my children learn how to build a home or grow their own food. I attach much greater value to these abilities than acquiring telephone skills in a call centre or, as I was recently required to do by a new work contract, learning how to place oneself correctly at a desk.

Gradually, I found myself the owner of a range of tools which were frequently hand-me-downs or purchased second-hand. Kirsty's uncle - a very practical man - had renovated a house in Normandy and, upon deciding to sell up and move back to the UK, recognised it would be cheaper to drive to the Dordogne and pass his tool collection to our grateful hands than it would be to transport it back across *la Manche*. As you will have noticed, we are surrounded by good people.

There is a saying in the French countryside that the two most useful purchases you can make are a trailer and a chainsaw. Very soon after our installation, I recognised the truth in this. When we were able to change our heating system to one which was wood-based, I received frequent calls telling me of opportunities of cheap or free timber. Collecting this was manageable with an estate car, but the real deal would have been a trailer. When cutting logs to lengths of fifty or thirty centimetres, the only realistic tool is a chainsaw.

Tree-management is an essential part of land maintenance, especially if you have fruit trees which you hope will produce for you, so adequate tools soon become a necessity. Cutting our extensive area of grass is impossible with an electric mower - firstly, the motors needed to be at least twice as powerful and secondly, a 200-metre extension lead lacks a certain practicality.

The purchase of larger, petrol-driven machines became a necessity.

Of all my friends, the afore-mentioned James (he the ex-goat-owning banjo player) indulged in the most exotic of manly, mechanical activities. As part of his extensive portfolio of skills, James would repair machines such as tractor-mowers and quad bikes. He was always run off his feet and would especially bemoan the onset of spring. Upon the arrival of the fine season, several thousand landowners (myself included) would dust off their mowers from the back of the shed and attempt to start them. For reasons unknown to me, it appears that a period of inactivity for a machine leads to a mechanical breakdown. On the first sunny weekend in each calendar year, James' phone would be on fire.

"Why can't they test the bl***y things in January?!" he would blurt out during his banjo lesson, in between strained renditions of *The Irish Washerwoman*.

In the little spare time he had, James liked to buy wrecked vehicles from scrapyards and restore them to their former glory. He once showed me a vintage tractor he had lovingly pieced together inch by painstaking inch. I confess it was rather beautiful but, practically-speaking, it served as a kind of nostalgic garage filler. One of the more exciting purchases he made was an old Solex moped which he picked up for about 20€ at a *brocante*. These marvellous little machines are a hybrid between a pushbike and a 50cc twist-and-go scooter. As they require human pedal power to get going, they are technically-speaking a bicycle. James informed me riders needed no licence and also, a helmet was surplus to legal requirements.

James would enjoy cruising around the village centre (it took about twenty seconds to cover its entire length) waving jovially at acquaintances as the wind blew through his hair. With some justification, Jane, James' wife, disapproved of her husband's passion for helmet-free cruising. She insisted he purchased a helmet before continuing his *sorties* on the Solex. A few days later, they were at another *brocante* when James spotted an old

German WW2 steel military helmet. His eyes lit up and, within moments, he had made his purchase (the helmet cost him more than the Solex). Over the next few days, James was to be seen zipping around the village, proudly sporting his new headgear. The problem was apparently, it is legal to ride a Solex with *no* helmet but *illegal* to ride with one which is unfit for purpose. At least that's what the local *gendarme* told him.

James also purchased a Land Rover which he stripped to its bare bones. He then fitted it with a snorkel. When it comes to motor mechanics, I am as much use as a chocolate fireguard, but I understood James organised the air intake to the engine to be taken from the snorkel which poked out of the side of the bonnet and reached up above the roof of the car. I enquired why James might wish to do such a thing.

"So I can take it for a drive down the River Dronne," was his unpredictable response.

One of James' preferred hobbies was to drive his Land Rover into the river and see how far he could advance. I presume he reached an *impasse* well before la Dronne reaches the Atlantic Ocean. He told me that on one occasion, he managed nearly three kilometres.

In the summer months, the river is populated by fishermen and families who hire canoes in order to navigate its picturesque windings through the Perigord Vert. I would have paid good money to have seen their faces as a grim-faced, bare-chested bloke in shorts careered around the corner in an aquatic Land Rover, pushing fish and frogs from his lap, the wipers working overtime trying to clear his line of vision of duckweed.

By 2012, we were in a position to (reluctantly) return *le Tank* to its owner and purchase a more logical run-around vehicle for me. I became the proud owner of a bright yellow Renault Clio: *la Banane*. It was one of the Mark I models and over 20 years old when I acquired it. Like *le Tank,* it ran and ran without a hiccup. Also like *le Tank,* it had blowers which had never functioned. This meant it was perishingly cold in the winter and unbelievably hot in the summer. Upon one occasion I gave a friend's son a lift home from the station. It had been touching forty degrees all day and, as the car had been parked in the sun for eight hours, it was about fifty degrees inside the cabin of *la Banane*. A kind of baked banana. I chuckled when the lad enquired as to what a 'manual choke' was. I laughed out loud when he asked if we could 'flick on the air conditioning'. Upon learning the car had neither 'AC' nor functioning blowers of any kind, he started stabbing frantically at the electric window buttons. When that action yielded no obvious response from *la Banane*, he slowly turned his head to face me. Wordlessly, I shook my head at him. They hadn't worked since day one. By the time we reached home, he was having a mild panic attack coupled with heatstroke. He practically crawled out of the car, gasping for water, like a marooned man on a desert island.

Sadly, *la Banane* (and I) became the victims of *verglas d'été* (summer black ice). Having played at a wedding, I was making my way home through the snaking forest roads which I love so much, when a storm moved in. This is a common occurrence in the summer and soon the road was a torrent of water. We had just undergone a spell of very hot weather and the sudden change of temperature and conditions created the famous *verglas d'été*. This is when oil in the tarmac rises to the road surface and creates a glossy sheen. Before I knew it, the car was in a spin. I ended up deep in the forest, *la Banane* was reduced to a Banana Split.

Of course, the more serious the motor, the more potent the potential danger. Friends who like me found no obvious danger in using a chair (whereas many modern-day employers see this as a threat on a par with catching a cobra bare-handed, in the dark, smothered head-to-toe in snake treats) would adopt a very different attitude when using powerful petrol-driven tools on their land. When we shared labour they would turn up with full protective gear, from face-masks to steel-toed boots. Where there was genuine risk, safety was respected.

The dangers of power tools were brought home to us only too clearly through a terrible incident one innocuous February afternoon. As already mentioned, our neighbour André was a virtuoso gardener. He loved nothing more than to tend to acres of immaculate rows of produce and then to share his bounty amongst friends. André owned an impressive fleet of power tools, one of these being a rotovator. This giant tool looked like a lawn mower pumped with more steroids than The Russian Olympic Squad. It had vicious, rotating blades which would dig deep into the ground and turn over the soil. It was also self-propelled making it unnecessary to push the beast along.

When we created our vegetable patch from a corner of our garden, André came to *Chez Jones* with this monstrous machine and within half-an-hour, had dug over fifty square metres of rich brown soil ready for planting. I recall hopping foot-to-foot at the edge of the patch, desperate to have a go at this fun device, but André refused. This was particularly agonising as I found the sight of a man closer to ninety than eighty working my garden difficult to accept, but I suspect he enjoyed playing with a power tool as much as I do.

One Wednesday, we were having lunch *en famille* when Florence casually mentioned a number of her friends claimed to have seen a helicopter in our garden the previous afternoon. We had a laugh about the flights of fancy of schoolchildren, but then Sam noted his friends had reported the very same thing. Kirsty and I had been out at work and our house had been empty so it was, theoretically-speaking, feasible. It then dawned on me that helicopters were deployed in the event of medical emergencies; I wondered if there had been an incident nearby. I looked out of the window and saw André and Eliane's shutters were closed. They would normally, without fail, be out on their terrace drinking an aperitif at this hour so I became concerned. I went next door to check on things and met Eliane, looking red-eyed, exhausted and deeply stressed. There had been a serious accident involving André.

Over the previous months, Eliane had expressed concern about André's health and his gardening activities. He was putting in a good eight-hour shift every day and, for a man of his advancing years, that was pretty impressive. On a number of occasions during the preceding weeks, André had fallen in the garden and been unable to stand up again unassisted. One afternoon he had been left lying amongst his runner beans for about an hour before anyone noticed he hadn't come in for his early-evening glass of *vin blanc*. Whereas Eliane was concerned by these events, for André it was just another good story to share with the neighbours (i.e. us). Even if he'd been banned from gardening by every doctor in the land, André would have laughed in their faces, given each of them a sack of King Edwards and returned to de-slugging his lettuces.

This particular afternoon, André had been using his rotovator to prepare his land for the approaching spring season. As the self-propelling machine advanced he had temporarily lost control, causing it to swerve into a cherry tree. The machine had bounced off the trunk and knocked André over before turning and coming down on his legs. Unable to stand, he'd called for help but Kirsty and I were out, and Eliane had gone to a nearby town for an appointment. His wounds were very serious and he was slowly bleeding to death.

André would have died in his garden if it were not for an extraordinary stroke of good fortune. A local lady, who was occasionally employed to carry out some of the more labour-intensive domestic chores in their home, had chosen this moment to call in. Having arrived, she spotted the upturned machine in the garden and found André unconscious on the floor. He had been there for about fifteen minutes and was clinging to life by a thread. Had she arrived five minutes later, it would have been too late.

An air ambulance was deployed (thus the helicopter) which then flew André to Bordeaux. In later months we laughed about this as André couldn't remember a moment of the trip – only the noise of the engine - telling me he would have enjoyed the experience in other circumstances. He spent four months in hospital in Bordeaux having reconstructive surgery on his lower legs, and also receiving psychological treatment as the incident had left him deeply traumatised.

Obviously, legs which are nearly a century old struggle to recover in the same way as younger limbs do. As I was working in Bordeaux at this time, I was able to visit him on a number of occasions. He was as sharp as ever but every time a helicopter passed overhead (and this was quite frequently) he would have a stressful recollection of the events of that fateful day. It was awful to see him reliving flashbacks of the experience over-and-over again and it was clear to those of us who knew and loved him that he needed to be back in his village, where his heart and soul belonged.

***

Man and Machine – The Essential Tips

(1) Be manly. It's OK in rural France.

(2) Budget to purchase a chainsaw and a trailer. These two items will repay you 100 times over.

(3) Driving a car down a river is apparently an acceptable leisure activity in the French countryside.

(4) Be aware of *verglas d'été*. It's just as slippery as the winter stuff.

(5) When using serious tools, be careful. A chainsaw is *really* dangerous. Lifting a small box from a squatting position is just a little bit dangerous. Apparently.

18. Twenty-One Weddings and a Funeral

So next Sunday night, I mean to prepare
To comb out my locks and to curl up my hair
And six pretty fair maids, so neat and so trim
Shall dance at my wedding next Monday morning

Next Monday Morning – Traditional (England)

***

The day of the funeral it was a sad sight
Four-and-twenty young men and they all dressed in white
They bore him on their shoulders and to rest him did lay
Saying: Farewell to you, Willie, and they all walked away

The Lakes of Shallin – Traditional (Ireland)

In France, marriages are conducted as a civil ceremony – usually at *la mairie*. There is the option of a religious service, but this alone is insufficient to constitute a legal marriage. Same-sex marriages exist and gay couples enjoy the same rights as their heterosexual counterparts. There are though, at the time of writing, fewer rights for those who share the same roof in civil partnerships.

Post-ceremony, there is a convention of driving to the party venue in a festive convoy, cars decorated with ribbons and flowers, horns beeping loudly. Fellow road users will respond in kind creating an exuberant, cacophony of sound and colour.

Marrying in the rolling vineyards of France basking in summer sunshine - and with the promise of abundant low-cost wine to follow - is a prospect which appeals to many couples from overseas. The reality though is that the cultural passion for meaningless and oft painful paperwork in triplicate seeps, like a stubborn fungal infection, into the marriage process. This is, predictably, enough to scare off all but the most tenacious of lovebirds. It is, for this reason, many wedding agencies will offer couples the chance to 'marry' in French *châteaux* but actually, what is carried out is a kind of imitation event with all the trappings.

The key to getting the best of all worlds is to organise your wedding in France and, the week before, nip down to your local registry office with your best mate as a witness to complete the paperwork. You can then enjoy the main event with family, friends, over-excited children and fancy hats in the Dordogne - without needing to worry about keeping French *fonctionnaires* in employment for another few weeks at your expense.

There are many agencies in France who will organise these events for you, and an important source of employment for me is to be a guitarist at *château* weddings. The agents are highly-skilled and will create an event which will, for all intents and purposes, look like your proper wedding. They organise seating in the shade for Auntie Vera, create a floral arch as a centrepiece, and the celebrant will read all of the correct lines with or without reference to God as the couple request. There's even a signing of a register which looks terribly official but is really a kind of token memento (like a Cycling Proficiency certificate from junior school).

Consequently, I regard myself as a *connoisseur* of the *château* wedding having played at more than I can possibly remember. I love doing wedding gigs. People are happy, often silly, and it is a privilege to be part of the most important day of a couple's life. As part of my package, I will speak to the couple in the months leading up to the big day and discuss music choices in detail. As I carry out a lot of music arrangement, I can pretty much play whatever the couple request and have performed everything from *Tenacious D* to Schubert. As time passes, I see the couples becoming younger, or is it me getting older? I find myself being a reassuring voice in the weeks leading up to the big day, acting as a kind of music-guru. The vast majority of couples are adorable and I have remained in contact with many whose ceremonies I've been lucky enough to be a part of. I've learned there is no such thing as being fortunate or unfortunate on a wedding day. It is all about the couple's attitude and reaction to the events which are offered by the world at that moment.

A profoundly beautiful experience which remains in my memory is a wedding where a couple from the USA came to a *château* on the Dordogne/Charente border to celebrate their big day. The ceremonies at this venue take place about 200 metres away from the main building, under a massive, looming oak which seems to offer the wisdom of the ages - as well as much-welcome shade. There had been a severe weather warning issued in the morning, but the Michael Fish-inspired storm prediction anticipated it was due to hit in the late afternoon – long after the 3.00pm ceremony. As I set myself up under the oak at about 2.15pm, I glanced towards the horizon. There I noticed leaden-coloured clouds gathering, and they appeared to be moving towards us at some pace. Ten minutes later, I tracked down the celebrant and the couple. I proposed we moved the ceremony forwards by fifteen minutes as the wind was also picking up; it felt distinctly as if a tropical storm of biblical proportions was about to hit. This suggestion was agreed upon and the couple, resplendent in their finery, tore around the building, banging on doors, encouraging cousins and friends from their school days to get a move on.

At 2.45pm, I was *in situ* playing a few tunes to entertain the assembly. As the bride, looking as pretty as a thousand pictures, processed across the finely-manicured lawn towards her husband-to-be, the inevitable happened. There was an almighty crash of thunder and the heavens opened. Rain and hail hurled down at incredible speed in thick, dense sheets. Chairs, hats and small children blew across the lawn and as for the floral arch, I think it took off and was last seen heading up the *autoroute* towards Calais. Staff tore out of the building in a pointless attempt to rescue dignity and property, including my musical equipment which was electrified. It could have resulted in an impromptu fireworks display with me acting as Guy Fawkes. What a sight it was to see waiters, waitresses, porters and management sprinting around like *the Keystone Cops,* endeavouring to hold coats over their guests' saturated heads as they dashed towards the shelter of the main house.

For many couples, this would be firmly labelled as a *catastrophe.* For this inspiring and wonderful pair though, it was just another story to tell the grandchildren. The bride and groom, hooting with laughter, spoke to the celebrant and staff (including myself) and then called a meeting in the beautiful, wood-panelled drawing room. Everyone gathered, letting off steam both literally and metaphorically, drenched to the bone, and an early glass of champagne was served. It was agreed all should have an hour to restore whatever dignity could be mustered, and the couple would be married in a barn to the rear of the building.

At 4.00pm, all was in place. The guests, still slightly damp and sporting hastily re-applied makeup, sat on everything from beer barrels to hay bales. The couple had asked for a moment's prayer and meditation during the service during which I would play a Scarlatti Sonata in A major. That three minutes of baroque genius was just magical; here was a couple who would allow no obstacle to interfere with their happiness. The day oozed peace and love.

A great treat for Kirsty and me is that we are sometimes booked as a couple, or we go out as a quartet with our friend Stéphane - who plays accordion and saxophone - along with his daughter Charlotte who is a double-bassist. Stéphane takes these events hugely seriously (thankfully) so I enjoy behaving rather poorly, indulging in cheap stunts such as whispering rude remarks just as he is about to blow into his sax, resulting in a note which resembles a duck rather than a thing of musical beauty. At one such wedding, a beautiful Irish couple got married in what was the most unashamedly romantic ceremonies I've ever witnessed. They'd created their own vows and memorised them. These promises were lengthy, biographical and deeply spiritual words of extraordinary beauty which they recited, hands held, staring into one another's eyes.

The congregation, who I suspect had gone rather too early on the champagne front, were in floods of tears and I have to say, we had difficulty maintaining a professional demeanour. Charlotte, a young lady still in her teenage years, was in bits. It was fabulous. I worry the ensemble's performances at these classy and lavish events will have fuelled her inspiration for something similar, come her big day. I suspect the budget may have a few more restraints than those of the clients who tend to enjoy *château* weddings.

It's incredible that agents still find it necessary to bring function bands over from the UK to play at evening receptions. There are British bands in France trying to break into the market but their idea of being 'modern' is offering *The Police* or *U2* rather than *Elvis* or *The Kinks*. They neglect to observe most couples marrying today would not have been born when Sting and Bono hit the big-time. I have half-considered forming a group of my own to serve the purpose, but maybe my days of dragging amplifiers around at 2.00am have passed me by. There have been weddings when I have been waiting, pre-ceremony, in the kitchen of a *château* with rock musicians. Whereas I've arrived an hour-or-so before my spot and set up in fifteen minutes, they've been there since the morning and are anticipating a further ten hours on-site before their shift is over. I'll be calculating if I'll be home early enough for a game of footie with the kids before tea-time as they mentally prepare for the eight-hour night drive to Calais. Still, they are treated very well and handsomely reimbursed for their efforts.

Running a wedding agency can be deeply satisfying work for the planners and the host venues but inevitably, there are variables. On one occasion, Kirsty and I played in a magnificent *château* in the Dordogne for a ceremony and *aperitifs*. Having completed our shift, we found the couple, thanked them and made our way back to the car. We were crossing the beautiful gravel courtyard which surrounded the main entrance when I noticed something somewhat out-of-place. I spotted a pool of dark, offensive-smelling liquid about thirty metres away from where the party were quaffing champagne in the early evening sunshine. Being somewhat expert on raw sewage, due to my endless battles with our septic tank, my highly-trained eye and nose homed in on the pool and set off an alarm in my head. I turned back, found the planner and pointed out the problem. She turned a peculiar shade of green, spun on her heels and suggested to the party they should perhaps appreciate the evening shade among the mature trees to the rear of the *château.*

Two weeks later, I was playing for the same planner. I enquired what had been the cause of the unfortunate discovery. She wore an expression which suggested the event in question was one which had given her many sleepless nights and would probably necessitate therapy. On the morning of the big day, the evening's rock band had arrived and set up in the main function room. In order to make their toil less arduous, they had brought their trusty, fully-laden transit van across the courtyard and parked adjacent to the double doors to the function room. Once installed, they had zipped off into a nearby town to pass the day in an agreeable fashion. Unbeknownst to all, they had run over an insufficiently-deeply-buried sewage pipe which served the entire *château.* It had sat there unmolested for a couple of centuries, having been installed in an era when most people approached the building on horseback. The pipe had been crushed to dust by the van earlier in the day; its disagreeable contents gradually rising to the surface over the ensuing hours until my unerring instinct for such matters had spotted it. The remainder of the planner's afternoon had been spent telephoning portaloo companies, trying to persuade them to come out at short notice – no mean feat for a country whose businesses still prefer signed paper contracts, in triplicate, before lifting a finger.

The biggest enemy of the *château* wedding though is the lethal combination of high spirits, champagne and hot weather. I must avoid being a moral judge here because I love a wedding and, if I am fortunate enough to be invited as a guest, I'm partial to a glass or two of the bubbly stuff. I will never, ever though, be discourteous to a member of staff or fellow guest. If I make a fool of anyone, it will be myself when I fall off a chair or the like.

Some venues rather invite trouble as they identify the 'Summer French Wedding in the Sunshine' market as a potentially-lucrative one which can easily be tapped into. Generally speaking, these events require a serious financial outlay, but there are venues who run more of a budget package - supplying *gite* accommodation or placing 'glamping' facilities amongst the trees in the grounds. They will also strike deals with local wine producers ensuring no-one will go thirsty. Whereas the classier *châteaux* will advertise rooms which have been slept in by 17th-century French aristocracy and a feast produced by Michelin-starred chefs, others will promise enough *Prosecco* to sink a ship, and an abundance of barbequed foodstuffs at an affordable price.

Venues which are simply holiday complexes rather than *châteaux* also get in on the act. The results are stressful and painful for the venue and forgettable for the participants, not because they endure a mediocre weekend but because they suffer memory loss due to the effects of drinking industrial quantities of budget *rosé*.

As I pull up at a venue to play for a wedding, I can, within minutes, discern what kind of experience the afternoon promises, and react accordingly. Having arrived at one particular engagement, for example, I was ambling across the lawns of a historic *château* close to Bertric Burée when my eye caught the sight of around fifteen lads wearing only England football shorts, kicking a ball around, using 300-year-old oak trees as goal-posts. They had lagers-in-hands and the air was blue with alcohol-induced expletives.

Bearing in mind this was a couple of hours before the ceremony, I politely said my 'Hellos' and found a corner well out of the way to set up. One has to be careful with a choice of repertoire at such events as, if I play anything remotely 'pop', it risks generating raucous applause and the dreaded 'requests'. I'm up for doing a few familiar tunes on the classical guitar as much as the next guy, but when I'm asked to play Jay-Z, well, I know my limits. Problems can arise when the invisible barrier between client and guitarist is broken; this can lead to a scene, despite my efforts to be courteous and light-hearted. I've experienced lager-fuelled Brits becoming aggressive because I am unable to perform the latest offering from *Little Mix* spontaneously for their little girl. Funnily-enough, being a hairy middle-aged white bloke, I tend to learn other material in my spare time.

The footie-wedding described above was particularly farcical and seemed to simmer with aggression all afternoon. Luckily for me, I was due to zip away at 6.00pm as it felt as if the event was going to 'kick off' in more ways than one. As mentioned, I communicate at length with my couples before their big day. This particular couple had chosen Pachelbel's Canon in D for the processional (although the email had read 'Canon's Pachelbel in D') - a pleasant if not trailblazing choice – and, two hours prior to their ceremony, were yet to select a piece for the recessional. In the end, I promised a stressed groom I would bash out 'something good' for them, leaving him to quaff *Stella Artois* number seven before making his vows.

The ceremony itself passed off well enough. The congregation talked throughout, seemingly unaware that the weekend's *Strictly* results were of lesser importance than a couple vowing to give their lives to one another. During the *aperitifs,* I found a little corner and settled into playing my repertoire to some pleasant folks sitting on recliners in the shade of the building.

The father-of-the-bride was walking in peculiar zig-zag shapes having knocked back enough bubbly to flatten a herd of elephants. He had learned some French for his weekend away in the Dordogne, which was admirable, and was keen to try it on anyone unfortunate enough to be cornered. I was halfway through a bit of *Tarrega* when he stumbled over, sat next to me and, resembling Officer Crabtree from *Allo Allo,* attempted a bit of the lingo.

"Bonjourno guitarist. Comment allez vous today?" asked Mr Dad-of-Bride.

"Très bien merci," I replied unthinkingly, concentrating on my job.

"Comment tu-t'appellez vous your name innit?" he ventured further.

"Dan," was my ground-breaking reply.

"Je suis English. Anglais-like," offered Mr Dad-of-Bride.

'No s**t Sherlock.' I thought. "D'accord, c'est trés interessant," I said.

Of course, I was digging myself a very big hole and one which I was going to struggle to climb out of. The good gentleman, beaming all over his face at the marriage of his daughter and perhaps due to the lavish imbibing of cheap bubbly, *believed that I was French.* To make matters worse *I appeared to understand him.* Call me stupid (you wouldn't be the first) but I didn't have the heart to reveal my Welsh origins, because I felt it would burst his bubble (and his body contained enough champagne bubbles to make quite a pop, I tell you). He seemed so proud of his efforts.

Thus commenced a surreal series of encounters during which he would periodically approach me to try out new phrases, in between mingling amongst guests proudly proclaiming he could communicate with the locals. By divine intervention, he failed to approach anyone who had chatted with me in English beforehand. He sported a little *English/French* phrase book and, having 'mastered' a new phrase, would meander over to try it out on me.

"J'aime le football. Man United. Man City sont les Nancy-Boys," he offered profoundly.

"Ha ha! C'est trés drole Monsieur," I said, this being the necessary response.

"He understood me!" he announced to one-and-all with worrying vigour.

I cringed, praying no-one within earshot would reveal my Anglophone identity.

During one particularly arduous exchange, he was trying to tell me how beautiful the Lake District was. He felt a good way to illustrate this would be to introduce mime into the linguistic equation. To illustrate 'lake' he repeatedly drew a circular shape in the air with his hands, about six inches from my face. To the uninitiated, this could have been anything from an egg to the solar system.

"Moi – je aime le Lake District," he said for the eighteenth time.

"D'accord," I replied, simultaneously fighting with Bach's *Prelude in G major*.

Mr Dad-of-Bride then called out to no-one in particular.

"I don't think he understands me. Hey, Geoff! How do you say 'lake' in Froggie Lingo?"

'It's 'etang' I thought. *'Please go away before I'm busted'.*

He then used the uniquely British multilingual approach:

"Moi – je aime le Lake District!!!" he yelled as if attempting to communicate verbally with someone in the *actual* Lake District.

At this point, I made the suspiciously quantum leap from 'understanding nothing' to 'all becoming as clear as day', apparently via the means of volume and circular hand gestures.

"Aha! Ze Lake Deestreect, eet ees very… err… beau n'est-ce-pas?" I offered, unconsciously putting on a French accent.

Dad-of-Bride looked more astonished than anyone at this success and, had he been sober, probably would have had his suspicions aroused, but I seemed to dodge the bullet.

When I finish my work for the day, I usually find the happily newly-wed couple, thank them, and perhaps give them a little gift such as a CD. Relieved to have escaped with my unwitting deception undetected, I checked to see if Dad-of-Bride was within earshot and, seeing he was unconscious under a sun-lounger, approached the couple who were celebrating the early stages of their union with a booze-fuelled row.

"F***ing leave it out!" exclaimed the good young lady with some venom, in a manner which was somewhat at odds with the trail of delicate summer blooms flowing from her peroxide-blond hair.

This was not aimed at me I hasten to add but at her sweetheart, whose face was wearing an expression which some may have interpreted as, 'What the heck have I done?' At that point, I turned on my heels and went home.

The following year, I had another, altogether more *gentile* engagement at the same *château*. I know the proprietors well and was invited to come along early to share a pre-wedding sandwich. During the lunch-time conversation, I brought up the topic of the previous year's wedding and enquired whether it had all ended in tears. The owner's faces adopted expressions usually reserved for stubbing a toe against hardwood furniture at the recollection.

Predictably it had done exactly that. Miraculously, there were only minor scuffles (I think the bride knocked her new husband's front teeth out) and no ambulances were necessary but at midnight, about thirty plastered guests had decided to work off their *fromage* course by leaping a safety fence and diving into the swimming pool. The *château* had made it very clear from the outset such actions were forbidden (and illegal - everyone knew that) and, upon ejecting the bathers, a vibrant, foul-language peppered and alcohol-fuelled dispute had ensued. There was no problem with the actual swimming; it's just no-one was wearing Speedos. I also learned the bill had been settled in used notes. Heaven only knows where the cash came from.

Just occasionally though, *château* owners get it horribly wrong. In 2017, *L'Ensemble Arisan* was booked to play for the ceremony and champagne reception of a wedding not far from the pretty town of Le Bugue in the Perigord Noir. Upon arrival, the owner grumpily protested about the parking space I'd selected for our vehicle (I'd erroneously believed the car park to be a reasonable choice) and, having moved six feet to a neighbouring space, watched as he sulkily shifted benches, sighingly picked up bits of confetti and micro-managed his guests' every move. It appeared that, despite his chosen profession, the crux of it was that he objected to the presence of people on his property.

As we approached the moment of the ceremony, he set up a little altar and seating for guests at the foot of the steps immediately adjacent to the main entrance of the *château*. This was in contrast to the set-up which I have witnessed at dozens of similar venues. Bearing in mind that the bride is preparing herself inside the *château,* the normal approach is to hold the ceremony fifty or so metres away from the building, in a small purpose-built garden. This allows the bride to exit the main door of the building in a theatrical fashion - to the appreciative 'oohs', 'aahs' and emotional sniffles of the assembly - and to glide regally down the steps, along a pathway and into the flora, accompanied by the music of her choice.

In this case, the owner insisted that the bride approach the ceremony *from* the garden, *towards* the *château*. This presented a logistical problem - how to get the said bride from the house to the garden without being seen by the assembly. The host's 'solution' was to herd the guests like cattle into a small, windowless room, which had presumably been used as a solitary confinement cell in the days of The Revolution, and slam the door shut. Once it had been resolutely locked, there followed an eerie silence, punctuated only by the wails of a confused, small child from behind the oak door. We continued playing our rendition of the waltz which, only moments before, the guests had been enjoying, whilst staring at one another with wide eyes. We felt like the band of the *Titanic* - abandoned by diners scrambling for the lifeboats and left playing to a scene of desertion - our remaining listeners being a few waiting staff bearing pained expressions and the house dog. To make matters worse, *Mademoiselle* the bride had very little English or French, so the wedding planner was forced to explain the sudden disappearance of her family and friends, along with the need to climb a tree in her frock, by means of mime and Google Translate.

After what seemed like three hours, the main door creaked open and the bride, complete with her *entourage,* scampered inelegantly across the lawn, train flapping in the breeze, to a copse where they concealed themselves in a bush. Only at that point were the guests released from their imprisonment and invited to take their seats facing the *château*. When the bride was eventually able to emerge from her hiding place, the chief bridesmaid was obliged to pluck bits of twig and bird poo from her veil as she processed down the aisle.

Other settings are refreshingly unpretentious about the whole market sector. One venue where I play every summer has no *château* at all to speak of. It is, in fact, a collection of converted barns with a swimming pool and horses for neighbours. Their publicity reads along the lines of: 'Come and celebrate your special day at affordable rates amongst the sun-kissed, rolling vineyards of the Charente'. This is thinly-veiled code for 'We'll put eight people in each room, give you a swimming pool, a decent chance of good weather and a *drink-one-bottle-get-two-free* deal with a wine producer of dubious legality in the woods. Discreet staff assured.'

When playing this venue in 2015, I witnessed the rarely-seen spectacle of a groom, at a flower-laden altar, holding a pint of lager for his *actual vows*. For this occasion, *Monsieur le Maire* came along in a show of support for local business. I bet he secretly thought perhaps *le Brexit* was actually not such a bad idea after all. It was a painful day to be British.

Another day at the same venue, I was asked to play on a balcony overlooking the spot where the ceremony would take place. In order to access it, I had to pass through the rooms where the bride-to-be and her adult bridesmaids were getting ready. They were ambling around in their nighties, or less, already attacking the sweet but deceptively potent *rosé* (in unmarked bottles I noted) as I set up my equipment. My multiple passages through their suite led to a series of exchanges where the air was full of blue banter. Whereas some menfolk would enjoy this kind of thing, I'm afraid I find such humour of a frankly sexual nature with drunk ladies I have known for twenty-three seconds more than a little challenging. It was decidedly cringe-worthy, akin to mishearing the theme for an evening out as a 'lady-boys night' -

and dressing accordingly - when it was actually a 'mainly boys night'.

Château weddings attract clients from all over the world. In order to enjoy such an event a certain amount of disposable income is a prerequisite, so many of the couples are active in the financial sectors of their home countries and are frankly, loaded. I have no problem with this - they pay me well - yet I think one *can* have too much of a good thing. I've worked for ceremonies where everyone seems to have a 'not another one' attitude. Maybe couples from these circles are under pressure to dream up some fresh novelty to amuse their friends. Call me old-fashioned but I think it should be about love rather than novelty. There is also the ever-lasting issue of 'today's cool being tomorrow's naff'. School photos of me with the mother of all mullets attest to that phenomenon.

The modern-day obsession with smartphones and social media can also be detrimental to the main event. We've all heard 'Please can you ensure your mobile phones are switched to 'silent' before the ceremony starts' (it's too much to ask them to be switched off or even left at home, perish the thought). Nowadays I hear 'Please refrain from taking photos during the ceremony' and 'Please refrain from posting photos to social media before the bride and groom have had a chance to do so themselves'. A further side effect is when the ceremony reaches the 'Please be upstanding to receive your bride and groom' bit, people find it a challenge to applaud with a phone in their hands – and ninety per cent of the congregation feel it necessary to film the moment. Instead, they resort to the modern-day whooping which we old-fashioned types find insufferable.

I love children at weddings. I have actually memorised a little repertoire of TV themes from children's programmes to entertain kids if they are becoming fractious. As they interact with me, the temptation for the wedding party to snap the 'cute shot with little Billy and guitarist' is too much, and I feel like Lady Di leaving a gymnasium as one hundred camera lens are directed at me. A problem arises if the child crosses a boundary. It seems the perfect photo remains the priority, irrespective of whether the child is *(a)* messing with my amplifier, *(b)* hitting me repeatedly in the face with a plastic toy or *(c)* pouring a bowl of jelly over my head. Bearing in mind my hands tend to be somewhat occupied when playing classical guitar, I have to stop doing my job if I am to intervene.

Of course, the cycles of life bring sadness as well as joy. There have been births, marriages and inevitably, those who have passed on. I experienced a French funeral in the most unlikely of circumstances, courtesy of my dear *Franglais* speaking friend, Huw.

One evening, I was out playing a gig, and Kirsty was at home with the children. At about 9.00pm, there was a sharp rap at the door. Kirsty answered to be confronted by Huw, in a state of advanced agitation, demanding to see me as a matter of some urgency. Kirsty invited him in, gave him a stiff drink, and asked him to explain his behaviour.

The story which transpired was that Huw had received a phone call earlier in the day from a French friend to tell him the sad news his mother had died. Huw, quite naturally, passed on his sincere condolences and said the fateful words we all utter without considering the consequences.

"If there's *anything* I can do, just let me know."

Now Huw is a keen amateur guitarist and singer. For what he lacks in technique, experience and basic musicality, he more than compensates for in good spirits and enthusiasm. The French friend whose mum had passed away, Paul-Henri, is a farmer whose musical experience I suspect has been limited to the local accordionist and a bit of *Europop.* He regards Huw's inimitable talents as genius of Beethoven-esque proportions. As a consequence of Huw's rash offer, he received a second call an hour later asking him if he'd be kind enough to play at the funeral.

Let's be clear. Huw's offerings are an absolute joy in a pub environment - his limitations and modest demeanour only adding to the charm of his programme. Playing for a funeral though is a different kettle of fish altogether. To intensify matters somewhat, as Huw sat at home digesting the consequences of his hasty actions, he received a phone call from the priest who would be conducting the service.

The priest informed Huw that the 300-or-so guests would listen to him play solo for half an hour as they reflected upon the life of the deceased, and then process around the coffin. *le Reverend* proposed some unaccompanied Bach or perhaps a transcription of a late Mozart Sonata. Huw, whose repertoire was limited to a handful of songs by The Kinks, Bob Dylan and The Who, turned a shade of off-white, squeaked 'Okay' and sought out a bottle of *eau de vie.*

To compound this lamentable situation, folk in the French countryside don't hang around when it comes to burying their dead; the funeral was scheduled for 2.00pm the following day. It was for this reason Huw was to be found hammering at my door at 9.00pm, looking as if his world had collapsed around him. Which it had actually.

Revived with comforting words and a camomile tea (probably with a sedative slipped in), Kirsty packed Huw on his way assuring him I was available the following afternoon and to come over in the morning. I arrived home from my gig at 2.00am and, as Kirsty was asleep, knew nothing about Huw's dilemma until I heard the same sharp rapping at the door at 7.30am. Bleary-eyed, I answered. I was more than a little surprised to be greeted by Huw, who appeared to have aged a decade or so since I'd last seen him three days previously.

He explained the situation to me over a reviving *espresso*. As if the web could become any more tangled, the family had now added a request to Huw's already over-burdened workload, in the form of an obscure French religious song – an apparent favourite of French ladies over ninety years of age. They had omitted to provide him with sheet music for the song - which would have been as much use as an ashtray on a motorbike to Huw anyway, as he can't read a note of music.

Together, we made a plan. Firstly, we found the requested song – what did we do before YouTube? I jotted out the chords for Huw (in his preferred key of C major) and worked out the tune. We then made the decision that I would field the pre-ceremony meditative music as I already had the appropriate repertoire under my fingers. As we were going to be playing for the lowering of the coffin into the grave, we decided Huw could join me at this point for the favourite song. At the end of the day, it was Huw's presence with a guitar which would be meaningful to the family; what he did with it was irrelevant. I then indulged in half an hour's tasteless humour, teasing Huw by suggesting a series of entirely inappropriate pieces we could play: The Jam's *Going Underground,* Simon and Garfunkel's *Slip Sliding Away,* The BeeGees *Stayin' Alive...* The list is endless. In the event of a cremation, a whole new world of possibilities can be uncovered.

So that afternoon, suited up in black and wearing serious expressions, we made our way half an hour south to the ceremony. I was installed metres away from a coffin containing a lady I had never even heard of a few hours earlier, such is the strange nature of my life.

The French family and friends slowly processed around the coffin, some stopping to say a little prayer of thanks. It was very emotional and rather beautiful. I was playing Bach (Jimi Hendrix definitely would have been an error) and I was interested to note everyone was casually dressed. Jeans, trainers and T-shirts were the order of the day. In the thirty-five-degree heat, Huw and I were the only ones wearing suits.

There followed a lengthy eulogy given by *Monsieur le Reverend* and then a call to the graveside. Mustering up as much dignity as possible, Huw and I tore out of a side door, guitars and chairs flapping wildly at our sides, and, pantingly installed ourselves next to the freshly-dug plot 200 metres down the road. Once the mourners and the deceased had arrived, we started to strum the requested song. Huw had a massive attack of nerves and I could see he was all over the place. His fingers were shaking like sausage-shaped jellies in the wind as he tried, in vain, to find the ever-elusive strings of his instrument. I found myself side-mouthing chords at him in an effort to keep the ensemble together.

"C … two… three… four…, D minor…. two… three… four…"

The more observant listeners would have noted this unusual verbal counterpoint to the musical offering being plucked away in the afternoon heat. Thankfully, no-one seemed to mind.

"Thanks, Dan, I owe you one," sighed a greatly-unburdened Huw on the way home.

In fact, Huw owes me nothing at all. His kindness and energy have been a constant source of inspiration to *la Famille Jones*. His unfailingly positive disposition has lifted me out of some bleak places over the years. The world needs more Huws.

Some years later, Kirsty and I were looking for some second-hand electric fencing so we could rotate the location of the goats on our land. I found some equipment for sale online and, after a phone call, the vendor invited us around to view it *en famille*. The gentleman was a farmer and kindly offered us an *aperitif* followed by a tour of his colossal farm machinery. The latter was a treat for Sam as he was permitted to clamber into the cabins of various impressive vehicles, from sower to harvester, each equipped with the latest farmers' toys such as video cameras and GPS. For the modern-day large-scale farmer, lunar rhythms have taken a back seat and the all-encompassing wisdom of Google is placed firmly at-the-wheel. Eventually, I reminded myself of the purpose of our visit and inspected the supply of fencing, posts and cable up for sale. It was high-quality stuff and I feared it would be well out of our budget. Bracing myself, I enquired about the asking price.

"It's free," he replied. *Gratuit.*

The vendor was Paul-Henri, the son of the deceased lady. He was only too happy to give us the equipment as a gift (unnecessarily so) as a 'thank you' for playing at the service. I have learned in this life, good things come to you if you are open in heart and do your best to be kind.

It was at about the same time that our neighbour, André, returned home following his accident. This announcement was met with great rejoicing all round and a number of *aperitifs* of a most convivial nature were necessary to properly mark the occasion. *'Il faut'* I insisted. One particular evening, we were just finishing off some local cider when I couldn't help noticing Eliane was giggling like a schoolgirl. She seemed desperate to tell us something. I was examining the label of the bottle to check its alcohol content when she suddenly burst like a bottle of champagne.

"André, I must tell them, I have to!" she exploded.

André smiled.

"D'accord, if you must, you can," he said.

Eliane turned to *la Famille Jones,* glassy-eyed and beaming.

"André and I are going to be married!" she announced.

A bewildered silence followed this proclamation and I found myself wondering if I'd translated this somewhat arresting statement correctly. There was though, no mistake. I had, reasonably I think, presumed they were already legally man-and-wife but it turned out, unbeknownst to us, they were both second-timers. Despite having been an item for pretty much the entire duration of my life, they'd never got around to tying the knot formally.

This beautiful announcement was bitter-sweet as upon later reflection, we realised André and Eliane must have had a serious conversation about mortality and our finite time in this world. Legally-speaking, they figured were one of them to pass away, life would be far less complex for the surviving partner if they were married, particularly as there were children from their first marriages. French law has a field-day at any opportunity for bureaucracy and inheritance law is more of a minefield than the Somme in 1917.

The couple decided on a relatively short engagement and a quick, functional ceremony with very few guests. They wanted no fuss so we respected that. I asked though if they would pass by *Chez Jones* one evening to have a little celebratory *aperitif* with us and our musician friends, Stéphane, Valérie and their teenage children.

This offer was accepted so, on a beautiful summer's evening, we gathered under the branches of our fir tree and brought in some bubbly as well as a few decent bottles of Saint Emilion. We wanted to give André and Eliane a wedding gift, but choosing a meaningful present for a couple who placed next-to-no value on material goods was a stiff proposition. I then struck upon the idea of writing them a little piece of music to mark the occasion so I created *La Valse d'Elan* (a mix of their names) which was a pastiche of the large body of French waltzes of which I knew André was particularly fond.

Being aware of how much the newly-weds enjoyed the accordion, the piece was scored for a trio of accordion, violin and guitar. That evening, I remember André, now in a wheelchair, was full of hilarious anecdotes. Both the laughter and wine flowed freely as he speculated when the newly-weds' first baby may come along, and also recounted for the fiftieth time a prank he had played on Sam some years previously. On that occasion, André was closing up his chickens for the night and having spotted Sam and me playing in our garden, concealed himself behind a tree where he emitted a strikingly-realistic wolf-howl. Sam had sprinted back to the house at lightning speed, his young legs almost invisible to the naked eye such was the urgency with which they had been stirred into action.

As the evening progressed, Stéphane caught my eye and the moment came for a little *musique*. We presented the couple with a copy of the score, artfully bound with red ribbons by Kirsty. Our instruments had been hidden behind a cherry tree, and we revealed them to delighted applause.

You must understand the idea was to play a light-hearted waltz and enjoy a good laugh together, yet as we started playing the notes, the atmosphere became charged with powerful emotion. I became intensely aware of the balmy late-day sunshine; the bleating of goats and the clucking of hens accompanying the melody. It seemed in this moment of song, despite our differences in life-experience, culture, age and background, we were bound together by our shared beliefs in good living, love and respect.

I glanced up from my score and caught the sight of both André and Eliane with tears streaming down their weather-beaten faces. Before I knew it, the entire group was fighting to reach the end of the piece, being all-consumed by a near-telepathic and overwhelming sense of something indefinable, yet truly profound. It was a deeply-spiritual experience which will stay with me for the rest of my days.

***

Twenty-One Weddings and a Funeral – The Essential Tips

(1) If you are going to marry in the French countryside, do the legal thing in the UK first and then go to France to have the party of your lives. I know a guitarist in the area who offers an incomparable personalised service and charges excellent rates.

(2) If tying the knot in a *château*, please behave in a reasonable fashion post-ceremony. Be exceptionally pleasant to your musicians (who incidentally, accept tips and beer-shaped gifts).

(3) Reveal your Anglophone identity at the earliest opportunity to clients. Otherwise, you may find yourself having to adopt a false persona for three hours.

(4) Please, leave your phone in your room for the wedding ceremony.

(5) In the event of you being required to attend a French funeral, dress down.

(6) Beware of making rash offers. You may be taken at face value and find yourself doing an impromptu performance at the graveside.

(7) Joy follows sadness.

19. Saying *Au Revoir*

Oh fare thee well, I must be gone
And leave you for awhile
Wherever I go, I will return
If I go ten thousand miles my dear
If I go ten thousand miles.

The True Lover's Farewell – Traditional (England)

For a whole academic year, Florence attended a private school in Bordeaux where she was permitted to leave classes early in order to attend a dance academy in the afternoon. During the week, she boarded with her teacher. On a Friday, I was in Bordeaux for work so I would walk to the academy to collect her and we would take the train home together. Most of her weekend was spent catching up on her missed classes, although being able to do this lying on a blanket under the cherry tree made up a little bit for the lost free time.

As the year progressed, so did Flo's standard of dance. The arrangement worked to a certain extent, but the fees were crippling, Flo was exhausted and *Madame Dinosaur* was driving me to distraction. It became apparent she needed to be at a specialist dance school as a boarder. With the invaluable insight of Flo's dance teachers, we were able to research various options. Florence could have tried for dance schools In England, but as we'd been out of the UK for nearly seven years, we were ineligible for grants. Flo did attract the attention of one major dance and theatre school in the UK. It was a great compliment to her when the director phoned us regarding the possibility of accepting her, and we were deeply grateful to the school for having taken the time to contact us. When I was asked outright if

I had the £50,000 tuition fees at my immediate disposal, I choked spectacularly on the plum I was nibbling and, having gathered three euros and twenty centimes from behind the sofa and the ashtray of the car was forced to accept defeat and decline the opportunity.

There was the option of trying for dance schools in France, such as those in Toulouse and Paris. The latter, in particular, suffers a reputation for being very aggressive towards young dancers – the teaching style historically being of the nature employed by *Monsieur L'Arsole* and his cronies. Although I'm certain this will have changed in this protective age, Flo's teacher was adamant her style would be better suited to the British system.

Speculatively, Flo tried for a dance school in Scotland particularly as the successful applicants would be given a bursary to cover both their tuition and lodging. Kirsty and Flo nearly didn't make it to the audition as, *en route* to the airport, our trusty Vectra half-exploded on the Bordeaux Ring Road. Whilst awaiting the breakdown service, Kirsty had asked Flo to text me to inform me of the hiccup in our carefully-laid plans; consequently, I was confronted with a series of worryingly-vague messages.

'HELP!' read the first one closely followed by *'Call me now!!!'*

What was this? My wife and daughter were meant to be on a plane to Edinburgh at this point. Had the unthinkable happened? I scrambled to open the next message.

'BIG problem!' it read, followed by a perhaps-unnecessary repeat of text number two, emphasised by the prolific employment of the upper case.

'CALL ME... NOW!!!'

Later that day, Flo and I had a little conversation about clarity when sending text messages.

Happily, an understanding mechanic and his taxi-driving buddy drove them at speed to the terminal, arriving with minutes to spare.

A few weeks later, we received a letter. Almost inevitably, it congratulated Florence as she had won a coveted place at the school and was to start in mid-August. The only teensy-weensy challenge was that she needed a Scottish address, and we happened to live in South West France.

Initially, we congratulated Florence on her formidable achievement, but to go to Scotland would be absurd. It rains. A lot. They eat haggis. Both battered Mars Bars and chicken tikka pizzas are welcomed to the world of the deep-fat fryer. Men are obliged to wear skirts. Bagpipes are played in public. Thus, we continued our search, yet upon speaking to teachers in the field of dance, it soon became clear that *not* to go would be absurd. We were warned that if we turned down this opportunity, a similar one would never emerge. Eventually, we came to the decision that, if we found work, we would leave France and try our luck in Scotland.

We sent CVs to every school in the land and applied for any music-related jobs which were up-for-grabs online. We were very lucky as we were both successful in being offered good, fulfilling employment, so it was all systems go for project *Ecosse.* We figured that the potential shock to our systems could be eased somewhat were we to live in a village environment; Sam was accustomed to having acres in which to burn off his seemingly unlimited reserves of energy so we needed green space nearby. A small school which shared our values was also critical and this needed to be within walking distance of our accommodation, so we could get by with a single car. Mindful of these factors, and a very tightly clipped budget, Kirsty set herself to task researching our options.

The month of July should have been spent calmly preparing for this sudden, unexpected turn of events in our lives but instead, we went on holiday to *Arcachon*, swam a lot, played gigs, made hooch and spent time with family and friends. Early August was charged with a mountain of DIY tasks so our home would be in order for the winter, and possibly suitable for short-term lets. Friends and family who came to *Chez Jones* for a lazy holiday had paintbrushes thrust into their hands rather than the habitual glasses of my latest brew. My brother-in-law, Ian, helped me load our goats into the car to their foster home in the forest.

So, it was early August when we locked up the house for the first time in many-a-year and climbed, *en famille,* into our Vectra, now with only one cat in tow, and took the road northwards. As was the case in 2010, we were treated to dinner by friends the night on our last evening and were consequently still packing at 3.00am. Whereas seven years earlier, the *plat* had been a takeaway curry – now officially the UK's favourite food - in the Dordogne we ate *une salade, une tarte aux courgettes* and washed it down with a local chilled white. There was a strange feeling of *déjà vu,* the familiar anxiety coupled with excitement, but this time we were wiser, more resourceful and had greater self-confidence.

As we passed Poitiers in Central France, I glanced in the rear-view mirror and then to my left. Everyone was asleep except for me (and the cat who was sulking). Without warning, I felt waves of emotion overcome my exhausted body. A deep sadness overwhelmed me and, before I could compose myself, I felt tears prick my eyes and trickle down my cheeks. There was quite a lot of snot as well, but that image is rather less poetic. As if to steal the last laugh, we were snapped by a traffic camera near Rouen *en route* to the ferry. More than six months later, a notification of our misdemeanour and demand for payment, headed with the *Tricolore* and the inevitable *Liberté, Egalité, Fraternité*, tracked us down to our first-floor flat in Perthshire.

We will return to this little corner of France, *Chez Nous,* which moulded our children, created our values, changed us for the better and stole our hearts. We are different people today from the family that set off in 2010; I can chop a log, Kirsty can grow vegetables, the children are truly bilingual, and we understand, respect and love the differences between our cultures.

Our short time in Scotland has, so far, been another exciting and enlightening chapter in our lives. I am living close to my brother once again (although he slides beers across the table nowadays rather than Panda Pops). Our souls though still regard *la France* as 'home'. Every time I feel pangs of nostalgia and longing for our village, its eccentric inhabitants, the animals and their fascinating characters, a glass of something strong and sweet, the sensation of sun on skin, the explosion of taste on the palate from a freshly-picked plum, a meaningless yet convivial staff meeting, laughing with friends over an *apero,* the need to burn a *pétassou* (and dodge the inevitable ensuing explosion), the cling of Speedos around my crotch (too much detail) or a cooling dip in the river, I only have to remember that *au revoir* is usually mistranslated as 'goodbye'.

In fact, it means 'until we see one another again'.

Figure 18 Flo and Sam at one of our favourite secret places.

Dan Jones hails from South Wales, but since experiencing a holiday in *la Belle France* in the early 1980's has felt he is a Frenchman at heart. He studied classical guitar in Wales' national conservatoire and went on to lecture there for twelve years. Dan's writing portfolio encompasses a range of music tutor books, including an audiobook for visually-impaired guitarists, and his performing career has taken him across Europe and Asia. A diverse teaching CV includes posts in national conservatoires, prisons, a major international school and écoles de musique in rural villages. In 2010, Dan, his wife Kirsty and their children Flo and Sam moved to France to experience a gentler mode de vie. During this time, the family's tendency to accept offers of abandoned fluffy creatures meant that their plot soon became home to goats, hens, cats, guinea pigs, rabbits and hamsters - indeed, a small petting zoo.

Dan continued his teaching, performing and recording career, and has loved the opportunity to collect the anecdotes and tips which make up *Extracting Goats...* Dan enjoys composing, musical arrangement, writing humorous poetry, road running, river swimming, homebrewing, chasing insomniac chickens and being butted by his goats. He presently passes his time between France and Scotland where, between performing, writing and composing, he lectures at The Royal Conservatoire of Scotland.

Printed in Poland
by Amazon Fulfillment
Poland Sp. z o.o., Wrocław